Step into Programming with Visual Basic .NET

Fourth Edition

Guity Ravai

Department of Computer and Information Technology - Purdue University, West Lafayette, Indiana

Ibrahim M. Baggili

Department of Computer Science - Tagliatela College of Engineering - University of New Haven, Connecticut

Kendall Hunt

publishing company

Dedication

Guity dedicates this edition of the book to her sons Ali and Amir.
Ibrahim would like to dedicate this edition to his sisters Mouna and Samiha.

CONTENTS

PREFACE

Step into Programming is written for those with no prior programming experience. The authors cover major programming concepts in a simple and concise language, with thorough explanation and ample examples. All the examples are in Visual Basic .NET 2012. This book is also a quick read for those who have prior programming experience and want to learn Visual Basic .NET.

The lead author, Guity Ravai, has been teaching Visual Basic at Purdue University since the fall of 1998. Throughout these years she has taught more than 6,000 students, most of whom were first-time programmers. Ibrahim Baggili, an assistant professor at the University of New Haven has taught the computer labs for this course, while a graduate student at Purdue, for more than three years and has been extremely successful in teaching the concepts to novice programmers. Together, the authors have a vast amount of experience dealing with the difficulties that first-time programmers might encounter.

It is a well known fact that learning how to program for the first time is an overwhelming task for most students. Therefore, having a readable textbook and an effective teaching approach is crucial. If taught well, programming can be fun and motivating. Over the years, we found that a lot of students become intrinsically motivated when they successfully complete and figure out programming assignments and projects. It is true that there are numerous Visual Basic .NET programming textbooks available, but relatively few are written by people who have spent years in the classroom clarifying programming concepts to raw beginners. Furthermore, most of the books are focused on teaching the programming language itself, and not the programming concepts. This book focuses on teaching the programming concepts and Visual Basic .NET is merely used as a tool to explain these concepts.

This is the fourth edition of the book. We have come a long way since the first edition published in 2007. Each edition was written to ensure that the book improves the students' learning experience.

The main reason that Guity wrote the book in 2006 was her struggle in finding the right textbook for the introductory programming course that she had been teaching for the past eight years. By 2006, the textbook for the course had been changed several times, but most of the students were unhappy with the book assigned at the time. With the help of her teaching assistants Ibrahim Baggili and Ting Zhuang, and collecting numerous feedback from her students, the first edition of the book was published in 2007.

The second edition of Step into Programming came out a year after the first edition. The authors (Guity and Ibrahim) queried students on the first edition and took into account the student comments and suggestions when writing the second edition of the book. The additions to the second edition included programming challenges at the end of each chapter and more tips throughout the book. Furthermore, the formatting issues that appeared in the first edition were resolved, making the text in the book more readable.

The third edition was introduced in 2010 because professors and instructors at academic institutions that adopted the book asked if it would be possible to have the same book using the recent version of the software, i.e., Visual Basic .NET 2008. In the third edition, the authors edited their past work, expanded some of the concepts, and added Appendix E on automating Excel using Visual Basic .NET.

While teaching her class using the third edition, Guity realized that Visual Studio .NET 2010 had slightly different features when compared to Visual Studio .NET 2008, so some of the text in the book would not apply to .NET 2010. Additionally, the trial version of Visual Studio .NET 2012 was being released. Therefore, the authors started working on the fourth edition. For the fourth edition, the entire book was reviewed, revised and edited by the authors. Additionally, the edits were reviewed and further edited by Byju Govindan, Guity's teaching assistant. In this edition, the authors elaborated on programming concepts, added more examples and topics. The authors have made sure that the examples are compatible with .NET 2012 and Contain more in depth explanations compared to previous editions.

As you can see - this book throughout its history was created based on instructor and student needs and if any future editions were to be written the authors would again ensure that these future editions would improve this book to enhance both the student and instructor experience in dealing with the challenges faced in programming.

Organization of the Book

The chapters in this book are organized in the order of their difficulty, starting with the most basic concepts and ending with the more difficult aspects of files and exception handling. The chapters may be read in the given order, but some chapters can be switched around. For example, the chapter on modularity may be covered before or after the chapter on selection. The exception handling chapter may be covered after the chapter on arithemetic operators, if preferred, and so on.

Each chapter covers one major programming concept and is divided into several sections. Each section explains a part of the main concept, with an example showing the concept's application. The authors also felt it was helpful to provide a more comprehensive example at the end of each chapter. Review questions are provided for the reader to assess their learning; the keys to review questions are provided in Appendix F.

Tips throughout the book are used to highlight certain programming rules and to emphasize the meaning of certain concepts. Boxes are used to emphasize and explain some of the important topics. Pitfalls illustrate common mistakes by novice programmers.

The book also contains six appendices that provide additional material for the reader to reference at any point while reading this book. The topics covered in the appendices are guidelines for designing the Graphical User Interface, coding standards, additional controls, debugging tools, integrating Excel into a VB .NET project, and the keys to review questions.

ACKNOWLEDGEMENTS

The authors would like to thank Byju Govindan for the time and efforts he has put to review the fourth edition of the book. Byju, has been Guity's teaching assistant for the past three years, teaching more than 100 students in computer labs each semester using the third edition of the book. Byju has a Master's degree in Computer Technology from Purdue University and is a PhD candidate in Forestry expecting to graduate in December 2013.

Guity, also thanks her students for providing valuable feedback on the third edition of the book throughout the past three years that she has been teaching Visual Programming. Their feedback has played a major role in the revisions made to the book.

Finally, the authors would like to thank Kendall Hunt Publishing Company for their cooperation in publishing the fourth edition and having it ready for the Fall 2013 semester. Our sincere thanks go to Amanda Smith, the Senior Regional Project Coordinator, who has been communicating with us in every step of this project, providing prompt responses, and being flexible with the deadlines. We would also like to thank Ray Wood, the Director of Author Relations. Ray was our initial contact with Kedall Hunt for this edition. He helped us with planning the deadlines and the official paper work. Last but not least, we would like to thank the behind the scene editorial staff at Kendall Hunt for proof reading and implementing our revisions and edits for the fourth edition of the book.

ABOUT THE AUTHORS

Guity Ravai has a Master's degree in computer science from the Department of Computer Science at Purdue University with a concentration in databases. She is a faculty member in the department of Computer & Information Technology at Purdue University, West Lafayette, Indiana. She has been teaching computer programming courses using Visual Basic, C, C# and C++ to undergraduate students since 1998. Currently, Guity teaches all the service programming courses offered in the department along with the first core programming course for the majors. On average she has more than two hundred students each semester.

Ibrahim Baggili received his PhD at the College of Technology at Purdue University. He has earned a Bachelor of Science degree in Computer Technology with a concentration in Network Engineering Technology and a Master of Science degree in computer programming for mobile platforms. Ibrahim is currently an Assistant Professor at the University of New Haven (UNH), CT at the Department of Computer Science - Tagliatela College of Engineering. His area of research and teaching expertise is in Cyber Forensics and Cyber Criminal investigations. Prior to his post at UNH, Ibrahim was an Assistant Professor at Zayed University in the UAE at the College of Technological Innovation, where he directed the Advanced Cyber Forensics Research Laboratory (ACFRL).

INTRODUCTION

In today's high-tech society, computers are a central part in running every industry. In the current job market, almost every job has some level of involvement with computers, and a lack of basic knowledge about computers is a big disadvantage for those seeking employment. Computers have come a long way in a short period of time, from the first computer built in 1945 by Electronic Numerical Integrator and Computer (ENIC), which weighed thirty tons and filled a large room, to the latest computers that come in sizes as small as a smartphone, with speed and power that is mind-boggling. No technology has made such a surge of improvement in such a short time period. In this section, we simply breeze through some basic terms that apply to computers in general. There are numerous sites on the Internet for further reading.

Computers consist of two main parts, the hardware and the software.

Computer Hardware: Computer hardware is the physical components of a computer, such as the monitor, the keyboard, the mother board, the hard drive, and so on.

Computer Software: Computer software is the program that instructs the computer to perform different jobs. Even the most expensive computer built with the latest hardware components would be worthless without the required software. Every computer comes with an Operating System, which is a type of software that is crucial for the computer to operate. There are several categories of software, such as system software, application software, and utility software, each designed for a specific purpose.

What Is a Computer Program?

A computer program is another term for computer software. It is a set of instructions that tells the computer what to do. In general, to solve a given problem, we must come up with an algorithm. An algorithm is a step-by-step logical solution for a given problem. In order to use a computer for solving a given problem, we must translate the designed algorithm into the programming language that is suitable for that problem.

There are many programming languages to choose from. Each language is useful for solving certain problems and has its own vocabulary, grammar, and syntax that must be followed. Unlike common belief, computers are not smart enough to distinguish between the right and wrong solution; they simply follow the instructions given in the program. Therefore, following the rules and syntax of a programming language is crucial for writing reliable programs.

A Brief History of Programming Languages

The early computers had to be programmed physically by turning switches on and off and storing data in different registers. Registers are used to accept, store, and transfer data and instructions that are being used by the computer during the program execution. After that came the machine language. Programming languages have come a long way since then. Below is a brief history of programming languages.

Machine Language: Computers do not understand anything but on and off switches. On or off state of a switch can be represented by ones and zeros. Everything is stored in the computer's memory as binary in terms of zeros and ones. The machine language, which is understandable by the computer, dates back to 1950s. Writing and reading such programs was extremely tedious.

Assembly Language: Assembly language is an improvement on the machine language; it uses English words to instruct the computer to perform certain jobs. Still an assembly language is a low-level language, meaning the instructions refer to the specific registers in the computer memory.

Procedural Languages: These high-level languages were developed in the 1970s and 1980s. These languages have English-like words incorporated in them, and do not work directly with the computer memory. The program is written with the focus on the tasks that need to be done. Normally a segment of code (e.g., function) is written to accomplish each task. Examples are: Fortran, Pascal, and C.

Event-Driven Languages: These are more modern languages developed in 1980s and 1990s. The programs written in these languages respond to the events that take place during the program execution, such as clicking on a button, entering some data, and so on. Most of these languages have a graphical user interface (GUI). Visual Basic is an event-driven language.

Visual Languages: These languages have a graphical user interface that the user of the program can interact with during the program execution. Visual Basic is a visual language.

Object-Oriented Languages: These languages came to existence in 1980s and have become very popular ever since. When writing a program in an object-oriented language, the main focus is on the objects involved in the problem, rather than the tasks. Objects have properties, which are like adjectives, and methods, which are like behaviors. Examples are: C++, Java, C#, and VB .NET.

How a Computer Understands a Computer Program

Source Code: The programming code written in a certain language is referred to as the source code. The computer cannot understand the program written in a high-level language. The program should be changed into a machine language for a computer to understand it.

Compiler: Compiler is a software that translates the code written in a specific language into the machine language. The translated code is referred to as an object code. The computer can understand and execute the object code. Every high-level language has a compiler, which must be installed on the computer in order to write and execute programs in that language.

Error/bug: An error or a bug is a mistake made in a computer program. Normally the computer program goes through several revisions before it can be properly compiled and executed to produce the right results. The name "bug" comes from early ages of the computers when a computer was the size of a room. In an incident, an actual bug was trapped in the tubes of the computer, causing it to malfunction. From that point on, the term bug has been used commonly to refer to a mistake in the computer program, and debugging has been used as a term for getting rid of the errors in a program.

Categories of Errors:

- *Syntax Error:* A syntax error occurs when the rules of a language are violated. Such errors are detected at compile time and are very easy to fix.

- *Runtime Error:* A runtime error occurs when the computer is unable to execute certain instruction written in the program, such as division by 0, using a non-existent function, etc. Such errors are detected during the program execution.

- *Logic Error:* Logic errors occur when incorrect logic or wrong formulas are used for solving a problem. Such errors can be detected by extensive testing of the program with different sets of data. The computer cannot detect logic errors, because a computer is clueless as to what the right logic is.

Debugging: As mentioned earlier, debugging is the process of getting rid of errors in a computer program. Visual Basic .NET contains a helpful built-in debugger provided in its Integrated Development Environment (IDE) that is readily accessible.

CHAPTER 1

Getting Started

After the completion of Chapter 1, students should be able to:

❑ Understand the basics of the IDE in Visual Studio .NET

❑ List and use the naming conventions for naming objects in the user interface

❑ Set and modify properties of user interface objects in Visual Basic .NET

❑ Understand the meaning of string literals/constants

❑ Use the assignment operator

❑ Set Tab Orders to user interface objects

❑ Understand the Program Development Life Cycle (PDLC), software development methodology

❑ Develop a simple application in Visual Basic .NET

1.1 Getting Visual Basic .NET

One can use VB .NET to program for different platforms (web, mobile, desktop). This book focuses only on desktop applications. To be able to program in VB .NET 2012, one has to install either the Professional edition of Visual Studio .NET (paid), or the desktop Express edition (free). You can download Visual Studio .NET Express for desktop applications from http://www.microsoft.com/express.

Visual Basic .NET is forward compatible. In other words, you can open a project developed in an older version in 2012; but it is not possible to open a a project developed in 2012 in an older version.

1.2 Visual Basic .NET Language

Microsoft developed the Visual Basic (VB) language in 1990 for the Windows Operating System (OS). The language has been through a number of changes since then. VB has become one of the most popular languages in business and industry. It is very powerful and easy to learn. VB .NET is often used in Rapid Application Development (RAD). RAD is a way of developing applications in an iterative manner.

An iterative manner means that changes can be made to the code and the application while it is being developed, if the user requirements change.

Visual Basic .NET 2012, is the latest version of the VB language, which is part of a bigger package called Visual Studio .NET 2012. Visual Studio .NET, contains few other languages such as Visual C++ and C# (pronounced C Sharp). The material covered in this book and all the examples are based on 2012 version of the software. However, there is little difference between the 2012 and 2010 version of the software at this level of programming.

.NET Framework

All the .NET languages work in the .NET Framework. They all compile to a common machine language called Microsoft Intermediate Language (MSIL). The MSIL code runs in the Common Language Runtime (CLR), which is part of the .NET Framework. In order to run the executable file of a Visual Basic project (example.exe), or any other language in .NET, one must have the .NET Framework installed on the computer.

Visual Basic .NET Programming Language is:

- A high-level and structured programming language. This means that English-like words are used in the language.

- A visual programming language. The programmer is able to visually design the Graphical User Interface (GUI). At runtime, the user interacts with the program through this visual interface.

- An event-driven programming language. A Visual Basic program may respond to different events during the program execution. An event is something that takes place during the program execution, such as clicking on a Button, clearing the text in a TextBox, hovering the mouse over an object, and so on.

- An object-oriented programming language. An object-oriented language is based on classes and objects. An object has properties and methods. Properties are like adjectives, and methods are like behaviors for the object. To fully discuss object orientation is beyond the scope of this book. However, everything in VB .NET is built on this concept.

A Visual Basic .NET program consists of two major parts:

1. A Graphical User Interface (GUI), which contains the Form and the objects placed on the Form. The user interacts with the application through the GUI objects during the program execution. That is the visual part of the language.

2. The code, which is the programming statements written in VB .NET language. The code is behind-the-scene (behind the GUI) logic that produces the expected result and functionality during the program execution.

It is also possible to write console applications (programs with no GUI) in VB .NET, but that is not the main purpose of this language. In this book, we discuss VB .NET applications that have a GUI.

Visual Basic .NET IDE

The Integrated Development Environment, also known an IDE, opens up when one starts VB .NET. The IDE has all the tools needed for designing a VB Windows Application integrated in one place and readily available to the programmer. It contains the tools needed for designing the graphical user interface, an editor to write the VB .NET code, a debugger to debug the program, and tools to compile and execute the program. Everything a programmer needs to develop a VB .NET application is usually available in the IDE.

Files Created in a VB .NET Project

When creating a new project, VB .NET creates a folder with the same name as the project in the specified location on the disk. In this folder, there are several folders and files that are created by VB .NET and are needed for the proper execution of the program. To open a VB .NET project from Windows Explorer, double-click on the Solution File (file extension .sln) or the Project File (file extension .vbproj).

One of the important folders is the Bin folder. In this folder, you will find the Debug folder which includes the executable file (file extension .exe) for the VB .NET project. A copy of the executable file can be placed on the desktop of the computer, or anywhere on the disk and the program can be executed by double clicking on this file. Among the other files created in the parent folder are the Form file with .vb extension and the Form Designer File, also with .vb extension. The Form file, contains all the code written by the programmer for this Form, and the Form Designer file, contains all the automatically generated code by VB .NET for GUI objects.

Solution File (.sln)

A VB .NET application, which is also referred to as a Solution, may consist of several projects. The solution file is a text file that holds data about the solution and projects it contains. In this book, we will work with applications that consist of only one project. One of the ways to open a VB .NET project is to double-click on the Solution file (.sln) in the Windows Explorer on your personal computer. This may not work if you are working in a lab computer with shared network drives.

Project File (.vbproj)

The project file is a text file that contains data about the project. One of the ways to open a VB .NET project, is to double-click on the Project file (.vbproj) in the Windows Explorer.

Form File (.vb)

The Form file is a text file that contains the code written by the programmer for that specific Form. The code written by the programmer is called the Source Code. Bear in mind that a VB .NET project may have multiple Forms; Each Form has its own code window and Form file.

 To move a VB .NET project to a different location on the disk, make a copy of the entire folder in the Windows Explorer, and paste it at the desired location on the disk. Or you may drag and drop the entire project folder to another location on the disk.

1.3 Getting Started with Visual Basic .NET

In order to develop VB .NET projects, you need to install Visual Studio .NET 2012, or its express edition on your computer. You may also consider installing Visual Basic .NET which is part of Visual Studio .NET. After installing the software, you can access it by going to Start at the bottom left of the screen, and then and selecting All Programs, then finding either Microsoft Visual Studio .NET > VB .NET 2012, or the Express Edition.

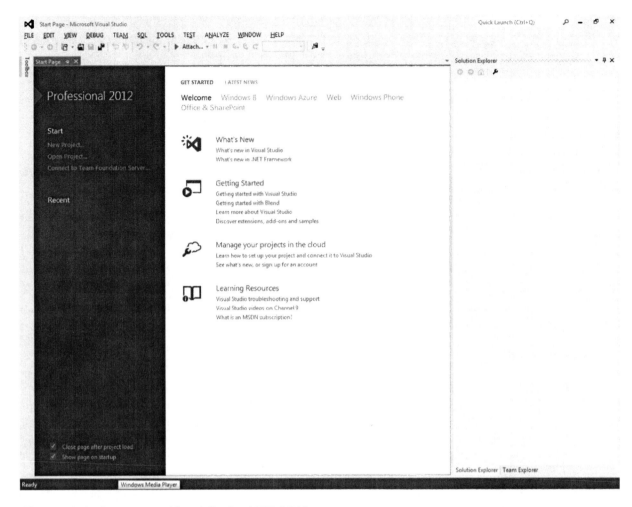

Figure 1.1 *Start page - Visual Studio .NET 2012*

To create a new VB .NET project, go through the following steps:

1. Start Visual Studio .NET 2012, or the Express Edition 2012. The Start Page shows up as shown in Figure 1.1. If Visual Studio 2012 was installed for the first time, the software might ask for the language option. In that case, choose VB Developers.

2. Click on Tools > Options on the menu bar. In the Options Window, click on Projects and Solutions, and then select General. Make sure the check box stating: "Save new projects when created" is checked. It is also helpful to change the default location for saving new projects in the top TextBox, to somewhere that is easy to find. This way if you forget to specify a location for saving a new project, it will be saved in the specified location on the disk See Figure 1.2.

3. Click on File on the menu bar, choose New Project. The window in Figure 1.3 will open up.

4. In the left panel, choose Windows under Visual Basic for Templates. In the right panel, choose Windows Forms Application. In the lower part of this window, enter a name for the project, and choose a location to save the project. The Browse button can be used to find the desired location on the disk to save the project. Do not enter a name for the Solution. VB .NET gives the solution the same name given to the project. Click OK. Figure 1.4, shows the screen capture when the name and location is specified for the new project.

5. The VB .NET Integrated Development Environment (IDE) will open up as shown in figure 1.5.

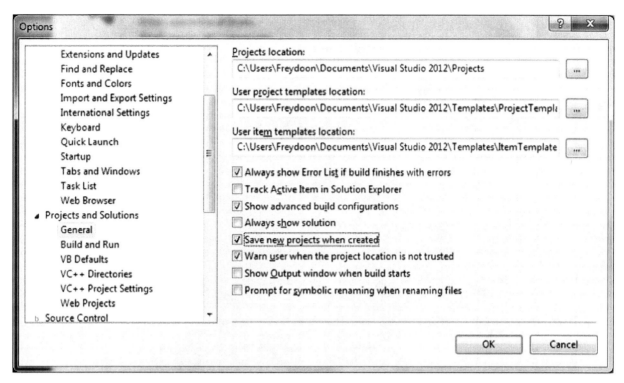

Figure 1.2 *Setting New Project Options*

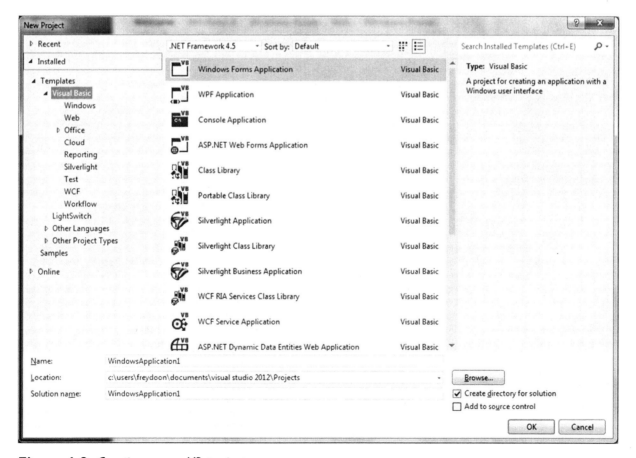

Figure 1.3 *Creating a new VB project*

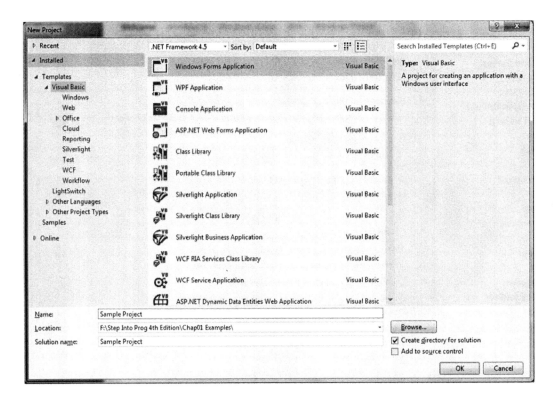

Figure 1.4 *Name of the New Project "Sample Project", and its location on the disk are specified*

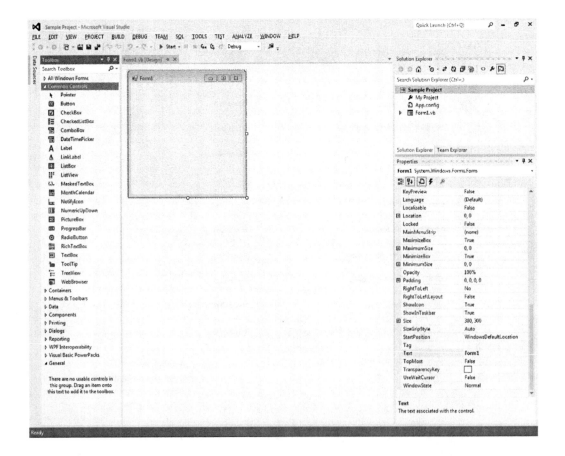

Figure 1.5 *The IDE of the Sample Project*

Getting Familiar with the IDE

Have a look at the different parts of the Integrated Development Environment (IDE) in VB .NET shown in figure 1.5. All the tools required for creating, compiling, running, and debugging a VB .NET project are included in this environment.

The IDE consists of several Windows, which provide important tools for designing a Visual Basic .NET project. If you cannot see one of the windows on your computer, choose View from the menu bar and select the desired window to have it displayed. Each window has a pushpin icon on its top right corner. To keep the window open, the pushpin should point downwards.

Toolbox Window

The Toolbox Window shown in Figure 1.6, contains all the built-in controls for VB .NET that can be used when designing the Graphical User Interface. Each control is a class that represents a group of objects that have similar properties and behaviors (methods). To place a control on the Form, you may double click on the control in the Toolbox, or left click on the control in the Toolbox to select it, then left click on the desired location on the Form; holding the left mouse button, drag the mouse to adjust the size. Once the control is placed on the Form, it is referred to as an object. An object has properties that describe the object and methods that perform an action for the object. After the object is placed on the Form, it can be resized or moved to the desired location on the Form. To re-size, delete, or move an object, left click on the object. Square handles appear around of the selected object. Then use the left mouse button, to re-size, delete or move the object on the Form.

Solution Explorer Window

The Solution Explorer Window is where all the files and folders comprising the solution and projects are listed. It appears on the top-right corner of the IDE. This window has been revised in 2012 version and has a different look. Figure 1.7 is an example of a Solution Explorer Window.

Properties Window

The Properties Window displays the properties of the selected object on the Form. To select an object on the Form simply left click on the object, square handles will appear around it. To deselect an object, click on another object or an empty space on the Form. Each object has many properties with default

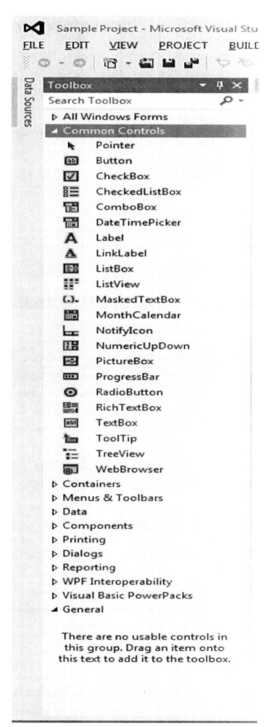

Figure 1.6 *The ToolBox Window*

View Code Window

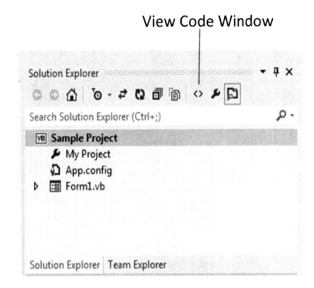

Figure 1.7 *The Solution Explorer Window*

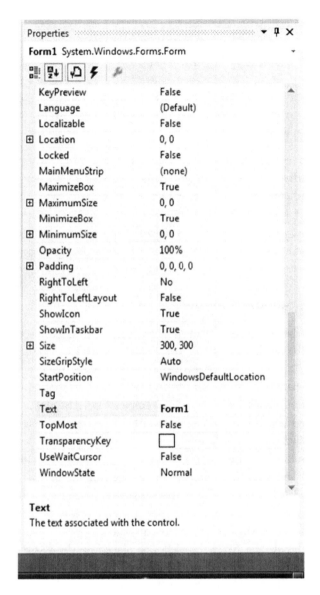

Figure 1.8 *The Properties Window*

values. The left column in the Properties Window is the name of the property, and the right column is the value of that property. You may change the property value of an object in the Properties Window during the design time, or inside the Code Window so that the changes will take place during the program execution. Figure 1.8 shows the Properties Window of a Form object.

Form Designer Window

The Form Designer Window is where the Graphical User Interface of the project is designed. Figure 1.9 shows a sample Form with few objects placed on it. Notice that the Form itself is an object with properties and methods.

Tool Bar and Menu Bar

The menu bar consists of useful options, such as saving, compiling and running the project. The tool bar is right under the menu bar. It consists of short cuts to the most common items on the menu bar. See Figure 1.10.

ToolTip, is one of the useful features in Visual Studio .NET. To learn more about any item on the design window, hover the mouse over the item for few seconds. A small box pops up with a brief description of that item.

Code Window

The Code Window is where the Visual Basic program statements are written. Figure 1.11, shows a sample Code Window.

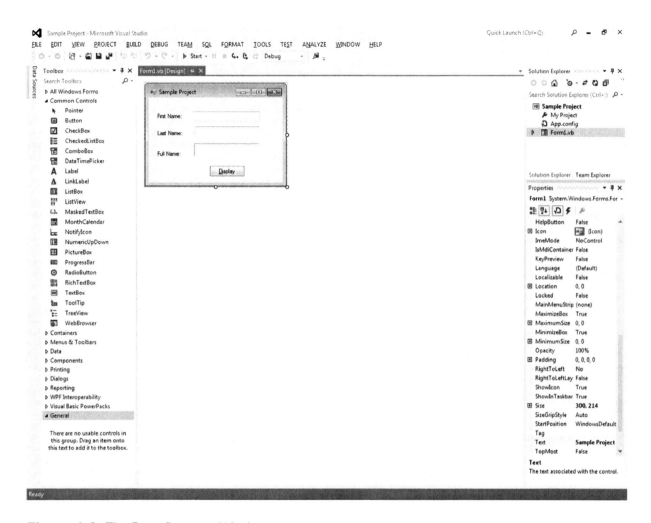

Figure 1.9 *The Form Designer Window*

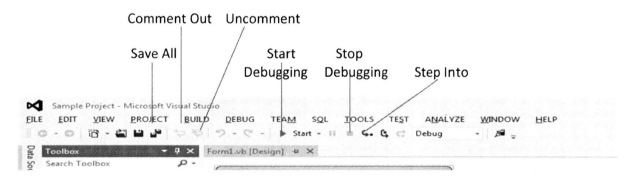

Figure 1.10 *The Standard ToolBar icons in Visual Studio*

To view the Code Window , select Form1.vb in the Solution Explorer Window and expand the tool bar at the top of this window. The Show Code icon, < > will appear on the tool bar. Click on < > to view the code window.

1.4 Three Basic Controls

The Toolbox Window contains many useful controls under the Common Controls for designing the GUI in a VB .NET project. In this section we cover the three major controls that are used in almost every Windows Application. These controls are the TextBox, the Label and the Button.

TextBox Control

The TextBox control is mainly used to get the user's input during the program execution. The user can enter the required data in the TextBox at runtime. After placing a TextBox on the Form, one may resize it and place it in an appropriate location on the Form. The TextBox object can only be resized horizontally.

Label Control

The Label control has two applications. 1) It is used to display program's output. 2) It can be placed next to another object to describe its purpose, in that case a Label is referred to as a descriptive Label. Once a label is placed on the Form, it can be resized only after its AutoSize property is changed to False. Unlike the TextBox

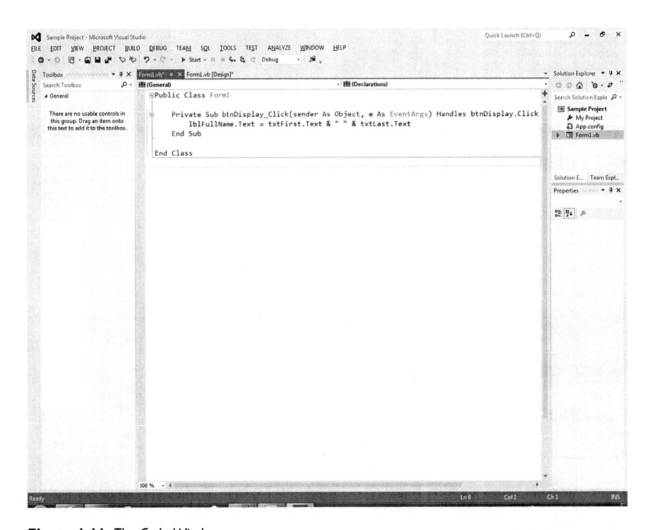

Figure 1.11 *The Code Window*

control, the user cannot enter any data in the Label control at runtime. When a Label object is used to display program's output, change the BorderStyle property of the Label to Fixed 3D so that it will be visible on the Form.

Button Control

The Button control is used to initiate an action. Normally, the user clicks on a Button during the program execution to get something processed. For example, to have the program calculate something and display the output, place a Button on the Form and write the code in the Click Event procedure of the Button to perform that calculation and display the result.

 Once a control is placed on the Form, it is referred to as an object.

1.5 Important Properties

Each object placed on the Form has many properties that can be viewed in the Properties Window as shown in Figure 1.8. All the properties have default values which you do not need to change. However, there are a few important properties that you have to modify in order to add to the clarity of the code and to make the program more meaningful.

Name Property

The Name property is the most important property of an object. To use an object in the code, you must use its name. It is important to give meaningful names to the objects so that it is easy to comprehend the purpose of each object placed on the Form. The most common naming standard for objects is Hungarian Notation, and the authors encourage you to follow this standard when naming the objects. To see the prefixes for naming objects, refer to the Appendix on Coding Standards.

Naming Convention for Objects

Start the object's name with a three-letter abbreviation (lower case) available for each control, followed by a meaningful name that describes the purpose of the object. If the name consists of several words, start each word with a capital letter and continue with lower case letters. This is known as Camel Case. Remember you may only use letters, digits, and underscores in the name. We suggest that you do not use any numbers or underscores when naming objects in VB .NET so as not to confuse the person reading the code. The three-letter prefixes for the controls we have discussed so far are as follows:

Control	3-Letter Prefix	Examples
TextBox	txt	txtName
Label	lbl	lblOutput
Button	btn	btnComputeAverage
Form	frm	frmMain

 You do not have to name descriptive Labels. They are usually not used in the code.

Text Property

The Text property is a property that is applicable to many controls. The Text property of an object is the text displayed on the object. The Text property can be changed at design time in the Properties Window, or at runtime in the code.

 Do not confuse the Text property with the Name property.

 IntelliSense, is a feature of Visual Studio that provides help and some automatic code completion when you are typing the code. For instance, as soon as you type the name of an object followed by a dot (e.g., txtName.), it displays all the properties and methods of the TextBox.

1.6 Accessing the Property of an Object in the Code

Once a control is placed on the Form, its properties may be accessed in the Properties Window. To access the property of an object in the code, use the dot operator (.).

```
ObjectName.PropertyName
```

For example, to access the Text property of a Label:

```
lblOutput.Text
```

Assignment Operator (=)

The assignment operator can be used to change the property of an object in the code. Its general syntax is as follows:

```
ObjectName.PropertyName = NewValue
```

The assignment operator works from right to left, which means that the value on the right-hand side is assigned to the target on the left-hand side of the operator.

Ex1: To display the name of your instructor in the Label, lblInstructor, change the Text property of the Label:

```
lblInstructor.Text = "Good Instructor"
```

Ex2: To clear the content of the TextBox, txtInput, change the Text property of the TextBox to the empty string:

```
txtInput.Text = ""
```

String Literal/Constant

A string literal is a group of characters, enclosed between double quotes that is treated as one piece of data, e.g., "Hello World!", "Visual Basic .NET is cool!" and "22".

The Text property of an object is of String data type. Data types are discussed in Chapter 2.

My First VB Program

Design a VB .NET project to display "Hello World!" when the user starts the program and clicks on a Button.

To design any program you should go through the following steps, which are collectively referred to as the "Program Development Life Cycle" (PDLC).

1.7 Program Development Life Cycle (PDLC)

Step 1: Analyze the problem and identify:

- Input requirements

- Output requirements

- Processing requirements

Step 2: Based on step 1, design the GUI. Place a suitable control for each input requirement, a Label or another control for the output requirement, and a Button for each of the processing needs of the program.

Step 3: Identify which objects should respond to which events.

Step 4: For each identified event, an event procedure must be written. Design the algorithm (step by step instruction) for each event procedure to produce the desired outcome.

Step 5: Translate each algorithm to VB .NET code in the corresponding event procedures.

Step 6: Debug and test the program. To debug a program you have to compile and execute the program. There are few ways to do so in the VB .NET environment. One way is to click on Debug on the menu bar, and select Start Debugging from the submenu. This will compile and run the program. The other way is to press the F5 key on the keyboard. Finally the easiest way is to click on the Start Debugging icon on the tool bar as shown in Figure 1.12. To test the program, you have to enter sample data at execution time, and see if the produced output matches the expected result.

Figure 1.12 *Start Arrow*

Follow the PDLC for This Example

Step 1.   Analyze the problem:
  a.   Input requirements: None
  b.   Output requirements: "Hello World!" should be displayed
  c.   Processing requirements: Display "Hello World!"

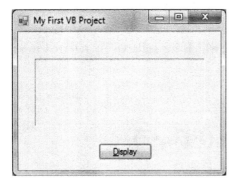

Figure 1.13 *GUI of my first project*

Step 2.   Based on analysis, the GUI design should contain one Label, and one Button as shown in Figure 1.13. Assign the following values to the properties listed below at design time:

Control	Property	Value
Button	Name	btnDisplay
Button	Text	Display
Label	Name	lblOutput
Label	AutoSize	False
Label	BorderStyle	Fixed 3D
Label	TextAlign	Middle Center
Label	Text	Nothing
Label	Font	Size = 10, Font = Courier New
Form	Text	My First VB Project

Step 3.   Only the Button should respond to the click event.

Step 4.   Develop the solution for the click event procedure of the Button. The solution is to display "Hello World!" in the Label. To display anything in a Label, one has to assign the string to the Text property of the Label.

Step 5.   Translate the algorithm developed in part 4 to VB .NET code. The code should be written in the Click event procedure of the Button. To write the code, double click on the Button; the code window will be opened with the first line and last line of the event procedure created for you.

```
Public Class Form1

  'Click event procedure of the Display button:

    Private Sub btnDisplay_Click(sender As Object, e As EventArgs)
        Handles btnDisplay.Click
      lblOutput.Text = "Hello World!"
    End Sub
End Class
```

Step 6.   Debug and test the program.

Start the program execution and click on the Button to see program's output. Figure 1.14 shows the screen capture at runtime, when the Button is clicked.

As a programmer, you should first get rid of all the syntax errors (errors that occur during the build or compilation) in the program. The Visual Studio .NET editor underlines all the syntax errors with a squiggly line which makes them easy to detect and fix. After fixing all the syntax errors, you should run the program with different sets of data and make sure that it produces the expected output. This example does not require any input data and always generates the same output. To learn more about debugging, refer to the Appendix-A on Debugging.

Figure 1.14 *Screen capture at runtime*

 To create the skeleton of the click event procedure of a Button, simply double-click on the Button on the Form. This will create the first line and the last line of the procedure in the Code Window. Write the code between these two lines.

1.8 What Is an Event?

As mentioned in the introduction, VB .NET is an event-driven language. At execution time, the user interacts with the program through the GUI objects by entering data in boxes, clicking on a Button, and so on. The project responds to some of the user interactions. An event is something that happens during the program execution by user initiation or by the system. Examples of an event are clicking on a Button, entering text in a TextBox, placing the cursor on an object, holding the mouse over an object, passage of the time, and many more. An object may respond to zero, one, or more events. The programmer decides which events require a response from the program, and writes code for those event procedures.

Depending on the application, the programmer decides which events the program should respond to. This is step 3 in PDLC. For example, an application may require the back color of a TextBox to change every time the cursor is placed on the TextBox. The event that the TextBox should respond to is the Enter event, therefore the programmer should write the code in the Enter event procedure of the TextBox in order to change the BackColor property of the TextBox during the program execution. The same way, if the program has to do some calculation when a Button is clicked, the proper code must be written in the Click event procedure of that Button.

 An event is something that happens during the program execution. Examples: clicking on a Button, entering text in a TextBox, or hovering the mouse over an object.

1.9 String Concatenation &, +

Two strings can be connected to form a longer string. This is called string concatenation. Both & and + operators can be used for concatenation. However, + operator is also used for adding two numbers. The authors recommend using one of these operators throughout the program for concatenation purposes. For example, "Purdue " & "University" results in "Purdue University".

As another example, assume that the user enters the first name "James" and last name "Bond" in txtFirstName and txtLastName. To create the full name, concatenate the Text entered in two TextBoxes:

```
txtFirstName.Text & txtLastName.Text
```

The result will be "JamesBond" with no space between the first name and last name. To fix this problem, concatenate a single space between the first name and last name:

```
txtFirstName.Text & " " & txtLastName.Text
```

The line shown above is not a complete VB .NET statement, but it can be part of a statement. For example, if you wish to display the full name in the Label, lblFullName, you have to assign the concatenated strings to the Text Property of the Label:

```
lblFullName.Text = txtFirstName.Text & " " & txtLastName.Text
```

Inserting a Line Feed in the Output String

Visual Basic provides several keywords that can be used to insert a line feed in a string. These keywords are vbLf, vbCrLf, and vbNewLine. To insert a line feed in a string, simply concatenate any of these keywords with the string at the desired point. The TextBox only accepts vbCrLf, or vbNewLine as a line feed. For example, to display "Hello" and "How are you?" on two separate lines in lblOutput, concatenate vbLf where you wish to insert the line break.

```
lblOutput.Text = "Hello," & vbLf & "How are you?"
```

How to Add Additional Text to the Existing Text in a Label

Suppose you wish to add more text to the content of the text displayed in a Label. To do this, you have to concatenate the Text property of the Label with additional text, and store the result back in the Text property of the Label. For example, to add a greeting message to the name displayed in the Label, lblFullName:

```
lblFullName.Text = lblFullName.Text & vbLf & "Good day!"
```

How to Clear the Text Displayed in a Textbox or Label

To clear the text displayed in a TextBox or in a Label, assign an empty string to the Text property of the object, as shown in the following examples. An empty string is two double quotes with no character in between, i.e.,"".

```
lblOutput.Text = ""
```

```
txtFirstName.Text = ""
```

1.10 Methods

Focus Method

Focus is a method of the TextBox and some other controls. It can be used to place the cursor in a TextBox at runtime. Like accessing a property of an object, the dot operator (.) can be used to access a method of an object. For example, the following statement will place the focus to the TextBox named txtFirstName:

```
txtFirstName.Focus()
```

Pay attention to () after the name of the method. It indicates that a method does something for the object. Some methods require input information to be passed to them inside the parenthesis.

 The Focus method may trigger security alerts during the program execution if the program resides on a network drive.

Clear Method

Clear is another method of the TextBox control. It clears the text displayed in the TextBox. For example, to clear the text displayed in a TextBox named txtFirstName:

```
txtFirstName.Clear()
```

Another way of clearing the TextBox is:

```
txtFirstName.Text = ""
```

Close Method

Close is a method of the Form object. It closes the Form by unloading it from the memory. If there is only one Form in the project, closing the form ends the program execution. The code for closing the Form is typically written in the click event procedure of a Button. In this statement, Me refers to the current Form.

```
Me.Close()
```

 The Label control does not have a Clear method. To clear the text displayed in a Label, simply assign "" to its Text property, e.g., lblx.Text = ""

Putting It All Together

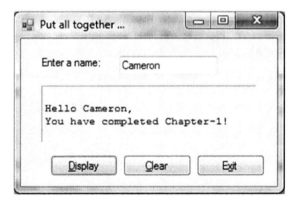

Figure 1.15 *Screen capture at runtime*

Let us expand "My first VB program" by adding a TextBox named txtName, a Button named btnClear, and another Button named btnExit. The user should enter a name in the TextBox and click on the Display Button to have a greeting message displayed to that name. The Clear Button should clear the TextBox, the Label, and place the focus to txtName. The Exit Button should end the program execution. To enhance the program output, change the font size of the output Label back to 8, and change its TextAlign property to MiddleLeft. Figure 1.15 shows the screen capture at runtime when a name is entered and the Display Button is clicked.

```
Public Class Form1

    Private Sub btnDisplay_Click(sender As Object, e As EventArgs)
                                    Handles btnDisplay.Click
        lblOutput.Text = "Hello" & txtName.Text & "," & vbLf
                        & "You have completed Chapter-1!"
    End Sub

    Private Sub btnClear_Click(sender As Object, e As EventArgs)
                                    Handles btnClear.Click
        txtName.Text = ""
        lblOutput.Text = ""
        txtName.Focus()
    End Sub
```

```
    Private Sub btnExit_Click(sender As Object, e As EventArgs)
                                            Handles btnExit.Click
        Me.Close()
    End Sub

End Class
```

The following is the Code Window for this example, with three click event procedures.

Setting the Tab Order of the Objects

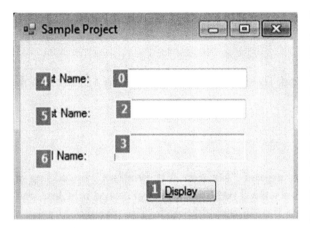

Figure 1.16 *View > Tab Orders selected*

Figure 1.17 *Tab orders are reset*

The Tab Order is the order in which the objects on the Form get focus when the user presses the Tab key on the keyboard. This order is determined by the object's TabIndex property which is a number that is assigned to each object on the Form. Setting proper Tab Order is very important in VB .NET projects. During the program execution, the user often presses the Tab key to move on to the next object on the Form. It can be very discomforting and user unfriendly to see the cursor move around as the Tab key is pressed. The first control placed on the Form has TabIndex of zero, the second one has TabIndex of one, and so on. If an application has many controls that are added in mixed order, the TabIndex of the objects should be reset. To change the Tab Order of the objects, select each object on the Form and change its TabIndex property to the desired number. The object with TabIndex 0 will get the focus when the program execution begins, and the Form gets loaded on the screen.

In a VB .NET project, you can also view and modify the TabIndex of the objects, by selecting view > Tab Order from the menu bar. Figure 1.16 shows a sample GUI with initial Tab Orders. You may change the TabIndex property, by clicking on the objects in the order you want them to get the focus. Figure 1.17, shows the GUI after the TabIndices are set to proper order. To remove the displayed indices on the objects, once again choose View > Tab Order from the menu bar. For more information about setting the Tab Order, refer to the Appendix-B on GUI Standards.

Review Questions:

1. Which control can be used to get user's input, e.g., name?
2. Which property of the Label control should be changed in order to allow resizing the Label object?

3. What are the applications of the Label control?

4. How do you clear the text displayed in a Label at runtime (VB .NET code)?

5. How do you clear the text displayed in a TextBox at runtime? Is there more than one way?

6. How do you set the cursor to a TextBox object at runtime (VB .NET code)?

7. What is an event? Give an example.

8. How can you make the VB .NET program respond to an event?

9. What is the Tab Order of the objects placed on the Form?

10. How can you change the Tab Order of an object?

PROGRAMMING CHALLENGES

1. Design a VB .NET project that allows the user to enter a name in a TextBox, and click on a Button to have a greeting message displayed to the name entered by the user on the Form.

2. Design a VB .NET project that allows the user to enter a name in the provided TextBox, and displays hello to the name entered in one of 3 languages, (e.g., English, French, and Spanish) depending on the user's preference.

    Hint: Go through the PDLC in order to design an appropriate GUI for this project.

3. Design a VB .NET project that can be used to display an acceptance letter or a rejection letter to the name entered in a TextBox. The user should enter a name in the input TextBox, and click on one of the Buttons to get the letter displayed to the user. Come up with your own message for acceptance and rejection.

4. Design a VB .NET project in which the user enters his / her first name, last name, address, phone # in provided TexBoxes, and click on a Button to get all the information displayed in a neat style in an output Label. Provide another Button that displays a generic email; myemail@ hotmail.com at the end of the displayed information in the Label. Provide a Button to clear the input and output boxes, and a Button to end the program execution.

5. Design a VB .NET project that displays the colors of traffic lights on the Form. Below is a screen capture for this project, when the Slow Button is clicked at runtime. As it is shown below, the word Slow is displayed in the middle of the Label, and the back color of the Label is changed to yellow. The program should display the corresponding colors and words when the user clicks on Stop and Go Buttons.

    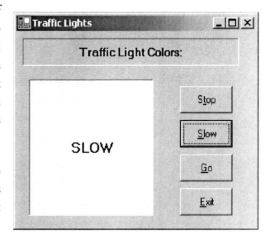

    Hint: To change the back color of a Label, one has to change its BackColor property. There is a Color class readily available in VB .NET that can be used as follows: lblColor.BackColor = Color.Yellow

CHAPTER 2

Variables

LEARNING OBJECTIVES

After the completion of Chapter 2, students should be able to:

- ❏ Define a variable
- ❏ Understand and list the naming conventions for variables
- ❏ List the various data types in VB .NET
- ❏ Understand the appropriate usage of the various data types
- ❏ Understand scope of a variable
- ❏ Understand lifetime of a variable
- ❏ Use comments in a program

2.1 Introduction

When writing a computer program, developers often need to get the user's input as numeric values (e.g., test scores) or textual data (e.g., student's name), store them for later use either in calculations or for simple display purpose. Furthermore, values calculated (e.g., Average score) may be stored for later use in other calculations (e.g., standard deviation), therefore a program needs a way to remember the intermediate results. A lot of times you need to change the data values during the program execution, for example the name entered for a student or the test score changes as the user enters different student's data in the program. Programming languages use variables to store and remember data values in a program.

2.2 Data Values in a Program

Generally, there are two kinds of data values used in a program: numeric data and string data. So far, we have only worked with strings (textual data). Stream of characters enclosed between double quotes is called a string literal or a string constant. Numeric data is also divided into two main categories: whole numbers (e.g., 12, −100, etc.) and real numbers (e.g., 2.55, −10.90, etc.). Furthermore, the data values used in a program can either remain constant or change (assume different values) during the program execution. Examples of constant values are: "Hello", 3.14, 1000. To use data values that can change during the program execution, we must use variables.

2.3 Variables

Variables are placeholders in the computer's random access memory, RAM. You may think of variable as a location in computer's RAM, with a designated name, where you can store a value that can be used or changed during the execution of the program. Variables can be used to store the data entered by the user during the program execution, the intermediate results in calculations and a program's output. To use a variable, you should introduce it to a program. Generally, in VB .NET the keyword Dim is used to define variables. Some find it easy to remember Dim by saying Data In Memory; although, that is not really the correct acronym, the correct acronym is Dimension, because by defining a variable several bytes get allocated in computer's memory. Below is the definition of a variable that can be used to store a course name.

```
Dim Course As String
```

Each variable is identified by the following characteristics:

Name

A name must be given to the variable at definition time. This name will be tied to the location in the computer's RAM that is allocated for the variable. In other words, variable's name is like the address of the variable in computer's RAM; it provides an easy access to that location in the memory. Instead of referring to the variable by its physical address in the memory, we use the variable's name to access the variable, to store a value in the variable, or to change the value stored in the variable.

Data Type

A data type must be specified for the variable at definition time. The data type specifies the kind of data values and the range of values that can be stored in the variable. Most programming languages have specific data types for different data values used in a program. Some examples in Visual Basic are String, Integer and Double. String data type is used for storing textual values, while Integer and Double are data types used for storing numeric values.

Value

Once a variable is defined, a value can be stored in that location in the memory. In Visual Basic, variables are initialized to a default value at definition time. For instance, the default value stored in variables of string data type is nothing and that stored in numeric variables is zero. The value stored in a variable can be changed as many times as needed by using the assignment operator (=).

Scope

Scope of a variable is the segment of code in which the variable is accessible. For example, a variable that is declared within an event procedure, has local scope, and is accessible only inside that procedure. A variable can be defined to make it accessible in all event procedures within a form (module scope) or across several forms (project or global scope). This concept is explained further in next chapter(s).

Lifetime

Lifetime of a variable is the time period during the program execution in which the variable lives in the computer's RAM. Some variables, like module scope variables, stay in the RAM throughout the program execution, and others, like local variables, exist only during the execution of the procedure in which they are declared. This is an important concept that will be discussed in Chapter-3.

2.4 Variable Naming Rules

Certain rules must be followed when naming variables in VB .NET:

- A variable name can only contain letters, digits, and underscores (_)

- A variable name cannot begin with a digit

- A variable name cannot be a VB .NET keyword such as Dim

- A variable name cannot have any spaces or special characters

Keywords | Reserved Words

Keywords, are special words in a programming language that are reserved for a specific purpose. Examples are: Dim, Private, End, etc. These words can be used only for designated purposes.

Suggested Naming Standards

It is very important to give meaningful names to variables, indicating the purpose of the variable in the program. Giving proper names to variables improves the clarity and readability of the program. Every corporation or industry has its own standards, that you need to learn and follow if you decide to work in that organization. In this book, we use the camel case naming standard for variables. For further suggested coding standards, refer to Appendix C on coding standards.

The following is a list of authors' suggested standards when naming a variable in Visual Basic:

- Start each variable name with a capital letter and continue with lower case letters

- If the name consists of several words, begin each word with a capital letter and continue with lower case letters

Legal Variable Names:

Count, Name, LastName, Ticket_Price, Code012, a, ThisIsLongButLegalVariableName

Illegal Variable Names:

2WayTraffic, Sub, First Name

2.5 Data Types in Visual Basic .NET

There are two main data values used in a computer program: numeric data and textual data. VB .NET has intrinsic (built-in) data types for representing different kinds of data values.

String Data Type

Any human readable data value that is not a number can generally be considered as textual data or string data such as a student's name, ID, address and so on. The Text property of the Label control and TextBox control are of String type. String data type is used to declare variables to store textual data, such as a name and address.

String Literals | Constants

A stream of characters enclosed between double quotes forms a string literal or string constant. We have already used string literals in our examples, i.e. "Hello World!".

You may also create an empty string "", by placing two double quotes next to each other. Empty string is used in the code to clear the text displayed in a Label or a TextBox.

String Variables

Sometimes, you need to use a string whose value may change during the program execution. For example, to process the students in a class, a string variable is needed to store different names during the program execution. To do this, declare a variable of type String to reserve a place in the computer's memory to store different names during the program execution. Notice that a variable can hold only one value at a time; therefore, when storing another value in the variable, it overwrites the existing value in the variable. Below is an example of defining a variable named StudentName that can hold a student's name.

```
Dim StudentName As String

StudentName = "George Goodall"
```

Data Types for Numeric Data

Numbers are divided into two main categories: whole numbers and real numbers. Whole numbers are the numbers without a fraction part, and real numbers are the ones with a fraction part.

Numeric Literals | Constants

Numeric literals or constants may contain only digits, a decimal point, a negative sign on the left-hand side for negative numbers, or a positive sign on the left-hand side which is hardly ever used. A numeric literal may not contain a dollar sign, a comma, or other characters.

```
Numeric literals:   22,   17,   -0.005,    340000
```

Data Types for Whole Numbers

Table 2.1 illustrates the data types for whole numbers, along with the number of bytes they allocate in computer's RAM and the range of values they can store. A byte is regarded as the standard unit of measurement for computer's memory. A single byte is made out of eight bits. A megabyte is made up of one million bytes which in turn is eight million bits. A gigabyte is made up of one billion bytes or eight billion bits.

Data Types for Real Numbers

Table 2.2 shows the data types that are used for real numbers in VB .NET.

Since the Decimal data type has no rounding problem, use it for storing monetary data values, e.g., price, salary and so on.

Other Data Types in VB .NET

Other data types in VB .NET are shown in Table 2.3.

TABLE 2.1 Whole number data types

Data Type Name	Bytes in Memory	Range
Byte	1	0 to 255
Short	2	−32,768 to 32,767
Integer	4	−2,147,483,648 to −2,147,483,647
Long	8	Larger whole numbers

TABLE 2.2 Real number data types

Data Type Name	Bytes in Memory	Accuracy
Decimal	16	Fixed point with 28 digits of accuracy
Single	4	Floating point with 6 digits of accuracy
Double	8	Floating point with 14 digits of accuracy

TABLE 2.3 Other data types in VB .NET

Data Type Name	Bytes in Memory	Range
Boolean	2	True, False
Date	8	1/1/0001 to 12/31/9999
Object	4	Any type of data
String	10 + (2 * string length)	0 to approximately two billion Unicode characters

2.6 Deciding Which Data Type to Use

When declaring a variable, you should think about the values it will hold. If the values are nonnumeric and are not used in calculations, the String data type should generally be used. If the values are whole numbers, you should think about the range of values the variable will hold and choose one of the data types for whole numbers. If the values are real numbers, then you should consider the range of values the variable will hold, and based on that, one of the data types for real numbers should be chosen. If the variable should assume only one of the two values to indicate on or off (True or False) the Boolean data type should be chosen. If the value is a date or time, the Date data type should be used. Generally, the rule of thumb is to choose the most appropriate data type that will consume the least amount of memory. The table below shows several examples on how to choose a proper data type for different data values.

TABLE 2.4 Example on choosing proper data types

Data Value	What kind of data?	Range of data	Data Type
Student name	Textual	—	String
Age	Whole number	1–120	Byte, Short, or Integer
Department name	Textual	—	String
Salary	Numeric	>0	Decimal
Power on/off	On–Off	True / False	Boolean
Class Average	Real number	0.0–100.0	Single | Double
Number of books	Whole number	>0	Short | Integer
Pounds of fruit	Real number	>0	Single | Double
Dean's List?	Yes/No	True/False	Boolean

2.7 Variable Definition

To define a variable inside a procedure, use the keyword Dim, which stands for Dimension.

```
Dim VariableName As DataType
```

Let us define a variable to store the pounds of apples purchased. Since pounds of fruit may be a number with fraction part, we will use one of the data types available for real numbers.

```
Dim PoundsOfApples As Single
```

We recommend that you define all the variables within a procedure at the beginning of the procedure, instead of in between program statements.

Multiple Declarations

Several variables of the same data type can be defined in a single statement. This is a feature available in VB .NET. However, the authors suggest that you do not define more than one variable in one statement. It is much easier to debug and read through the code when variables are declared separately.

How a Declaration Works

Let us define a variable to store the number of tickets purchased. Since the number of tickets is a whole number, the data type of such variable should be among the data types available for whole numbers:

```
Dim NumberOfTickets As Integer
```

With this declaration, the compiler requests enough space in the computer's RAM for an Integer, i.e. 4 bytes. The memory manager allocates 4 bytes in the RAM, and gives the name NumberOfTickets to that location in memory. Visual Basic compiler assigns the default value of 0 to that memory location. Later on, this name can be used to access and use the variable.

2.8 Assignment Operator (=)

The assignment operator is used to assign a value to a variable. Remember we also used this operator to assign values to the properties of objects in the code. It is important to understand that the assignment operator works from right to left. In other words, the value on the right-hand side of the operator gets assigned to the target on the left-hand side. Therefore, the left-hand side of this operator must be a location in the computer's memory, such as a variable name or an object's property where a value can be stored. For example, the following statement assigns 6 to the variable declared for the number of tickets:

```
NumberOfTickets = 6
```

It is also possible to store a value in a variable at declaration time. For example, the following statement defines a variable and initializes it to some value:

```
Dim PricePerPound As Decimal = 1.49
```

The process of storing a value in a variable for the first time is referred to as initialization. Initialization can be done at the time of definition or afterwards. Visual Basic initializes all the variables to their default value at the time of definition. This feature does not exist in some of the programming languages. In Visual Basic, the default value for numeric variables is 0, for Boolean variables is False, and for string variables is Nothing. Note that Nothing is different from an empty string "".

Default Values:

The default value stored in numeric variables is 0.

The default value stored in Boolean variables is False.

The default value stored in String variables is Nothing, which is different from an empty string.

2.9 Scope of a Variable

Scope of a variable is the segment of code in which the variable can be used. A variable's scope depends on where in the program the variable is declared. A variable that is declared inside a procedure has local scope and is only accessible within that procedure; variables as such are called local variables. We will look at module scope and project scope variables in later chapters.

2.10 Lifetime of a Variable

Lifetime of a variable is the duration within the program execution in which the variable holds its allocated memory, hence the value stored in it. Local variables have a short lifetime. They come to existence when the execution of the procedure in which they are declared begins. They are destroyed when the execution of that procedure ends. Later on, we will see that the module scope and project scope variables have a longer lifetime and live throughout the program execution.

EXAMPLE 1

Design a VB .NET project that displays an invitation message to the name entered on the Form. The user should enter a name in the TextBox, and click on a Button to view the invitation message on the Form.

Let Us Follow the PDLC to Design This Application

Step 1: ANALYZE THE PROBLEM:

- Input needs: The user should enter a name

- Output needs: The output is an invitation message

- Processing need: The program should display a message to the user

Step 2: DESIGN THE GUI: Based on analysis, there should be a TextBox, txtName to enter a name; a Label, lblMessage to show the program's output, and a Button, btnDisplay to do the processing. There should also be a descriptive Label in front of txtName with the Text property: "Enter a Name:". Figure 2.1 shows the GUI for this example.

Step 3: DETERMINE THE EVENTS THAT THE PROGRAM SHOULD RESPOND TO: Only the Button responds to the click event.

Step 4: DESIGN THE ALGORITHM (LOGICAL SOLUTION) TO DISPLAY THE INVITATION:

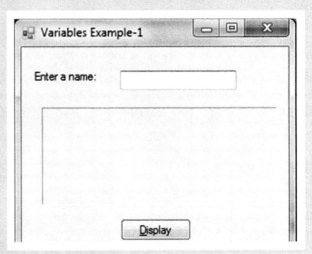

Figure 2.1 *GUI for Example-1*

The pseudocode for the click event procedure of btnDisplay:

1. Define a variable to store the input name.

2. Define variables to store the invitation message and the entire message.

3. Store the entered name in the variable.

4. Store the invitation message in the corresponding variable.

5. Concatenate the name and the invitation message variables, store the result in the output variable.

6. Display the output variable in the output Label.

Step 5: TRANSLATE THE LOGIC TO VB .NET CODE:

```
Private Sub btnDisplay_Click(sender As Object, e As EventArgs)
        Handles btnDisplay.Click
    Dim Name As String
    Dim Message As String
    Dim Invitation As String

    Name = txtName.Text
    Invitation = "Please come to my graduation party" & vbLf &
        "On: Sunday May 12th" & vbLf &
        "At: Eagles Country Club" & vbLf &
        "Time: 6:00 PM to Midnight" & vbLf &
        "Hope to see you there! "
```

```
        Message = "Dear " & Name & "," & vbLf & Invitation
        lblMessage.Text = Message
    End Sub
```

Step 6: DEBUG AND TEST THE PROGRAM:
After typing the code, debug and test the
program. First you should get rid of the compile errors (that occur during the compilation
of the program). The next step is to run the
program and test it by entering different
names, and see if the program produces the
expected output. Figure 2.2 is the screen capture of the program at runtime.

Figure 2.2 *Screen capture at runtime*

 The solution for Example 1 can be developed without using any variables. However, variables
were used in order to clarify the code.

EXAMPLE 2

Create an application to display the name of the teams in a college football game. Display the name of your favorite team
in the winner Label, and the name of your least favorite team in the other Label. Provide a way in the program to switch the
names of the teams in the Labels.

Let Us Follow the PDLC to Design This Application

Step 1: ANALYZE THE PROBLEM:

- Input needs: None

- Output needs: Name of two teams

- Processing: Swap the team names

Step 2: DESIGN THE GUI: Based on step-1, there should be two Labels to display the teams' names,
and one Button to do the swapping. The teams' names should be entered in the Labels at design
time, and the code in the Button will switch them at runtime. Let us name the Labels lblWinner and
lblLoser. Name the Button btnSwap. Notice that besides the two Labels required for displaying the
teams, there should be two descriptive Labels describing the winner and loser Labels. Figure 2.3 is the
GUI designed for this example.

Step 3: DETERMINE WHICH OBJECTS ON THE FORM SHOULD RESPOND TO EVENTS: Only the Button
should respond to clicking.

Step 4: Design the algorithm (logical solution) for swapping the names:

The pseudocode for the click event procedure of btnSwap:

1. Define a variable of type String.

2. Store the text displayed in lblWinner in the variable.

3. Copy the text displayed in lblLoser into lblWinner.

4. Copy the value stored in the variable into lblLoser.

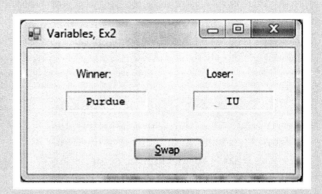

Figure 2.3 *Screen capture at runtime*

Step 5: Translate the algorithm designed in step 4 to VB .NET statements:

```
Private Sub btnSwap_Click(sender As Object, e As EventArgs)
          Handles btnSwap.Click
    Dim Team As String
    Team = lblWinner.Text
    lblWinner.Text = lblLoser.Text
    lblLoser.Text = Team
End Sub
```

Step 6: Debug and test the program: At design time, enter Purdue in lblWinner and IU in lblLoser. Click on the Button and see if they are swapped as expected.

 The solution for Example 2 cannot be developed without using a variable.

EXERCISE

Create Example-02 on a computer and see how it works.

2.11 Comments

Comments are very important when writing computer programs. Comments are entirely ignored by the compiler, and are merely used for documentation purposes. A programmer should always include his/her name, the date the program was developed, and a brief explanation of the program at the beginning of the Code Window. One may also add comments between the lines to explain the purpose of each section. A comment may also be added at the end of a statement to clarify the logic. In VB .NET, a comment starts with a single quote. Any text to the right of the single quote on the line will be considered as comment, therefore, ignored by the compiler. In the Code Window of a VB .NET project, the comments appear in a different color. In this book, the comments are shown in a different font. For example, the following lines are comments:

```
'This document was developed by Guity Ravai.
'Today's date is August 27, 2013.
```

A comment may also be added at the end of a statement to explain its purpose:

```
Dim N As Integer
    'To store number of items
```

Review Questions:

1. What is a variable?

2. What is the keyword for defining variables inside a procedure?

3. Which data type is recommended for holding monetary values?

4. What is the smallest data type (bytes in memory) in VB .NET?

5. Name three data types used for storing real numbers.

6. Define a variable to store the population of Lafayette, Indiana. Initialize the variable to 125,000.

7. Define a variable to store your name. Store your full name in it.

8. Define a variable to store your home address. Store your address in it.

9. Is this a valid name for a variable?

```
Dim It_IS_Snowing_Out_There As Boolean
```

PROGRAMMING CHALLENGES

1.   Design a VB .NET Project that allows the user enter a name, address and phone number in the provided TextBoxes, and click on a Button to have all the input data displayed in the output Label on separate lines. Go though the PDLC explained in this chapter to design an appropriate GUI for this project. In the code for the click event procedure of the display Button, declare three variables to store the entered data, and use those variables to display the program's output.

     Hint: Notice that using variables adds to clarity of the code.

2.   Design a VB .NET project similar to example-2 in this chapter with some changes. In this project, place three Labels on the Form and display the names of the three Olympic medalists at design time. Place a descriptive Label next to each Label, with the text: Gold, Silver, and Bronze. Add three Buttons to the GUI. One Button should swap the names of the gold and silver winners. The other Button should swap the names of silver and bronze winners. The third Button should swap the names of the gold and bronze winners. Go through the PDLC to complete this project.

     Hint: Notice that using variables in this project is a must.

CHAPTER 3

Arithmetic Operators

LEARNING OBJECTIVES

After completing Chapter 3, students should be able to:

☐ Understand and use arithmetic operators in VB .NET

☐ Understand and interpret arithmetic expressions

☐ Convert string data to their numeric equivalents

☐ Convert numeric data to string form

☐ Format numeric output

☐ Understand the functionality of Option Explicit and Option Strict

☐ Use named constants

☐ Understand the application of module scope identifiers

3.1 Introduction

So far we have worked with string data in a program, such as getting the name entered in a TextBox, or displaying a message in a Label and so on. However, we often have to work with numeric data. Some numeric data such as age, zip code, or a flight number need not necessarily be used in calculation. But more often than not, numeric data is used in some sort of computation. For example, a program that computes the monthly payment on a loan uses the loan amount, the duration of the loan, and the interest rate applied to the loan in a formula. A program as such can compute the monthly payment on a loan as its output. Likewise, a program that computes the total electrical resistance in a parallel circuit with a few resistors uses the resistance value of the resistors in the appropriate formula. Programming languages have a list of arithmetic operators that make such computations possible. Although all the languages have similar operators for the four basic arithmetic operators, i.e., addition, subtraction, division, and multiplication; each language has a set of other arithmetic operators that must be studied when programming in that language.

TABLE 3.1 VB .NET Arithmetic Operators

OPERATOR	MEANING	EXAMPLE
^	Power	2 ^ 5 results in 32
*	Multiplication	2 * 90 results in 180
/	Real Division	15 / 4 results in 3.75
\	Integer Division	10 \ 3 results in 3
Mod	Modulus	25 Mod 8 results in 1
+	Addition	12 + 6 results in 18
−	Subtraction	33 − 50 results in −17

3.2 Arithmetic Operators in VB .NET

There are seven arithmetic operators in VB .NET. All these operators are considered binary operators, meaning they operate on two numbers, which in turn are referred to as Operands. Table 3.1 depicts the arithmetic operators in VB .NET in the order of their precedence. The operators' precedence rules will be discussed in the next section.

Let us have a closer look at these operators.

Power Operator (^)

VB .NET has a power operator (^) that operates on two operands. The operand on the left-hand side of the operator gets raised to the power of the operand on the right-hand side. For example, 5 ^ 2 raises 5 to the power of 2. Notice that the first operand (the one on the left-hand side) can be a whole number or a real number (a number with a fraction part). The second operand may be positive, or negative, a whole number, or a real number. For example, to take the square root of a number, one has to raise it to the power of 1/2 or 0.5. In this case, the operand on the left-hand side cannot be a negative number. For example, 9 ^ 0.5 computes the square root of 9 which is 3. Note that, since ^ has higher precedence than unary minus, −10 ^ 2 will result in −100.

 VB .NET has a Math class with many useful methods, such as pow, sqrt, and etc. Math.Pow (2, 10) will compute 2 ^ 10.

Multiplication Operator (*)

The asterisk (*) is the operator for multiplying two numbers. The result of multiplication is the product of the two operands. The result may be a whole number or a real number, depending on the data type of the operands. For example 1.2 * 3 results in 3.6.

Real Division (/)

The forward slash is the operator for dividing two numbers. It divides the operand on the left-hand side of the operator by the one on the right-hand side. The result of this operation is a real number of type Double. For example, 17/2 results in 8.5. Each operand may be a whole number or a real number.

Integer Division (\)

The backward slash is the operator for Integer Division. The outcome of an Integer Division is the number of times the Operand on the right-hand side goes into the operand on the left-hand side. For example, 22\5 results in 4, because 4 times 5 is equal to 20. The outcome of an Integer Division is always a whole number. If either or both of the operands were real numbers, VB .NET implicitly rounds them up or down to whole numbers, and then performs the Integer Division. To round a real number means replacing the number with the closest Integer value. For example, 2.67 gets rounded up to 3, whereas 2.25 gets rounded down to 2.

Modulus Operator (Mod)

The Mod Operator (pronounced modulus) is used to find the remainder of a division. The outcome of the Mod is the remainder of dividing the operand on the left-hand side of the operator by the one on the right-hand side. For example, 14 Mod 5 results in 4 which is the remainder of dividing 14 by 5 and 12.25 Mod 3 results in 0.25. One has to realize that, if the operand on the left-hand side is smaller than the one on the right, the remainder of division will be the operand on the left-hand side. For example, 4 Mod 10 will result in 4. The reason is that there is 0 times 10 in 4, therefore the remainder of this division will be 4.

Addition and Subtraction Operators (+, −)

The addition and subtraction operators are self-explanatory. The result of adding or subtracting two numbers may be a whole number or a real number. For example, 4 + 6 results in 10, 12 − 16 results in −4, and 2.50 + 5.25 results in 7.75.

3.3 Arithmetic Expression

Any meaningful combination of numeric literals (e.g. 5), variables, and arithmetic operators form an arithmetic expression. An arithmetic expression is not a complete statement; therefore, it has to be part of a statement. The following are the examples of arithmetic expressions. Assume that variable Data has been declared as Integer with some value stored in it.

```
3 + 4 * 120
Data * 0.06 + 100
(12 - Data)\8 + 10
```

Precedence Rules

An arithmetic expression is evaluated from left to right, respecting the precedence order of operators, similar to algebraic expressions. Arithmetic operators have different levels of precedence. To evaluate an arithmetic expression, one has to know the precedence order of the operators. The precedence order indicates which operator takes precedence over the other operators in the order of operations. The operator with higher precedence operates before the operator with lower precedence. For example, 3 + 4 * 2 gets evaluated from left to right, but since * has higher precedence than +, multiplication takes place before addition, hence this expression evaluates to 11. If there are several operators with the same precedence in an expression, then VB .NET evaluates the expression from left to right. The only exception to the precedence rules are parentheses. Any expression enclosed in parentheses must be evaluated first. If there are several levels of nested parentheses, the expression in the innermost parentheses must be evaluated before the ones surrounding it, and so on.

The precedence of arithmetic operators in VB .NET from highest to lowest:

1. Expression enclosed in parentheses ( ) has the highest precedence.

2. Power operator: ^

3. Unary minus: −

4. Multiplication and real division: *, /

5. Integer division: \

6. Modulus operator: Mod

7. Addition and subtraction: +, −

8. Assignment operator = has lower precedence than all the arithmetic operators.

There is one operator in the box above that was not explained among the arithmetic operators; that is the unary minus, which operates on one operand only. It can be placed on the left-hand side of a numeric literal (e.g. −6) or on the left-hand side of a numeric variable (e.g. −N), to change the sign of the number. It is interesting to note that the unary minus has lower precedence than the power operator; therefore, −5 ^ 2 results in −25, however (−5) ^ 2 results in 25 because parenthesis has higher precedence than power operator.

Let us evaluate the following arithmetic expressions respecting the precedence of operators:

Ex1: `3 + 5 * 3`

The expression is evaluated from left to right. But since multiplication has precedence over addition, addition has to wait.

    3 + 15

Now the addition is performed, and the result will be:

    18

Ex2: `12 * 4 Mod 10`

Again the expression is evaluated from left to right. Since * has higher precedence to Mod, it is performed first:

    48 Mod 10

Now the Mod operator takes effect, resulting in 8:

    8

Ex3: `-10 ^ 2 + 1`

Looking at the expression from left to right, you see that ^ has the highest precedence. Therefore, 10^2 is evaluated first:

    -100 + 1

Between the unary minus and addition, the unary minus has higher precedence, therefore 1 will be added to negative 100:

    -99

Ex4: `4.90 + 8 - 1.5`

Since addition and subtraction have the same precedence, the expression is evaluated from the left, by first adding 4.90 to 8:

`12.90 - 1.5`

Finally, 1.5 is subtracted from 12.90 resulting in 11.40:

`11.40`

3.4 Arithmetic in VB .NET

An arithmetic expression is not a complete statement; it has to be part of a program statement in order to be executed. For example, one may store the result of an arithmetic expression in a variable. The following assignment statement stores the outcome of an arithmetic expression, which is 5.80, in variable Result.

```
Dim Result As Double
Result = (12 + 2.5) * 4 / 10
```

Lvalue and Rvalue

It is very important to understand the way the computer views a variable when the variable name appears on the left-hand side or on the right-hand side of an assignment operator.

Lvalue

When a variable's name appears on the left-hand side of an assignment operator, it represents an Lvalue or a location in the computer's random access memory (RAM). In other words, the Lvalue, is an address in the computer's memory, where a value of proper data type can be stored. In the example below, variable Count is declared as Integer and is initialized to some value. Notice that in the assignment statement, the variable's name appears on the left-hand side of the assignment operator; hence it represents a location in the computer's RAM where a value can be stored:

```
Dim Count As Integer
Count = 20
```

 There should always be an lValue, or a variable name on the left-hand side of an assignment operator.

 A constant value cannot appear on the left-hand side of an assignment operator, or it results in a Build error, ex: 20 = Count is wrong and cannot be compiled.

Rvalue

When the variable's name appears on the right-hand side of an assignment operator, it represents an Rvalue, also known as the register value. It provides the value stored in the variable in the computer's RAM. Consider the following example, in which the variable Count from the previous example is being used.

```
Dim Price As Decimal
Price = Count * 1.5
```

In this example, the variable Count on the right-hand side of the assignment operator represents the value stored in Count, which is 20. It is multiplied by 1.5 and the result 30 is stored in variable Price. Note that, since variable Price is on the left-hand side of the assignment operator, it represents an Lvalue or an address in the computer's RAM.

Changing the Value Stored in a Variable

To change the value stored in a variable, it should appear on the left-hand side of the assignment operator. On the right-hand side of the assignment operator, there can be a constant value, another variable or an expression. Consider the variable Count declared in the previous example. To increment the value stored in Count by 1, one has to write the following statement:

```
Count = Count + 1
```

It is important *not* to think of this statement as an algebraic equation. The variable Count on the right-hand side of the assignment operator represents the value stored in Count, which is 20. Since the assignment operator has lower precedence than the addition operator, the value in Count is added to 1 and then the sum of 21 is assigned to variable Count on the left-hand side of the assignment operator. Therefore, after this statement, the value stored in Count will be changed to 21. You can use the same way to increment, decrement, multiply, or divide a variable by any value. For example, the following statement subtracts 5 from variable Count, changing the value stored in Count to 16.

```
Count = Count - 5
```

What Happens When Operands Are of Different Data Types?

The result of an arithmetic expression will be of the data type that is more precise or that consumes more bytes in the memory. For example, if you are adding an Integer and a Short, the result will be an Integer, because Integer data type allocates more bytes than Short in the computer's RAM. Multiplying variables of types Decimal and Integer will result in Decimal, because Decimal can store digits after the decimal point and is more precise. VB .NET does what is referred to as implicit-type conversion when assigning a data value of smaller (number of bytes) data type to a wider data type and vice versa. Implicit conversion is performed internally by VB .NET. Consider the following examples:

```
Dim Result As Double
Result = 500                  '500 is converted to Double and stored in Result
Dim Count As Integer
Count = 10 / 3                '3.33333 is rounded down to 3 and stored in Count.

Dim N As Integer = 12.78 '12.78 is rounded up to 13 and stored in N
```

3.5 Combined Assignment Operators

Combined assignment operators can be used when the variable's name appears on both sides of the assignment operator. This syntax is also available in other languages such as C and C++. The combined assignment operators exist for all the arithmetic operators: +=, −=, *=, /=, \=, Mod=, ^=. For example, consider the variable Number declared below. All the statements may be written using the combined assignment operators:

```
Dim Number As Integer
Number = 5
```

`Number = Number + 2`	*Can be written as:*	`Number += 2`
`Number = Number - 6`	*Can be written as:*	`Number -= 6`
`Number = Number ^ 3`	*Can be written as:*	`Number ^= 3`
`Number = Number * (12\5)`	*Can be written as:*	`Number *= 12\5`

Note that the combined assignment operator applies to string concatenation as well. For example the following statement:

```
lblShow.Text = lblShow.Text & vbLf & " More text"
```

can be written as:

```
lblShow.Text &= vbLf & " More text"
```

Option Explicit On

Option Explicit means that every variable must be declared before it can be used in the program. In VB .NET, Option Explicit is always *on* by default.

Option Strict On

Option Strict enforces the type compatibility when storing data in a variable, meaning the data value on the right-hand side of the assignment operator must be of the same data type as the variable on the left-hand side. One may turn this option on by typing Option Strict On at the beginning of the code window before the Form's generated code. Option Strict checks for the type compatibility and does not allow implicit type conversion between different data types.

In the example shown in Figure 3.1 the Option Strict On has been typed at the beginning of the code window, hence the program generates two compile errors. In the first statement, the outcome of 7 ^ 4 is of type Double and cannot be stored in an Integer variable; in the second statement, an Integer variable is being assigned to the Text property of the Label. In both statements, the type mismatch is causing the compile error. To fix these errors, you need to use explicit-type conversion, as shown in Figure 3.2. Notice that one can change the data type of a numeric variable in an expression to another data type, by using one of the conversion functions available in VB. Some of these conversion functions are CInt, CShort, CDbl, CDec, and so on. By removing the Option Strict On, VB .NET does an implicit type conversion and the program generates no errors.

Figure 3.1 *Option Strict On, does not allow implicit type conversions*

Figure 3.2 *Build errors are resolved by using explicit type conversions*

3.6 Explicit-type Conversion

Whether Option Explicit is on or off, it is a good practice to do an explicit type conversion when mixing the numeric data with the string data.

Converting a String to Its Numeric Equivalent

In a VB .NET program, you often need to get the user's input from a TextBox. The data entered in a TextBox at runtime is stored in the Text property of the TextBox; hence, it is of String data type. Even if the data entered in the TextBox is a number, it will be in string form, e.g., "25". To retrieve the numeric data entered in a TextBox, and store it in a numeric variable, you have to convert it from the string form, i.e., "25" to its numeric equivalent, i.e. 25. This is made possible by the Parse method.

Parse ( ) Method

All the numeric data types in VB .NET are classes and they all have a Parse method. The Parse method takes a numeric string as input and changes it into the number of the specified data type. Notice that the Parse method cannot parse a non-numeric string such as *"Bell"* into a number. An attempt to parse such a string to a numeric value will result in a runtime error, which causes the program to halt. This method is useful when converting a numeric string to its numeric equivalent.

Assume that the user enters the number of items purchased in the TextBox, txtItems. The following statement will store the entered data in the Integer variable Count declared below:

```
Dim Count As Integer
Count = Integer.Parse(txtItems.Text)
```

Converting the Numeric Data to String

To display numeric data in a Label, the data has to be stored in the Text property of the Label; therefore, it has to be converted to string form. Every numeric data type has a method called ToString which can be used to convert the numeric data, e.g., 34 to its string equivalent, i.e., "34".

ToString( ) Method

All the numeric data types have the ToString() method. This method converts a numeric data to its string equivalent.

Assume that the monthly payment on a loan has been computed and stored in variable Payment of type Decimal. The following statements display this variable in the Label, lblOutput:

```
Dim Payment As Decimal
Payment = 120.9
lblOutput.Text = Payment.ToString()
```

3.7 Formatting the Numeric Output

ToString() method can be used with or without an input argument. Without an input argument, it converts the numeric data to string form without any changes in the appearance of the data. However, a lot of times programmers want the converted string in a specific format, for example, with no digits after the decimal point, with 4 digits after the decimal point, with currency format and etc. ToString() method accepts a string argument that specifies how the converted string should be formatted. For example, 90.ToString("C") will result in string $90.00. Table 3.2 displays few of these format strings. Assume the following declaration. The value stored in the variable Price can be formatted and displayed as shown in Table 3.2.

```
Dim Price As Decimal = 1200
```

TABLE 3.2 Format strings

FORMAT STRING "?"	EXAMPLE	OUTCOME STRING
C or c	Price Tostring ("c")	$1,200.00
N or n	Price ToString ("n")	1,200.00
Nx or nx	Price ToString ("n3")	1,200.000
P or p, percent	0.05.ToString("P")	5.00 %

3.8 Translating Formulas to VB .NET

Often, you have to use a formula to solve a given problem, such as computing the volume of a sphere, or the monthly payment on a loan. For example, to compute the volume of a sphere with a given radius, you have to use the formula $V = 4/3\pi R^3$. To translate this formula to VB program statement(s), one has to declare variables to store the radius and the volume of the sphere, and then store a value in the radius. Finally, those variables have to be used in the given formula to calculate the volume. In the example below, variables are declared, Radius is initialized to 1, 3.14 is used for pi, and the volume is computed and stored in the variable Volume:

```
Dim Radius As Double
Dim Volume As Double
Radius = 1
Volume = 4/3 * 3.14 * Radius ^ 3
```

As another example, let us look at a generic formula that does some calculation:

$$Z = \frac{(a + b)^{-n}}{b}$$

To translate this formula to VB .NET, one has to declare variables to represent *a, b, n,* and *Z,* and use them in the formula. Since this is a generic formula, variables are declared with generic names that match the ones given in the formula.

```
Dim a As Integer
Dim b As Integer
Dim n As Integer
Dim Z As Double
```

Store some values in *a, b,* and *n,* and use them in the formula. Note that b cannot be 0, otherwise it will result in division by 0.

```
Z = (a + b) ^ -n / b
```

 Additional parentheses may be added to improve the clarity of the operations.

$$Z = ((a + b) \wedge (-n)) / b$$

EXAMPLE 1

Design a VB .NET project to compute the volume of a cylinder. Allow the user to enter values for the radius and height on the Form, and have the program compute and display the volume. The volume of a cylinder is computed by multiplying the area of the base by the height of the cylinder, as given in the following formula:

Volume $= \pi R^2 H$

Where R is the radius of the base, and H is the height.

Let us go through the PDLC (Program Development Life Cycle)

Step 1: ANALYZE THE PROBLEM:

- Input needs: radius and height

- Output needs: calculated volume

- Processing needs: Compute the volume

Step 2: DESIGN THE GUI: Based on step 1, there should be two TextBoxes, to enter input data, one Label to display the volume, and a Button to compute the volume. Let us name the objects as: txtRadius, txtHeight, lblOutput, and btnCompute. Besides these objects, there should be few descriptive Labels to describe other objects. There is no need to name descriptive Labels. Change the Text property of each object to show its purpose on the Form. Figure 3.3 shows the GUI designed for this example.

Step 3: DETERMINE WHICH OBJECTS ON THE FORM SHOULD RESPOND TO EVENTS.

Only the Button should respond to the click event.

Step 4: Design an algorithm (logical solution) for the event procedure. The pseudocode of the click event procedure of btnCompute:

1. Declare variables to store the entered data.

2. Declare a variable to store the output.

3. Store the entered data in variables.

4. Plug in the variables into the formula given for volume, and store the result of calculation in the output variable.

5. Display the computed volume in the Label.

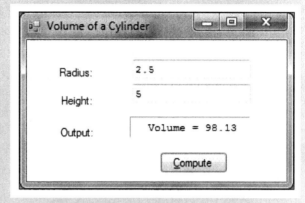

Figure 3.3 *Screen capture at runtime*

Step 5: Translate the algorithm designed in step 4 to VB .NET statements. To allow the user enter data values with a fraction part, declare the variables with Single or Double data type. Below is the translation of the given pseudocode to VB .NET code.

```
Private Sub btnCompute_Click (sender As Object, e As EventArgs)
                                     Handles btnCompute.Click
        Dim Radius As Single
        Dim Height As Single
        Dim Volume As Single
        Radius = Single.Parse(txtRadius.Text)
        Height = Single.Parse(txtHeight.Text)
        Volume = 3.14 * Radius ^ 2 * Height

        lblOutput.Text = " Volume = " & Volume.ToString("N")
End Sub
```

STEP 6: Debug and test the program: The last step of the PDLC entails debugging the program and testing it by entering different input values. There are tools in the VB .NET development environment to compile, run, and debug the program (refer to the Appendix A on Debugging). There are several ways to compile and execute a VB .NET program: by clicking on the F5 key on the keyboard, by clicking on the run icon (>) in the tool bar, or by choosing

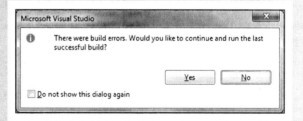

Figure 3.4 *Dialog box shown due to build errors in the program*

Debug on the menu bar, and Start Debugging from the submenu. Any of the ways will compile and execute the program. If there are compile errors in the program, a dialog Form shown in Figure 3.4 gets displayed, informing the user of the compile/build errors. A build error occurs if you violate the rules of the language; for example, if you forget to type the keyword As when declaring a variable, or misspell the name of the object, or do not use Text after the name of the TextBox or Label, the program will result in build errors, and the dialog box in Figure 3.4 will be displayed. Always close this dialog Form by clicking on the No Button. Fix the compile errors and run the program again until there is no build error in the program.

You should always test all the code in the program by entering varying sample inputs, and clicking on each Button. Verify the program's output with the expected results for the sample input data. If the program generates the right answer for all the sample data, one may assume that the program is working properly. Figure 3.3, is the screen capture of this project at runtime.

3.9 Named Constants

Often times, there are constant values in the program that have some significance and should not be changed in the code. For example, tax rate, value of pi = 3.14159, name of the president, and so on, are constant values in a program. It is a good idea to give a name to such constants. For instance, if the tax rate is a fixed value of 0.08, then it can be defined as a named constant with a meaningful name cTaxRate. This in turn will improve the clarity of the code. By giving a name such as cTaxRate, to the tax rate = 0.08, you can use cTaxRate instead of the constant value 0.08 in the code. This will improve the clarity of the code.

Declaration Syntax:

To use a named constant, it has to be declared with the keyword Const, and a value should be assigned to it at the time of declaration. The value assigned to the named constant can not be changed in the program. A named constant may be declared with local scope, module scope or project scope. The general declaration syntax is:

[Private] Const Identifier As DataType = Value

The keyword Private is used when declaring a named constant with module scope. It should be omitted when declaring the constant inside an event procedure with local scope. Module scope identifiers are explained at the end of this chapter. It is recommended to precede the name of a named constant with a lowercase *c*.

Examples:

Declare a local scope named constant to store the sales tax in Indiana.

```
Const cTaxRate As Double = 0.08
```

Declare a module scope named constant to store the name of the university.

```
Private Const cSchool As String = "Purdue University"
```

Advantages of Using Named Constants:

- Adds to the clarity of the program.
- It is easier to maintain and modify the program, if the value of the constant changes in future. For example if the tax rate changes in a few years, you can update the program, just by changing one single line of code.

■ It protects the constant value from accidental changes in the code.

■ It prevents the programmer from using any erroneous value in place of the constant. For example, the programmer might enter 0.6 for tax rate instead of 0.06.

 Tip A named constant is often declared with module scope, making it accessible to the entire code written for the Form.

EXAMPLE 2

Example 1 is a good candidate for using a named constant. Let us declare the value of pi = 3.14159 as a named constant, and use it in the click event procedure of the Button. Below is the entire code window of Example 1, modified using a named constant in the code.

```
Public Class Form1
    Private Const cPI As Double = 3.14159
    Private Sub btnCompute_Click(sender As Object, e As EventArgs)
                                        Handles btnCompute.Click
        Dim Radius As Single
        Dim Height As Single
        Dim Volume As Single
        Radius = Single.Parse(txtRadius.Text)
        Height = Single.Parse(txtHeight.Text)
        Volume = cPI * Radius ^ 2 * Height
        lblOutput.Text = " Volume = " & Volume.ToString("N")
    End Sub
End Class
```

EXAMPLE 3

Develop a VB .NET program to be used as a simple calculator. At execution time, the user enters two numbers (whole or real) in provided TextBoxes, and clicks on the desired operator. The program should then display the result in the output Label, and display the operator in the provided Label.

Let us go through the PDLC (Program Development Life Cycle):

Step 1: ANALYZE THE PROBLEM:

• Input needs: two numbers

• Output needs:

   a. The arithmetic operator used

   b. The result of the operation

• Processing needs: Perform addition, subtraction, multiplication, division, integer division, power, and modulus operations, and clear the input and output boxes, and end the program execution.

Step 2: Design the GUI: Based on step 1, there should be two TextBoxes to enter two numbers. Let us name these objects txtNum1 and txtNum2. Based on the output needs, there should be two Labels. Let us name them lblResult and lblOperator. The processing needs requires nine Buttons, one Button per operation; one button to clear the boxes, and one to end the program execution. The Buttons for arithmetic operators are placed in a GroupBox. GroupBox is one of the controls under the Container Controls that can be used to group together other objects on the form. Name the GroupBox grpOperators and change its Text property to Operators. Let us name these Buttons: btnAdd, btnSubtract, btnProd-

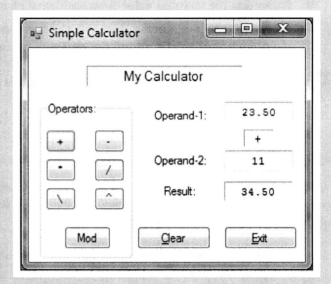

Figure 3.5 *Screen capture adding 2 numbers*

uct, btnDivide, btnIntDivide, btnPower, btnMod, btnClear and btnExit. Change the Text property of these buttons to convey their purpose, i.e. $+, -, *, /, \backslash, ^$, Mod, Clear and Exit. The descriptive Labels are used to describe the purpose of other objects on the Form. There is no need to rename descriptive Labels. The small box between the two TextBoxes is a Label which is used to show the selected operator. Figure 3.5 shows the screen capture at runtime.

Step 3: Determine which objects on the form should respond to events: All the Buttons should respond to their respective Click events. Therefore there should be a click event procedure for each Button placed on the Form.

Step 4: Design the algorithm for each event procedure: You must think about the way the finished project should respond to different events at execution time. Let us develop the algorithm or the step-by-step logic for the click event procedure of btnAdd (+).

Pseudocode of the Click event of btnAdd:

1. Declare variables to store the user's input.

2. Declare a variable to store the sum of two numbers.

3. Store the entered data in declared variables.

4. Display the operator "+" in the Label between the two TextBoxes.

5. Add the two variables and store the result in the output variable.

6. Display the result in the output Label.

The pseudocode for the Click event of other Buttons are very similar to the one provided for btnAdd.

Step 5: Translate the logic into VB .NET: This step of the PDLC entails translating the pseudocode to VB .NET code. The code for each operation should be written in the click event procedure of the corresponding Button. Below is the translation of the pseudocode for the click event of btnAdd.

```
Private Sub btnAdd_Click(sender As Object, e As EventArgs)
                                    Handles btnAdd.Click
        Dim N1 As Double
        Dim N2 As Double
        Dim Sum As Double

        N1 = Double.Parse(txtNum1.Text)
        N2 = Double.Parse(txtNum2.Text)
        Sum = N1 + N2

        lblOperator.Text = "+"
        lblResult.Text = Sum.ToString("N")
End Sub
```

The code for click event of btnClear and btnExit are as follows:

```
Private Sub btnClear_Click(sender As Object, e As EventArgs)
                                    Handles btnClear.Click
        txtNum1.Clear()
        txtNum2.Clear()
        lblOperator.Text = ""
        lblResult.Text = ""
        txtNum1.Focus()
End Sub
Private Sub btnExit_Click(sender As Object, e As EventArgs)
                                    Handles btnExit.Click
        Me.Close()
End Sub
```

Step 6: DEBUG AND TEST THE PROGRAM: The last step of the PDLC entails debugging the program and testing it by entering different input values. One should always test all the code in the program by entering varying sample inputs, and clicking on each Button. Verify the program's output with the expected results for the sample input data. If the program generates the right answer for all the sample data, one may assume that the program is working properly. In this example, beware that if the operator is division, the second operand should not be 0, or the result of division will be infinity.

3.10 Different Types of Errors

It is quite rare for a computer program to compile and run perfectly the first time. There are four kinds of errors that a computer program may encounter: compile error, run time error, logic error and a data entry error.

- Compile error also known as build error or syntax error, takes place at compilation time, when the rules of the language are violated. The compile error is among the easiest errors to fix. In VB .NET, such errors are underlined with blue squiggly lines in the code window. By placing the mouse cursor on the word that is underlined, VB .NET provides descriptive information about the nature of that error. This feature of VB .NET is referred to as IntelliSense technology, which guides the programmer when typing the program statements.

- Runtime error takes place during the program execution when the computer is unable to execute a statement in the program. Examples of such errors are converting a nonnumeric string to a number or using a nonexistent function in the program.

- Logic errors are the result of using the wrong formulas in calculations. Such errors may be difficult to find and fix because VB .NET does not detect logic errors. Having a good set of test data will be helpful in catching these errors.

- Data entry errors are the result of erroneous data entry by the user of the program, such as entering a wrong price, or erroneous student ID. Such errors are also hard to detect. The program should have tight data validations to reduce the chance of these errors.

3.11 Module Scope Identifiers

In chapter 2, we mentioned that, besides name, data type, and value, a variable also has a scope and a lifetime. Scope of a variable is the segment of code in which the variable can be used. A variable's scope depends on where in the program it is declared. A variable that is declared inside a procedure has local scope and is only accessible within that procedure; variables as such are called local variables.

A variable with module scope must be declared outside all the procedures (and functions) at the beginning of the code window, after the first line of the code generated by VB .NET; which is usually: Public Class Form1. The scope of a module scope variable is the entire code window. In other words, a module scope variable is accessible to all the procedures and functions in the code window of the Form. It is recommended that such variables be declared with the keyword Private, and their name be preceded with a lower case *m*. One may also declare a named constant with module scope, in that case the name of the constant is preceded with lower case c. Declaration syntax:

```
Private mTotal As Integer
Private Const cRate As Single = 0.08
```

Lifetime of Module Scope Identifiers

Another important asset of the identifiers with module scope is that their lifetime is the duration of the program execution (only if the program is made up of a single Form). In other words, these variables come to existence when the program execution begins, and get destroyed when the program execution ends. Hence the value stored in these variables remains in the memory throughout the program execution.

Counting and Accumulating

In general you must avoid giving an identifier a scope larger than is needed. The reason is that when a variable is accessible to all the procedures and functions in the program, it is prone to side effects, i.e. unintentional changes may happen to the variable. Nevertheless, there are typical two situations that qualify the declaration of module scope variables.

1. **Reduce redundancy:** If the variable is being used in several procedures, one may declare it with module scope, that way there is no need to declare the variable in every procedure. Example 3 in this chapter is a good candidate for this case. By declaring the variables for input

numbers with module scope, one can remove their declaration from the click event procedures of arithmetic operators and avoid redundant code.

2.   **Counting & Accumulating:** There are times in the program that you need to count the number of items processed, or number of times a button is clicked. This is referred to as counting. You may also want to keep track of the items kept in an inventory by adding the new items bought or subtracting the items sold. This is called accumulating. In either case, you need to declare variables of proper data type, with module scope to do the job. If a variable is used to count or to accumulate, it has to be declared with module scope. That way, due to the life time of module scope variables, the variable will remain in computer's RAM throughout the program execution and its value can be used and changed as needed. To better understand this concept, let us look at some examples.

EXAMPLE 4

Design a VB .NET project to count the number of times a Button is clicked. The GUI includes one Button and one Label to display the output. Let us name these objects btnClick, and lblCount.

The only object that should respond to an event is the Button, so the code should be written in the click event procedure of btnClick. To count the number of times the Button is clicked, an integer variable should be declared and be incremented by 1, in the click event procedure of the Button. The question is where to declare this variable?

■   The wrong approach is to declare the variable with local scope, in the click event procedure of the Button. Each time you click on the Button, the variable gets created, initialized to the default value 0, and incremented by 1. The variable gets destroyed at the end of the procedure. Hence, the program output will always be 1 no matter how many times the Button is clicked. The code and screen capture at runtime are shown below:

```
Public Class Form1
    Private Sub btnClick_Click(sender As Object, e As EventArgs)
                                            Handles btnClick.Click
        Dim Count As Integer     ' Wrong approach
        Count = Count + 1
        lblCount.Text = Count.ToString()
    End Sub
End Class
```

Figure 3.6 *Local scope counter does not work*

- The right approach is to declare the variable with module scope. The module scope variable gets created at the beginning of the program execution, gets initialized to the default value of 0, and remains in memory during the program execution. The variable gets incremented by 1 in the click event procedure of the Button, hence its value changes each time the button is clicked. Below is the code and the screen capture at runtime.

```
Public Class Form1
    Private mCount As Integer      ' Right approach
    Private Sub btnClick_Click(sender As Object, e As EventArgs)
                                    Handles btnClick.Click
        mCount = mCount + 1
        lblCount.Text = mCount.ToString()
    End Sub
End Clas
```

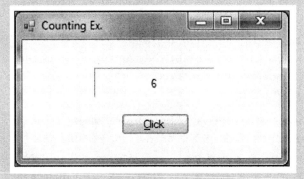

Figure 3.7 *Module scope counter works properly*

EXAMPLE 5

Develop a VB .NET project to process the quiz scores of students in a class. Allow the user to enter one score at a time, followed by a click on a Button to process the score. Also, provide a Button to display the number of scores entered and the class average. Assume that the quiz score is a whole number.

Let us go through the PDLC (Program Development Life Cycle)

Step 1: ANALYZE THE PROBLEM:

- Input needs: quiz score

- Output needs: Number of scores and class average

- Processing needs:

  a. Enter the score

  b. Display the count and the average

Step 2: DESIGN THE GUI: Based on step-1, there should be one TextBox for entering the score and one Label to display the program's output (one might use two Labels as well). The processing needs require two Buttons, one for entering the score in the program, and the other for displaying the results. Let us name these objects as: txtScore, lblOutput, btnEnter and btnDisplay. Change the Text property of the Buttons to display their objectives. Figure 3.8 shows the GUI designed for this example.

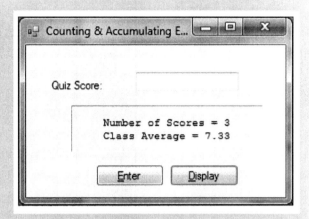

Step 3: DETERMINE WHICH OBJECTS ON THE FORM SHOULD RESPOND TO EVENTS: The two Buttons

Figure 3.8 *Screen capture at runtime*

should respond to the click event; hence we should develop the logic for those event procedures.

Step 4: DESIGN AN ALGORITHM (LOGICAL SOLUTION) FOR EACH EVENT PROCEDURE. One has to think about the task that each Button is responsible for. You need to declare a counter that gets incremented by one, each time a new score is entered by the user. There should also be another variable that adds up the scores. The Enter Button should count the number of quiz scores entered and accumulate total scores. The Display Button should compute the average by dividing the total scores by the number of scores and display the output. These variables are updated in the Enter Button, and used in the Display Button. Therefore, they must be available to both event procedures; hence be declared with module scope. Another reason for declaring these variables with module scope is that if they were declared with local scope inside the Enter Button, the variables would not stay in the memory from one click of the Enter Button to the next.

Pseudocode of btnEnter:

1. Declare a variable to store the input data.

2. Increment the number of scores entered.

3. Add the entered score to the total scores.

4. Clear the TextBox.

5. Set the focus to txtScore, for next data entry.

Pseudocode of btnDisplay:

1. Declare a variable to store the average.

2. Compute the average by dividing the total scores by the number of scores.

3. Display the number of scores in the output Label.

4. Display the computered average on the next line of the output Label.

Step 5: TRANSLATE THE ALGORITHM DESIGNED IN STEP 4 TO VB .NET: One has to declare two variables with module scope: one to count the number of scores entered, and another one to add up the scores.

The Code Window, with pseudocode translated to VB .NET code:

```
Public Class Form1

    Private mCount As Integer
    Private mSum As Integer

    Private Sub btnEnter_Click(sender As Object, e As EventArgs)
                                    Handles btnEnter.Click
        Dim Score As Integer
        Score = Integer.Parse(txtScore.Text)

        mSum = mSum + Score
        mCount = mCount + 1

        txtScore.Clear()
        txtScore.Focus()
    End Sub

    Private Sub btnDisplay_Click(sender As Object, e As ventArgs)
                                    Handles btnDisplay.Click
        Dim Mean As Double
        Mean = mSum / mCount
        lblOutput.Text = "Number of Scores:" & mCount.ToString()
        lblOutput.Text = lblOutput.Text & vbLf & "Class Average:"
                                    & Mean.ToString("N")
    End Sub
End Class
```

Step 6: DEBUG AND TEST THE PROGRAM: Let us enter three quiz scores: 7, 6, and 9 and click on Display button to see the output. The output should be three scores entered and average is 7.33. Figure 3.8, is the screen capture at runtime that verifies this outcome.

Abbreviation Notice: Since the first line of the Click event procedures have similar list of parameters (inside the parentheses), for brevity, we will replace the parameter list with ellipsis (. . .) in the majority of the text from this point on. In other words the first line of the Click event procedure for a Button, e.g., btnExit will be written as follows:

```
Private Sub btnExit_Click (. . .) Handles btnExit.Click
```

Please notice that you should *not* use the same shorthand when typing your code in a VB project, or it will result in a build error.

1. Evaluate the following arithmetic expressions.
   a. 23 * 2 / 5
   b. 3 + 5 * 2
   c. 2 * (12 + 5) Mod 9
   d. 1200 \ 2 ^ 3
   e. −10 ^ 2

2. Translate the following formula to VB .NET code. Assume variables X, Y, and Z are declared as Double, and (.) is used to show multiplication in the formula:

$$Z = \frac{X^2 + XY}{3Y}$$

3. Declare a variable to store the name of a student. In another statement, store the value entered in TextBox, txtName in this variable.

4. Declare a variable to store the number of students in a class. In another statement, store the number entered in the TextBox, txtNumber in this variable.

5. Declare two variables to store the area and the radius of a circle.

6. Store the value entered in txtRadius in the variable declared for radius.

7. Write a statement to compute the area of the circle and store the result in the variable declared for area. The formula is $3.14\ R^2$.

8. Display the area of the circle in lblOutput, with two digits after the decimal point.

PROGRAMMING CHALLENGES

1. Design a VB project to compute and display some statistics about a road trip the user has taken during a long weekend. The user should enter the following information:

   - Distance in miles,

   - The gallons of gas used,

   - Price per gallon,

   - The number of minutes it took to drive to destination.

   When the user clicks on "Compute" Button, the program should compute and display the following information in one large Label, on three separate lines:

   - The mileage (miles per gallon),

   - The average speed on this trip (miles per hour),

   - Cost of gas.

   The program should have Buttons to clear the input and output boxes and to end the program execution.

2. Design a VB project for a local car rental agency that calculates rental charges. The agency charges $40 per day and $0.15 per mile. The user should enter the customer's name, beginning odometer reading, ending odometer reading, and number of days the car was rented. The program should compute the miles the car was driven, and the due amount when the car is returned. The program output should be displayed in one Label, starting with a descriptive message, e.g., "Charger for customer's name:" followed by the miles driven, and the amount in due currency format on separate lines. The program should have a way to clear the I/O boxes and end the program execution. Go through the PDLC to design a suitable GUI for this project. You might consider placing the input boxes in a GroupBox.

3. Design a VB project to study the gas prices on the pump for the past four months in the local market. In this project the user should enter the regular gas prices of the first day of each month in the provided TextBoxes. There should be Buttons to perform the following:

   - Clear the I/O boxes.

   - End the program execution.

   - Display the entered regular gas prices in two columns in the output Label, i.e.,

   - Compute and display the average price of the regular gas in 4 months.

MONTH	PRICE/GALLON
01	$1.98
02	$2.25
03	$2.95
04	$2.09

- Display the regular, super, and premium gas prices at the beginning of each month. Assume that the super gas price is 5 % more than the regular and price of the premium gas is 12 % more than the regular gas.

- Compute the financial index required for projecting the future gas prices. Assume that the financial index is computed using the following formula, where P1 . . .P4 are the regular gas prices at the beginning of the first . . . fourth month.

$$\text{Index} = \frac{P1^2 + P2^2 + P3^2 + P4^2}{P1 \; * \; P2 \; * \; P3 * P4}$$

CHAPTER 4

Selection

After completing Chapter 4, students should be able to:

- ☐ Understand selection
- ☐ Produce pseudocode for selection
- ☐ Interpret flowchart symbols
- ☐ Construct a flowchart to illustrate selection
- ☐ Select and use the correct relational operators
- ☐ Compare String data
- ☐ Construct and interpret the syntax for If / Else statement
- ☐ Construct and interpret the syntax for If / ElseIf statement
- ☐ Construct and combine Nested If statements
- ☐ Construct a Select Case Statement

4.1 Introduction

There are three major coding structures in high-level programming languages: sequential, selection, and repetition. So far, we have learned the sequential structure, in which the program statements are executed one after another in sequence. Sometimes the problem's logic requires that different statement(s) be executed based on the outcome of some decision. The selection structure provides a way for the programmer to write such code. For example, the cost of a movie theater ticket may depend on whether a customer is a student, a senior citizen, or a child. To charge the right ticket price, a decision has to be made based on a customer's status.

To be able to make decisions, a selection structure is used. Using a selection structure is quite simple. People make decisions in their daily lives. For example, if your hair is out of shape, you decide to get a haircut, or if the weather is cold, you wear a jacket, etc. Below are some examples of simple decisions anyone may make in their daily lives:

- If *it is cold outside,* then wear your scarf and coat.

- If *you have free time,* then go out and party, otherwise, stay home and study.

- If *you study hard,* you will ace the exam, otherwise, you will fail.

Note: the conditions that lead to different decisions are italicized.

4.2 Using Pseudocode to Write Selection Structures

Pseudocode, is writing the step-by-step solution in human understandable language, e.g. English, Spanish, Chinese, and etc. Writing pseudocode is a good idea, because it helps the programmer to organize and lay out his or her thoughts and logic for solving a problem. There are two main selection structures that will be discussed in this section: the If statement and the If / Else statement. Below examples are explained in pseudocode.

EXAMPLE 1

Determine the price of the theater ticket for a customer. Assume that students get a 50 % discount. For this example, a one-way decision is used.

Pseudocode:

1. Find out whether the person is a student

2. Find out the regular ticket price

3. If the *person is a student* then
         Apply a 50% discount

4. Display the ticket price.

EXAMPLE 2

Determine the price of the theater ticket based on the time of the show. If the time is before 4:00 pm, the charge is $6.00, if it is 4.00 pm or later, the charge is $8.00. This example requires a two-way decision.

Pseudocode:

1. Find out the time of the show

2. If the *time is less than 4:00 P.M.* then
         The ticket is $6.00
     Otherwise
         The ticket is $8.00

3. Display the ticket price

In the above examples, the conditions are italicized. As shown so far, writing pseudocode is a simple way of explaining the logic of the decision making. Another way of depicting the logic is through the use of flowcharts.

4.3 Using Flowcharts to Depict Selection Structures

Flowcharts have been used for many years by programmers to illustrate a graphical solution to a given problem. As the saying goes, a picture is worth a thousand words. Let us use flowcharts to show the logic of the solution for the two examples given in the previous section.

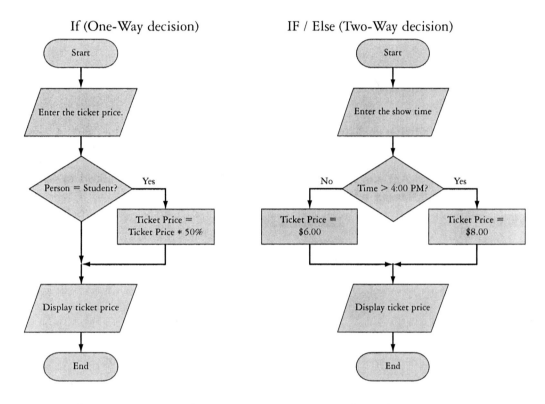

Each shape has a specific purpose in the flowchart diagram. Some of the flowchart shapes and their corresponding   meaning are portrayed in Figure 4.1.

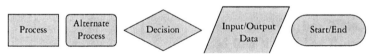

Figure 4.1. *Flowchart symbols*

4.4 Relational Operators

To make a decision in a computer program, two values of similar data types are compared. Relational operators are used to compare two values and form a condition. The relational operators are listed in Table 4.1.

Relational Expression or Condition

A relational expression or a condition is formed by a meaningful combination of literals (constant data values), variables, and relational operators. For example, $5 < 12$, $A < B$, $Age > 21$, $A + B > C$ are all relational expressions, or conditions. The outcome of a relational expression is either yes or no, i.e., the value stored in the variable Age is either greater than 21 or it is not. In programming

TABLE 4.1 Relational Operators

OPERATOR	MEANING
>	Greater than
<	Less than
=	Equal to
<=	Less than or equal to
>=	Greater than or equal to
<>	Not equal to

terms, we say, a condition evaluates to either True (i.e., yes) or False (i.e., no). A condition is not a complete statement, but it can be used in selection structure such as an If / Else statement.

Assume that variables Age and Size are declared as Integers, and are initialized to 40 and 100, respectively. Evaluate the following relational expressions (conditions):

Condition	Resulting Value
Age > 21	True
Age <= 40	True
Age < 40	False
Age >= 30	True
Size = Age	False
"Abe" < "Ali"	True *(Will discuss later)*
Age = "Hello"	Illegal *(Can't compare a number to a string)*

4.5 If Statement (One-Way Decision)

General Syntax and Flowchart

The bold words are the keywords in VB .NET and must be used as specified. The statements enclosed between If and End If will be executed if the condition evaluates to True.

> **If** *condition* **Then**
>
> ...
>
> ...
>
> **End If**

4.6 If / Else Statement (Two-Way Decision)

General Syntax and Flowchart

The bold words are the keywords in VB .NET and must be used as specified. The statement(s) placed under the If keyword will be executed if the condition evaluates to True, otherwise the statement(s) under the Else keyword will be executed.

If *condition* Then

...

Else

...

End If

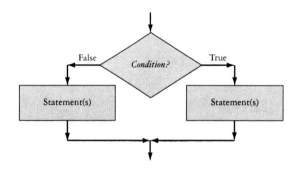

EXAMPLE 1

Let us go back to the first example discussed in Section 4.2, and design a VB .NET project to solve that problem.

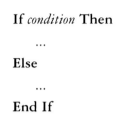

Figure 4.2 *One-Way Decision Ex.*

The Form shown in Figure 4.2 may be used as the graphical user interface (GUI) for this problem. There are two TextBoxes on the Form to get the user's input; a Label to display the program's output and a Button to process the entered input and produce the output. The objects on the Form are named txtCustomer, txtPrice, lblOutput, and btnCalculate. The user should enter the word Student or Non-student in txtCustomer, and the ticket price in txtPrice, and then click on btnCalculate to get the price of the ticket calculated and displayed in the Label. Students get a 50 percent discount. The logic of the solution for determining the price of the ticket has been given using a pseudocode and a flowchart in Sections 4.2 and 4.3. Below is the translation of the logic into VB .NET code:

```
'Click event procedure of the btnCalculate:

Private Sub btnCalculate_Click(...) Handles btnCalculate.Click
    Dim TicketPrice As Decimal

    TicketPrice = Decimal.Parse(txtPrice. Text)
    If txtCustomer.Text = "Student" Then
        TicketPrice = TicketPrice - 0.50 * TicketPrice
    End If

    lblOutput.Text = TicketPrice.ToString("C")
End Sub
```

EXAMPLE 2

Now, let us go back to the second example discussed in Section 4.2, and design a VB .NET project to solve that problem.

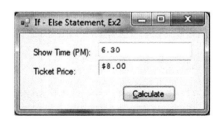

Figure 4.3 *Two-way Decision Ex.*

The Form shown in Figure 4.3 may be used as the GUI for this problem. There is one TextBox on the Form to input the show time, one Label to display the ticket price, and one Button to process the entered input and produce the output. The objects on the Form are named txtTime, lblOutput, and btnCalculate. In this example, the user should enter the time of the show in the txtTime, followed by a click on btnCalculate to have the ticket price calculated and displayed. Tickets are priced based on the time of the show. If the show is before 4:00 p.m. the charge is $6.00, if it is at 4:00 p.m. or later, the charge is $8.00. The logic of the solution for determining the price of the ticket based on time of the show has been given using pseudocode and a flowchart in Sections 4.2 and 4.3. Below is the translation of the logic into VB .NET code:

```
Private Sub btnCalculate_Click(...) Handles btnCalculate.Click
    Dim TicketPrice As Decimal
    Dim ShowTime As Double
    ShowTime = Double.Parse(txtTime.Text)
    If ShowTime >= 4.0 then
        TicketPrice = 8.0
    Else
        TicketPrice = 6.0
    End If

    lblOutput.Text = TicketPrice.ToString("C")
End Sub
```

4.7 Nested If Statement

An If statement can be written in the If part, or Else part of another If statement. In programming terms, this is referred to as nested If statements. There can be several levels of nesting. This might be needed when there is more than one possible situation that needs to be evaluated.

EXAMPLE 3

Consider the following scenario. If a student walks into a campus bar, he or she needs to be 21 in order to get in. If that student is wearing the school team shirt, there is no cover charge, otherwise, there is a five dollars cover charge. Below is the pseudocode used to explain the logic of this decision process.

Pseudo-code:

If the *student is 21 or older*
    If the *student is wearing a school team shirt*
        There is no cover charge
    Otherwise,
        The cover charge is 5 dollars
Otherwise,
Don't allow the student to enter

The GUI presented in Figure 4.4 consists of a TextBox to input student's age, a CheckBox, to check if the student is wearing the school's team shirt, a Label to display the output message, and a Button to process the entered input. The objects on the Form are named as txtAge, chkTeam, lblMessage, and btnProcess. The CheckBox control has a Checked property that is equal to True, if the CheckBox is checked, and False otherwise. CheckBox control is explained in Apendix-D. Below is the translation of the pseudocode to VB .NET code.

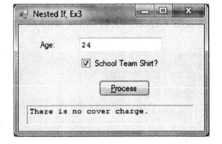

Figure 4.4 *Nested If Statement Ex.*

```
Private Sub btnProcess_Click(...) Handles btnProcess.Click
      Dim Age As Integer

      Age = Integer.Parse(txtAge.Text)

      If Age >= 21 Then
          If chkTeam.Checked = True Then
              lblMessage.Text = "There is no cover charge."
          Else
              lblMessage.Text = "Cover charge is $5.00."
          End If
      Else
          lblMessage.Text = "You cannot enter the bar."
      End If
  End Sub
```

If / ElseIf Statement

The If / ElseIf statement is a special kind of the nested If statement. If the Else part of an If statement is another If statement, we can use the ElseIf keyword which simplifies the indentation of the code, and requires fewer End Ifs.

EXAMPLE 4

Consider the business case of determining the price of a pizza depending on whether the pizza is small, medium, or large. The small pizza is $6.00, the medium pizza is $9.00, and finally, the large pizza is $12.00. Consider the GUI shown in Figure 4.5 with a TextBox named txtPizzaSize, a Label named lblPrice, and a Button named btnCalculate. The user should enter the size of the pizza as Small, Medium, or Large in txtPizzaSize, followed by a click on btnCalculate. Below is the pseudocode of the logic for determining the price of a pizza based on its size.

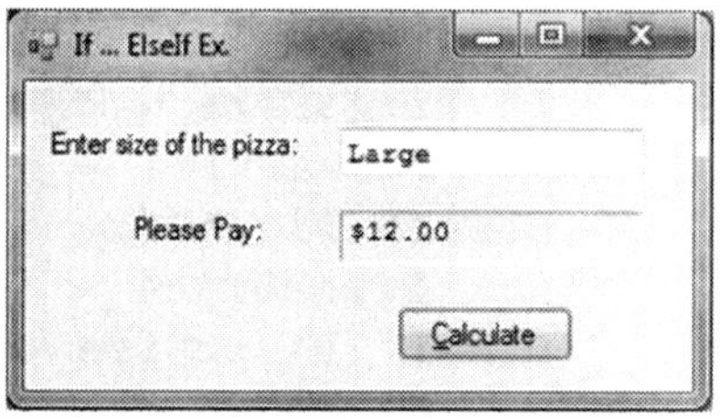

Figure 4.5 *Screen Capture of If - ElseIf Ex.*

Pseudocode

If the *pizza is small* Then
    Price is $6.00
Otherwise, if *the pizza is medium* Then
    Price is $9.00
Otherwise if *the pizza is large* Then
    Price is $12.00

Below is the translation of the pseudocode to VB.NET code:

```
Private Sub btnCalculate_Click(...) Handles btnCalculate.Click
    Dim PizzaPrice As Decimal
    Dim PizzaSize As String

    PizzaSize = txtPizzaSize.Text
    If PizzaSize = "Small" Then
        PizzaPrice = 6
    Else
        If PizzaSize = "Medium" Then
            PizzaPrice = 9
        Else
            If PizzaSize = "Large" Then
                PizzaPrice = 12
            End If

        End If

    End If

    lblPrice.Text = PizzaPrice.ToString("C")
End Sub
```

```
'Revise the code using ElseIf:

Private Sub btnCalculate_Click(...) Handles btnEnter.Click
    Dim PizzaPrice As Decimal
    Dim PizzaSize As String

    PizzaSize = txtPizzaSize.Text

    If PizzaSize = "Small" Then
        PizzaPrice = 6
    ElseIf PizzaSize = "Medium" Then
        PizzaPrice = 9
    ElseIf PizzaSize = "Large" Then
        PizzaPrice = 12
    End If

    lblPrice.Text = PizzaPrice.ToString("C")
End Sub
```

 Only one of the branches in the If / ElseIf statement gets executed. At runtime, each branch is examined starting from the top. Once the condition in a branch evaluates to True, the statements in that branch get executed and the execution moves to End If.

4.8 Select Case Statement

Another important selection structure is the Select Case statement. Any Select Case statement can be written as a nested If statement, but not every nested If statement can be written as a Select Case. You may use a Select Case statement when checking one variable (or an expression) against the different values it may assume.

General Syntax

The bold words are keywords. The Expression on the first line can be a variable or an expression. The Expression is evaluated and compared against values presented in each Case from top to bottom. Once a match is found, the statement(s) in that Case get executed and the execution moves to the last line, End Select. Case Else is optional and takes care of the situation where there is no match found. Notice that you can also check the range of the values if needed.

Select Case (Expression)   'Parentheses () are optional
    Case Value1
        Statement(s)
    Case Value2 **To** Value3   'Checking for a range of values
        Statement(s)
    Case Is < Value4   'If it is less than some value
        Statement(s)
    Case Is > Value5   'If it is greater than some value
        Statement(s)
    Case Else   'Default case
        Statement(s)
End Select

EXAMPLE 5

In this example, the user enters the type of the medal (i.e., Gold, Silver, Bronze) the athlete has won and clicks on the Button to see the placement of the athlete. Assume the GUI presented in Figure 4.6 with a TextBox named txtMedal, a Label named lblMessage, and a Button named btnRanking. Below is the pseudocode of the logic for determining the athlete placement based on the type of medal won.

Figure 4.6 *Screen Capture of Select ... Case Ex.*

Pseudocode

1.   Acquire the athlete's medal type

2.   Examine the medal, if it is
      • *Gold,* display "First Place"
      • *Silver,* display "Second Place"
      • *Bronze,* display "Third Place"
      • *Otherwise,* display "No ranking"

Below is translation of the pseudocode to VB .NET code using Select Case statement:

```
Private Sub btnRanking_Click (...)...
    Dim MedalType As String
    MedalType = txtMedal.Text

    Select Case MedalType
    Case "Gold"
        lblMessage.Text = "First Place"
    Case "Silver"
        lblMessage.Text = "Second Place"
    Case "Bronze"
        lblMessage.Text = "Third Place"
    Case Else
        lblMessage.Text = "Not Ranked!"
    End Select
End Sub
```

 Use Select Case when checking a variable or an expression against different possible values.

EXAMPLE 6

Assume that a pizza place will give a 25 % discount to customers that purchase a large pizza and a large Soda. Also, assume that the pizza place will give a 10 % discount to customers that purchase a medium pizza and a large soda. Furthermore, students get a flat 5 % discount in addition to other discounts on anything that is purchased.

Figure 4.7 *Compute the discounted price*

With this business scenario, we present the GUI in Figure 4.7.

- A TextBox named txtPriceBeforeDiscount, to input the Price.

- A TextBox named txtDrinkSize, to input the drink size.

- A TextBox named txtPizzaSize, to input the pizza size ("Small", "Medium", or "Large")

- A CheckBox named chkStudent, to check if the customer is a student.

- A Label named lblPrice, to display the price after discount.

- A Button named btnCalculate, to do the processing.

Below, is the pseudocode of the solution logic for determining the price of the pizza based on the user's input.

Pseudocode

If the *Customer purchases a large pizza* Then
    If the *customer purchases a large* soda
        Give the customer a 25 percent discount
    End If
End If

If the *Customer purchases a medium pizza* Then
    If the *customer purchases a large soda*
        Give the customer a 10 percent discount
    End If

End If

If the *Customer is a student* Then
      Give the customer an extra 5 percent discount

Translate the pseudocode to the VB .NET code in the Click event procedure of the Button. Notice that the VB code for this problem requires a couple of nested if statements.

```
Private Sub btnCalculate_Click(...) Handles btnCalculate.Click
    'Declaration of variables
    Dim BillablePrice As Decimal
    Dim SodaSize As String
    Dim PizzaSize As String
    'Assign values to the variables from input:
    BillablePrice = Decimal.Parse(txtPriceBeforeDiscount.Text)
    SodaSize = txtDrinkSize.Text
    PizzaSize = txtPizzaSize.Text
    If PizzaSize = "Large" Then
        If SodaSize = "Large" Then
            BillablePrice = BillablePrice - (BillablePrice * 0.25)
        End If
    End If
    If PizzaSize = "Medium" Then
        If SodaSize = "Large" Then
            BillablePrice = BillablePrice - (BillablePrice * 0.1)
        End If
    End If
    If chkStudent.Checked = True Then
            BillablePrice = BillablePrice - (BillablePrice * 0.05)
    End If
    lblPrice.Text = BillablePrice.ToString("C")
End Sub
```

4.9 Comparing String Data

String literals and variables can be compared using relational operators. To understand how the program compares two strings, you need to understand how the characters are stored in the computer's memory. There are many examples where two strings need to be compared. For example, you may want to compare the name of the college entered in a TextBox against "Purdue", or compare an employee name against a specific name, e.g., "Simpson", and so on. We have already used string comparison in a few examples in this chapter.

How Are Characters Stored in the Computer's Memory?

Each character has an internal numeric representation in the computer's memory. The American Standard Code for Information Interchange (ASCII) was developed by a group of experts. ASCII code is the numeric representation for each character (printable/nonprintable) used in most languages. You may find the complete ASCII character set through Internet resources. Below is a subset of the ASCII set.

Character	ASCII Code
A	65
B	66
C	67
F	70
...	...
a	97
b	98
c	99
...	...
0	48
1	49
2	50
...	...
9	57
Space	32
+	43
[	91
&	38
;	59
#	35

Luckily, you do not have to memorize the ASCII code of 255 characters in the character set. All you need to know is that the ASCII code of the letters of alphabet increase in sequence, i.e., the ASCII code of uppercase letters "A" to "Z" are 65, 66, . . . 90, and the ASCII codes of lowercase letters "a" to "z" are 97, 98, . . . 122. The same applies to the ASCII codes of the characters representing the digits "0" to "9" which are 48, 49, . . . 57. ASCII code of the space " " character is 32.

When comparing strings, the ASCII code of the characters forming the strings are compared, starting with the leftmost character. For example, to compare "Sina" and "Brenda," the ASCII codes of "S" and "B" are compared and the outcome is immediately clear that "Sina" is greater than "Brenda," because 83 is bigger than 66. As another example, consider comparing "Ed" and "Edna." The first two characters from the left-hand side are the same, but the first string has fewer characters. In this case, VB .NET pads the shorter string with spaces. Since the ASCII code of the space character is smaller than the ASCII code of any letter, the outcome will be "Ed" is smaller than "Edna". This is similar to the process you follow when searching for a name in the phone book.

Examples on String comparisons:

String Comparison	Result	Comments
"Arian" < "Nita"	True	ASCII code of "A" is less than "N"
"David" <> "david"	True	"D" is not equal to "d"
"Bear" > "Bee"	False	ASCII code of "a" is less than "e"
"Tia" < "Tiamin"	True	Tia is the shorter string
"463-7755" = "463-7465"	False	Some characters are different
"1000" > "70"	False	ASCII code of "1" is smaller than "7"
"Bob" < "nancy"	True	Not a proper comparison. Both strings should be in similar case.
"12**" > "Hello"	False	Meaningless comparison
txtCity.Text = "Rome"	?	Depends on the text entered in txtCity

How to Perform a Case-Insensitive Comparison

Since the ASCII codes for lowercase and uppercase letters are not the same, the condition "Purdue" = "purdue" results in False. To perform a case-insensitive comparison, you need to change all the letters in both strings to either uppercase or lowercase letters, and then perform the comparison. There are two methods of the String class can be used for conversion of cases.

■ **ToUpper()** is a method of the String class. It returns the same string, with all the letters in the string changed to uppercase letters. None of the other characters in the string will change. For example, assume the user has entered "com 101" in txtCourse. The following statements will display the course name in the Label in uppercase letters.

```
Dim Course As String
Course = txtCourse.Text.ToUpper()      'Stores COM 101 in Course
lblShow.Text = Course
```

■ **ToLower()** is a method of the String class. It returns the same string, with all the letters changed to lowercase letters. ToLower does not make any changes to the other characters in the string. For example, the execution of the following statements will display: "good fellow" in the Label.

```
Dim Name As String
Name = "Good Fellow"
lblShow.Text = Name.ToLower()      'Displays "good fellow" in the label
```

Therefor, to compare the school name to "purdue" in a case insensitive manner, one can write the following code:

```
If txtSchool.Text.ToLower() = "purdue" Then
...
```

4.10 String Manipulation Methods

Besides ToUpper and ToLower methods, String class has many useful methods and properties. We discuss some of these methods and properties.

Length Property

The Length property determines the number of characters in a string. It can be used on a string variable, string literal, or the Text property of an object. Let's look at few examples:

■ `"Blue Skies".Length`   'Outcome is 10
■ Assume the following declarations:

```
Dim Fruit As String
Dim Count As Integer
Fruit = "Apple"
  Count = Fruit.Length      'Stores 5 in variable Count
```

■ Assume the user has entered White Horse in the TextBox named txtInput. The following statement will store 11 in the variable:

```
Count = txtInput.Text.Length
```

Note that using the Length property on an uninitialized string will result in runtime error.

Trim() Method

The Trim method can be used to remove the leading and trailing spaces in a string; it produces another string. For example, the following statements will display "Hello Sara!" in the Label:

```
Dim Message As String

Message = " Hello Sara! "

lblOutput.Text = Message.Trim()
```

Note that the method does not change the content of the string variable.

SubString Method

The SubString method can be used to retrieve a sub string within a string. This method takes 2 input arguments. The first argument is the starting position of the substring, and the second argument is the number of characters in the substring.

```
StringName.SubString (position, length)
```

Note that, the position of the first character in a string is 0, the position of the second character in a string is 1, and so on. For example, the following statement will extract and display the string "semi", without the quotes, in the Label.

```
lblOutput.Text = "Yosemite Park".SubString (2, 4)
```

IndexOf Method

The IndexOf method can be used to find the location of a character or a substring within a string. The general syntax is:

```
StringName.IndexOf ("xyz")
```

Note: If the StringName does not contain the substring "xyz", the method returns -1 as outcome. Example:

```
Dim Position As Integer
Position = "Blue Jay".IndexOf(" ")      'Outcome is 4
Position = "Garden".IndexOf("c")        'Outcome is -1
```

Note: The IndexOf method does a case sensitive comparison to find a substring within a string.

 To read more about string methods, refer to MSDN web site at:
http://msdn.microsoft.com/en-us/library/system.string_methods(v=vs.71).aspx

4.11 Logical Operators

Sometimes, the logic of the problem requires combining several conditions and forming a more complex condition. For example, checking whether an employee is a female and her salary is below $45,000, or whether a student is in a certain department, and the GPA is greater than 3.0, and so on. In every programming language, there are logical operators that are used to combine several conditions and come up with a more complex condition.

TABLE 4.2 Logical operators

LOGICAL OPERATOR	MEANING	UNARY/BINARY
And	Logical and	Binary operator*
Or	Logical or	Binary operator*
Not	Logical not	Unary operator**

*A binary operator is an operator that operates on two operands.
**A unary operator is an operator that operates on one operand.

Logical Expression

A logical expression is a meaningful combination of conditions and logical operators, e.g., Score $>= 60$ And GPA $>= 3.0$. A logical expression evaluates to True or False.

Logical And

Logical And operates on two conditions. The outcome of a logical And is True, only if both conditions evaluate to True. The outcome of a logical And is False, if either or both of the conditions evaluate to False.

TABLE 4.3 Logical And Truth Table

CONDITION 1	CONDITION 2	CONDITION 1 *AND* CONDITION 2
True	True	True
True	False	False
False	True	False
False	False	False

For example, let us evaluate the following logical expression. Assume that variables Age and Salary are properly declared and have values 54 and 55,000 stored in them, respectively. To evaluate a logical expression, you have to evaluate each condition, and then apply the logical And, Ex:

```
Age < 50 And Salary > 45000

    False And True

    Outcome: False
```

Logical Or

Logical Or operates on two conditions. The outcome of a logical Or is True, if either one or both conditions evaluate to True. The outcome of a logical Or is False, if both conditions evaluate to False.

TABLE 4.4 Logical Or Truth Table

CONDITION 1	CONDITION 2	CONDITION 1 *OR* CONDITION 2
True	True	True
True	False	True
False	True	True
False	False	False

For example, let us evaluate the following logical expression. Assume that variables Age and GPA are properly declared and have values 20 and 3.75 stored in them, respectively. Again, to evaluate a logical expression, you have to evaluate each condition separately, and then apply the logical Or:

```
Age < 20 Or GPA > 3.5

    False Or True

    Outcome: True
```

Logical Not

Logical Not operates on one condition. It negates the value of the condition.

TABLE 4.5 Logical Not Truth Table

CONDITION	NOT CONDITION
True	False
False	True

For example, to evaluate the following logical expression, one has to evaluate the condition, and then apply the logical Not which negates the value of the condition.

```
Not(12 > 100)

Not False

Outcome: True
```

To evaluate a more complex logical expression such as $120 - N >= 100$ And $M < N$, you have to know the precedence order of the operators, meaning which operator is stronger.

Precedence Rule

The precedence rule is the order in which operators operate in an expression. The operators with higher precedence operate before the others. Anything placed inside parentheses should be evaluated first. The arithmetic operators have the highest precedence, then the relational operators, and then the logical operators. The logical operators have different precedence order amongst themselves; the logical Not has the highest precedence, followed by logical And, and then logical Or. Notice that the assignment operator has the lowest precedence.

Evaluate the following logical expressions. Notice that these expressions are not complete statements, but can be part of another statement such as an If statement. Consider the following declarations:

```
Dim Data As Integer = 200

Dim Student As String = "Hanson"

Dim GPA As Single = 2.85
```

Logical Expression   **Value**

```
a. Student = "Brown" And GPA > 2.0                                  False
   →  False And True
   →  False

b. Data * 10 > 1000 Or Data / 2 < 100                              True
   →  2000 > 1000 or 100 < 100
   →  True Or False
   →  True

c. Not Data < 100                                                  True
   →  Not False
   →  True

d. Student = "Smith" Or Student = "Hanson" And GPA > 3.0           False
   →  False Or True And False
   →  False Or False
   →  False

e. GPA >= 2.5 And GPA <= 3.5                                       True
   →  True And True
   →  True

f. Not GPA > 3.0                                                   True
   →  Not False
   →  True
```

Tip A Logical expression is not a complete VB .NET statement; therefore, it must be used as part of another statement, such as an If statement, for example:

```
If Age < 16 Or Age > 95 Then
    lblOutput.Text = " You may not drive!"
End If
```

Often students factor out the variable used in a logical expression, for example:

`Age < 16 Or > 95.` This is wrong. Both sides of a logical operator must be a complete condition, i.e., `Age < 16 Or Age > 95`

Review Questions:

1. What is the relational operator for equality?

2. What is the relational operator for less than?

3. Write an If statement to check if a test score is greater than 60, in that case display a message. Assume:
   `Dim Score As Integer`

4. Write an If statement to check if an employee's salary is between 4500 and 7000 dollars. Given:
   `Dim Salary As Decimal`
   Assume that some value is stored in Salary.

5. (T/F) Any nested If statement can be written as a Select Case statement.

6. (T/F) Any Select Case statement can be written as a nested If statement.

7. Assume that the program accepts only certain department names, e.g., CGT and MET, entered by the user in txtDepartment. Write an If statement to check if the user has entered a valid department name. The user may enter the department name in mixed-case letters.

PROGRAMMING CHALLENGES

1. Design a VB .NET project that determines the income tax rate based on the employee's salary. The program should let the user enter the salary in a TextBox, followed by a click on a Button. The program should then compute and display the applied tax, based on the following break down. Assume that the tax rate for salaries higher than 350,000 is 30 %, the tax rate for salaries above 200,000, and less than or equal to 35,000 is 25 %, the tax rate for salaries between 100,000 and 200,000 is 15 %, and for anything below 100,000 is 10 %. Use a Select Case statement to determine the applied tax for a given employee.

2. Design a VB .NET project that allows the user to enter the test score of a student and click on a Button, to display the letter grade for the student in the output box. Assume that the test score is a number between 0 and 100, and the cutoff for A, B, ... is based on a straight-line scale, i.e., score of 90 and more is an A, 80 to 90 is a B, etc. The program should also display the number of test scores processed at all times.

3. Design a VB .NET project to compute the weekly pay of the workers in a factory. Assume that each worker is paid the regular hourly pay if he/she works 40 hours or less in a week. For additional hours beyond 40, the worker should be paid an overtime, which is 1.5 times the regular hourly pay. Allow the user to enter the worker's name, hours worked, and hourly wage on the Form, and click on a Button to get the worker's pay displayed in the output box with a descriptive message that includes the name of the worker. The program should also display the number of workers processed and total wages paid.

4. Design a VB .NET project that can be used to do all the arithmetic operations on two real numbers. Allow the user to enter two numbers in TextBoxes, and one of the arithmetic operators; +, -, *, /, \, ^, Mod in a smaller box provided for operator. The user should click on a Button to have the operator perform its job. The logic for this project requires a chain of If / ElseIf statements to determine which operator is entered by the user, and to perform the required operation. Make sure not to perform division by zero if the second number entered is 0, and the operator is division.

CHAPTER 5

Data Validation

LEARNING OBJECTIVES

After completing Chapter 5 students should be able to:

☐ Interpret the importance of data validation

☐ Apply and understand the correct MessageBox characteristics

☐ Construct and perform the following validations

- Existence check
- Type check
- Range check
- Pattern check
- Code check
- Selection check

5.1 Introduction

Our programs thus far have been simple. They did not take into account that the data the end users enter can be erroneous. For example, if a user has to enter a number into a TextBox, and instead enters a name, our program should be able to detect it and let the user know that the entered data is not valid. The process of checking for the incorrect user input is known as data validation. Data validation is an important part of a reliable Windows application.

If you have ever bought anything online, you have experienced data validation. For example, when entering the credit card number, if you entered an invalid number or an invalid expiration date, you would get a message explaining that the credit card is not valid. The program will then give you a chance to enter a valid number. Imagine if the data validation did not exist, then random credit cards could possibly be charged!

5.2 Why Use Data Validation

Data validation is important for many reasons. First, businesses need correct data to perform reliable processing. Data validation allows only the correct data to be stored and processed. Second, without data validation, the program may result in runtime error and crash.

EXAMPLE 1

In this example, the user is expected to enter two real numbers in the provided TextBoxes and click on the Button to get the sum of the two numbers computed and displayed. Refer to figure 5.1. The GUI for this example requires two TextBoxes, an output Label, and a Button. Let's name the objects txtNum1, txtNum2, lblSum, and btnAdd. The GUI is shown in Figure 5.1. Among these objects, only the Button should respond to the click event. Below is the code written for this example without validating the input data.

```
'The click event procedure of the button Add
Private Sub btnAdd_Click(...) Handles btnAdd.Click
  'Declare Variables:
     Dim Num1 As Single
     Dim Num2 As Single
     Dim Sum As Single
  'Assign values to variables:
     Num1 = Single.Parse(txtNum1.Text)  'Explicit Type conversion
     Num2 = Single.Parse(txtNum2.Text)  'Explicit Type conversion
  'Compute the sum:
     Sum = Num1 + Num2
     lblSum.Text = Sum.ToString("N2")  'Display to 2 decimal places
End Sub
```

Suppose, the user starts the program and enters 2.90 for Num1 and 4 for Num2, and clicks on the Add Button. Sum of the two numbers will be computed and displayed, as shown in Figure 5.1. Now let us examine what would happen if the user forgot to enter one of the data values, or entered a non-numeric input in one or both TextBoxes? Assume that the user starts the program and enters "five" for Num1 and "ten" for Num2 as shown in Figure 5.2.

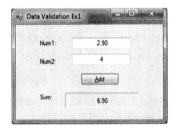

Figure 5.1 *Screen capture with valid data*

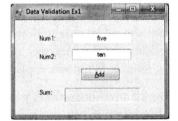

Figure 5.2 *Screen capture with invalid data*

The code remains the same. Now, if the user clicks on the Add button, the program will result in runtime error and program execution will stop, as shown in Figure 5.3. A diagnostic message will be displayed by .NET, pointing to the line that caused the crash, explaining the nature of this error. See Figure 5.4.

Notice that there is an arrow to the left of the line that results in runtime error, and that whole line of code is highlighted. Additionally, the title bar of the diagnostic message displays "*FormatException was*

Figure 5.3 *Program execution stops at highlighted line, due to invalid input entered in txtNum1*

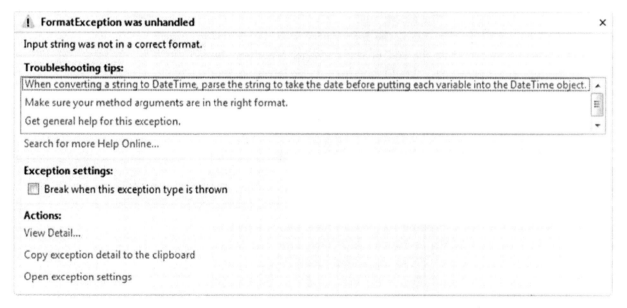

Figure 5.4 *The diagnostic error message displayed by .NET*

unhandled." "Input string was not in correct format." This basically says that you cannot enter a word in place of a number and expect the program to Parse that into a number; in fact, it does not make sense to convert "five" to a number. This is why data validation is important. Therefore, as a rule of thumb, programmers should always validate the input data before assigning them to variables to avoid runtime errors, and to ensure that the correct data gets processed.

5.3 Using a MessageBox

Although you can display a message to the user in an output Label, a MessageBox provides a better way to capture the user's attention. As shown in Figure 5.4, a MessageBox was used by .NET to display the error message to the user. In a VB .NET project, a MessageBox is used to inform the user of something important. MessageBox.Show () displays a dialog Form, which stays on the screen until the user clicks on one of the Buttons on the MessageBox to close it. You may add different Buttons and icons to the MessageBox when displayed; however, there should be a reason for adding additional Buttons or a certain icon to the MessageBox. There are different types of MessageBoxes that are used for various reasons. The two main MessageBoxes that will be discussed in this chapter are: 1) the OK only MessageBox and 2) the Yes/No MessageBox.

The OK only MessageBox is used to inform the user when validating the input. The following code is used to display an OK only MessageBox with all 4 arguments:

```
MessageBox.Show("A custom message.", Application.ProductName,
        MessageBoxButtons.OK, MessageBoxIcon.Information)
```

As shown in Figure 5.5 the first argument within the parentheses is the message to be displayed in the MessageBox upon display. The second argument within the parentheses is the caption shown in the title bar of the MessageBox. We recommend using the default Application name, i.e. Application.ProductName for the caption. ProductName is the name that you give to your VB project when designing the project, ex: DataValidation Ex1. The third argument within the parentheses specifies the Button (s), in this case, it is an OK Button. The fourth argument within the parentheses specifies the icon, which in this case is the Information icon. Furthermore, notice that there is a period at the end of the message. Messages always have to be very descriptive, and should not include exclamation marks. Additionally, some programmers try to use the word "Please" in their message. An application is not supposed to have etiquette! A message is used to simply inform the user of what is wrong so that the user can fix the problem.

Figure 5.5 *OK Only MessageBox*

The other type of MessageBox is a Yes/No MessageBox. A Yes/No MessageBox is used to pose a question to the user. The MessageBox function returns an output, which corresponds to the Button clicked by the user to close the MessageBox. In the case of Yes/No MessageBox, you need to know the user's response to the question, i.e., whether the user has clicked on Button Yes or Button No. Therefore, the output of the function must be examined in an If statement. The output of the MessageBox is DialogResult.Yes, if the user clicks on Button Yes, and DialogResult.No, if the user clicks on Button No. This version of MessageBox is shown in Figure 5.6.

Figure 5.6 *Questioning MessageBox*

For example, the code below is a way to determine whether the user is certain of the input entered:

```
MessageBox.Show("Are you sure?", Application.ProductName,
MessageBoxButtons.YesNo, MessageBoxIcon.Question)
```

After asking a question using a MessageBox, it is important to know user's response to our question. Therefore, this kind of a MessageBox should be used in an If statement, so that you can check user's response:

```
If MessageBox.Show("Are you sure?", Application.ProductName,
        MessageBoxButtons.YesNo, MessageBoxIcon.Question) =
        DialogResult.Yes Then
    ...
Else
    ...
End If
```

Notice in Figure 5.6, the message has a question mark at the end of it rather than a period when compared to Figure 5.5. Also notice that a question mark icon is shown on the MessageBox.

 Using the correct punctuation in a MessageBox is a Windows GUI norm.

5.4 Data Validation

There are different types of data validation. The following list represents the most common data validation techniques used in a program:

1. Existence check

2. Type check

3. Range check

4. Pattern check

5. Code check

6. Checking if a RadioButton (*) is selected

7. Checking if something has been selected from a ComboBox (*)

    (*) These controls are covered under Additional Controls in Appendix D.

Let us explain each of these validations in depth.

Existence Check

In the existence check, the goal is to check whether the user has entered any data in the input object, which is normally a TextBox. For example, to perform an existence check for data entered in the TextBox named txtName, you have to check the Text property of the TextBox, and compare it to an empty string "". If the user has not entered any input, i.e., if input is an empty string, then the condition in the If statement evaluates to true. Consequently, the MessageBox.Show() is executed to informs the user of missing data, the focus is set to txtName, and the user gets a chance to enter a valid data.

```
If txtName.Text = "" Then
    MessageBox.Show("Enter a name.",
        Application.ProductName, MessageBoxButtons.OK,
        MessageBoxIcon.Information)
    txtName.Focus()
Else
    ...
```

Type Check

This kind of validation is used to check the data type of the numeric data entered by the user. Typically, when the program expects a numeric data to be entered, this validation is performed before processing the input data.

There are different ways to check for numeric data. One of the functions provided in VB .NET is the IsNumeric function that checks if the input string is numeric. The other way to perform type check is by using TryParse method. Both of these ways are explained in this section.

IsNumeric Function

IsNumeric is an intrinsic function in VB .NET that takes a String data as an input argument, and checks it for being a numeric string. The function returns a Boolean output. If the input argument is a numeric string, e.g., "45" or "2.90", it returns True, otherwise, if the input argument is not numeric, e.g., "ten" it returns False. In general, you may think of a function as a closed box that takes zero or more inputs, does some processing, and returns a result (output) back:

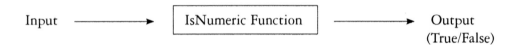

Input ⟶ | IsNumeric Function | ⟶ Output (True/False)

Often, the IsNumeric function is used to check the data entered in a TextBox for being a numeric string. For example, to check the data entered in the TextBox, txtData, for being a number, you may use the IsNumeric function in an If statement. If the output of the function is False, it means the data entered in txtData is not a numeric string; therefore, the user should be informed:

```
If IsNumeric(txtData.Text) = False Then
    MessageBox.Show("Enter numeric value.",
            Application.ProductName, MessageBoxButtons.OK,
            MessageBoxIcon.Information)
    txtData.Focus()
Else
    ...
End If
```

TryParse Method

Sometimes the user has to enter a specific kind of data, e.g., a whole number or a real number as input data. In such cases, the IsNumeric function cannot perform the proper validation and check whether the entered data is a whole number or real number, and this can create a problem. For example, assume that the user has to enter a whole number for the number of tickets purchased in the TextBox, txtTickets. The following segment of code will result in a runtime error if the user enters 2.5 in txtTickets. The error occurs at the line before End If.

```
Dim Tickets As Integer
If IsNumeric(txtTickets.Text) = False Then
    MessageBox.Show("Enter numeric value.",
            Application.ProductName, MessageBoxButtons.OK,
```

```
        MessageBoxIcon.Information)
    txtTickets.Focus()
Else
    Tickets = Integer.Parse(txtTickets.Text)
...
End If
```

The reason is that Integer.Parse cannot parse 2.5 into a whole number. Hence, TryParse method is a good alternative in such cases.

TryParse is a more object-oriented way of the type check. In VB .NET, every numeric data type like Short, Integer, Double, Decimal, and etc. has a TryParse method. Methods are like functions, they take zero or more inputs, perform some processing, and return an output. The TryParse method takes two input arguments, e.g. DataType.TryParse (Argument1, Argument2). The DataType, is the data type we expect the input string to be. Argument1, is the string to be parsed to the desired DataType. Argument2, is a variable of desired data type that will store the parsed value, if the string was of proper data type. TryParse tries to parse the first argument, which is a string, into the specified data type, namely DataType. If the string was of proper data type, it will be parsed and stored in the second argument. Otherwise, the string will not be parsed, and the second argument will not change. The TryParse method returns a Boolean output. It will return True if the parse is successful and will return False if the parse is not successful. Therefore, the output of the TryParse method can be used in an If statement to check if the input string is of desired data type. For example, assume that the user is to enter a whole number in the TextBox, txtTickets, for the number of tickets purchased. We can use the following code to validate the input data:

```
Dim Tickets As Integer
If Integer.TryParse(txtTickets.Text, Tickets) = False Then
    MessageBox.Show("Enter a whole number.",
        Application.ProductName, MessageBoxButtons.OK,
        MessageBoxIcon.Information)
    txtTickets.Focus()
Else
    'Process the valid data stored in variable Tickets
    ...
End If
```

The main difference between the Parse method and TryParse method is that, the TryParse method is used to validate the input string for being of a specified data type; It tries to parse the input string, it may succeed or fail, depending on the string. whereas the Parse method is used to parse a valid string into a number of the specified data type.

Range Check

Sometimes the numeric data should be within a certain range. For example, the range for a test score may be between 0 and 100, the range for an employee's age may be between 21 and 80, and so on. The range check must be done after the type check. One should not attempt to perform the type check and the range check in one If statement. To validate the range of a certain variable, one should use an If statement and logical operators. In the above example, if the user input is valid, the TryParse statement stores the number of tickets purchased in an Integer variable Tickets. Assume that the valid range for the number of tickets one can purchase is 1 to 10, both inclusive. To validate the range of the tickets purchased, we will check whether the value stored in variable Tickets is outside the expected range (i.e., less than 1 or greater than 10), and in that case, inform the user. The following code shows this kind of data validation:

```
If Tickets < 0 Or Tickets > 10 Then
    MessageBox.Show("Valid range is 1 to 10.",
        Application.ProductName, MessageBoxButtons.OK,
        MessageBoxIcon.Information)
    txtTickets.Focus()
Else
 ...
End If
```

In above example, assume that the user enters 5 in txtTickets, but that the range check is not preceded by the type check.

In that case the range check will fail, prompting the user to enter valid input in txtTickets. This is because value stored in variable Tickets is still the default value 0, which falls outside the expected range.

Using logical And instead of logical Or when checking for invalid range is a big mistake. For example the following If statement: If Tickets < 0 And Tickets > 10 Then, will never display the MessageBox, because it is impossible for Tickets to be both less than 0 and greater than 10.

Pattern Check

The pattern check is used when the input data should satisfy a certain pattern. For example, the program may accept the telephone number in a certain pattern with the area code inside parentheses followed by three digits, a dash, and four more digits. There is a Like operator in VB .NET that facilitates the pattern check.

Like Operator

The Like operator is used to compare two strings and determine whether they are alike, i.e., have similar patterns. The outcome of the Like operator is a Boolean. The outcome is True if the two strings have similar patterns, and False, otherwise. There are certain characters that can be used to form the string that represents a pattern. For example, character "#" represents one digit, character "?" represents any character, and character "*" represents any number of characters. To check for a specific character in a pattern, include that character in the string pattern at the desired location. For example, the pattern "A*", matches any string that starts with letter "A", followed by zero or more characters. Pattern "###-##-####" matches any string that contains three digits, a dash, two digits, a dash, and four more digits, such as a Social Security Number, e.g., "222-33-4455". For example, the following If statement, validates the data entered in txtID for being a valid social security number.

```
If txtID.Text Like "###-##-####" = False Then
   MessageBox.Show("Enter a valid SSNO.",
      Application.ProductName,
      MessageBoxButtons.OK,
      MessageBoxIcon.Information)
   txtID.Focus()
Else
   . . .
```

Code Check

The code check is used to make sure that the user has entered one of the acceptable choices in the TextBox. For example, the program might accept only the department names "Math" and "Stats". To make sure that the user has entered one of these names in the TextBox, txtDept one has to use an If statement and a logical operator; if the input data is not equal to any of the acceptable departments, then inform the user and set the focus. The following shows such validation:

```
If txtDept.Text < > "Math" And txtDept.Text < > "Stats" Then
   MessageBox.Show("Valid data is Math or Stats.",
      Application.ProductName, MessageBoxButtons.OK,
      MessageBoxIcon.Information)
   txtDept.Focus()
Else
   . . .
End If
```

 Using Logical Or instead of logical And in a code check. In other words, the   If statement: `If txtDept.Text < > "Math" Or txtDept.Text < > "Stats" Then` will always display the message, no matter what the user enters. Why?

Notice that in this example, data validation is case sensitive, i.e., if the user enters "math" in the TextBox, the program will not accept it as a valid department name. Case-insensitive checks can be performed by using the ToUpper or ToLower methods of the String class, as discussed in chapter 4. To perform a case-insensitive check, convert the input data to uppercase or to lowercase letters and then compare it to the uppercase or lowercase version of the valid data. For example the following code is the case insensitive version of validating the department name:

```
If txtDept.Text.ToUpper <> "MATH" And txtDept.Text.ToUpper <> "STATS" Then
      MessageBox.Show("Enter Math or Stats.", Application.ProductName,
      MessageBoxButtons.OK, MessageBoxIcon.Information)
   txtDept.Focus()
Else
```

Another way is to declare a variable of type String to store the entered data in upper case or lower case, and then use that variable in an If statement:

```
Dim Department As String
Department = txtDept.Text.ToLower()
If Department <> "math" And Department <> "stats" Then
    MessageBox.Show("Enter Math or Stats",
    Application.ProductName, MessageBoxButtons.OK,
    MessageBoxIcon.Information)
    txtDept.Focus()
Else

...
End If
```

Checking if a RadioButton Is Selected

Usually, when there are a group of RadioButtons on the Form, the user has to select one of them. This validation ensures that one of the RadioButtons is selected. Refer to Appendix D on Additional Controls for further reading on RadioButtons. To check whether the user has selected one of the RadioButtons, examine the Checked property of the RadioButtons, in an If statement. The Checked property of a RadioButton is equal to True, if it is selected, and False, otherwise. The user should be informed if no RadioButton is selected. For example, assume that the user has to select one of the RadioButtons that represents colors red, blue and white. Assume that RadioButtons are named radRed, radBlue and radWhite. The following If statement checks if none of the RadioButtons is selected and informs the user.

```
If radRed.Checked = False And radBlue.Checked = False And
        radWhite.Checked = False Then

    MessageBox.Show("Choose a color.", Application.ProductName,
        MessageBoxButtons.OK, MessageBoxIcon.Information)
Else
...
End If
```

Validate Selection in a ComboBox

Often, when there is a ComboBox on the Form, the user should select one of the items displayed in the ComboBox. Refer to Appendix D to learn more about the ComboBox control. A ComboBox has a property called SelectedIndex, which is available at runtime. This is a zero-based index property in which if the first item in the ComboBox is selected, the SelectedIndex will be equal to 0, if the second item in the ComboBox is selected, the SelectedIndex will be equal to 1, and etc. The SelectedIndex property will be equal to −1 if no item is selected from the ComboBox.

5.5 Major Steps in Validating the Data

Data validation is one of the important applications of the Selection Structure in programming languages. In order to validate the data entered by the user, one has to use an If statement. There are four major steps when validating the entered data:

1. Examine the input data in an If statement.

2. Inform the user of invalid data using an OK only MessageBox.

3. Set the focus to the object with invalid data (except for RadioButtons).

4. Allow the user correct the mistake and try again.

Exit Sub

Exit Sub is a statement that can be used inside an event procedure or a general procedure. The purpose of Exit Sub is to end the procedure execution before its normal termination. In other words, Exit Sub branches the program execution to End Sub, the last line in the procedure, and ends the procedure execution. Some programmers are against using such statement(s) that make a jump in the program execution, without using one of the structured statements in the language, such as Selection or Repetition structures. However, in the example below, the authors use Exit Sub to simplify the code and avoid a lengthy nested If/ElseIf statement when validating the input data. For example, to perform a type check in Example 1, you may write the code in a cascading If / ElseIf statement, or use simple If statements and Exit Sub. Both versions are shown below. The advantage of using Exit Sub is that the code for processing the valid data will not be trapped in the Else clause of the cascading If / ElseIf statement.

```
'Validation Code without using Exit Sub.
    Private Sub btnAdd_Click(...) Handles btnAdd.Click
        Dim Num1 As Single
        Dim Num2 As Single
        Dim Sum As Single

        'Validate the input before processing:

        If Single.TryParse(txtNum1.Text, Num1) = False Then
            MessageBox.Show("Enter a real number for Num1.",
                    Application.ProductName,
                        MessageBoxButtons.OK,
                        MessageBoxIcon.Information)
            txtNum1.Focus()
        ElseIf Single.TryParse(txtNum2.Text, Num2) = False Then
            MessageBox.Show("Enter a real number for Num2.",
                    Application.ProductName,
                        MessageBoxButtons.OK,
                        MessageBoxIcon.Information)
            txtNum2.Focus()
        Else
            'Valid data is stored in Num1, and Num2

            Sum = Num1 + Num2
            lblSum.Text = Sum.ToString("N")
        End If
    End Sub
```

```
'Validation Code using Exit Sub.

    Private Sub btnAdd_Click(...) Handles btnAdd.Click
        Dim Num1 As Single
        Dim Num2 As Single
        Dim Sum As Single

        'Validate the input before processing:

        If Single.TryParse(txtNum1.Text, Num1) = False Then
            MessageBox.Show("Enter a real number for Num1.",
                Application.ProductName,
                    MessageBoxButtons.OK,
                    MessageBoxIcon.Information)
            txtNum1.Focus()
            Exit Sub
        End If

        If Single.TryParse(txtNum2.Text, Num2) = False Then
            MessageBox.Show("Enter a real number for Num2.",
                Application.ProductName,
                    MessageBoxButtons.OK,
                    MessageBoxIcon.Information)
            txtNum2.Focus()
            Exit Sub
        End If

        'Valid data is stored in Num1 and Num2, add them up:

        Sum = Num1 + Num2
        lblSum.Text = Sum.ToString("N")
    End Sub
```

EXAMPLE 2

This example contains an input object for each of the validations discussed in this chapter. The program will validate the input data once the user clicks on the provided Button. Consider the illustration shown in Figure 5.6. The business rules specify the following when entering data:

FIGURE 5.7 *Data Validation Ex2*

A. Name is required. (Existence check)

B. A whole number must be entered for age. (Type check)

C. Age must be between 18 and 90 (Range check)

D. A student ID has to be entered in the following format "00###-#####" (Pattern check)

E. A department name has to be entered into a TextBox. The only departments allowed are Tech, Eng, Sci, and Bus in a case-insensitive manner (Code check)

F. A RadioButton (*) needs to be selected for gender (Selection check)

G. A year has to be selected from the drop down ComboBox (*). (Selection check).

* These controls are explained in Appendix D.

In the click event procedure of the Validate Button, the following code is written in order to validate the user's input according to the provided rules.

```
Private Sub btnValidate_Click(…) Handles btnValidate.Click
    Dim Age As Short
    Dim Dept As String

     'A: Existence Check

    If txtName.Text = "" Then
        MessageBox.Show("Name is required.", Application.ProductName,
                    MessageBoxButtons.OK, MessageBoxIcon.Information)
        txtName.Focus()
        Exit Sub
    End If

      'B: Type Check

    If Short.TryParse(txtAge.Text, Age) = False Then
        MessageBox.Show("Enter a whole number for age.",
            Application.ProductName, MessageBoxButtons.OK,
                MessageBoxIcon.Information)
        txtAge.Focus()
        Exit Sub
     End If

      'C: Range Check

    If Age < 18 Or Age > 90 Then
        MessageBox.Show("Valid range is 18 to 90.",
                Application.ProductName, MessageBoxButtons.OK,
                MessageBoxIcon.Information)
        txtAge.Focus()
        Exit Sub
    End If

     'D: Pattern Check

    If (txtStudentID.Text Like "00###-#####") = False Then
          MessageBox.Show("Enter a valid ID like: 00###-#####.",
                Application.ProductName, MessageBoxButtons.OK,
                MessageBoxIcon.Information)
        txtStudentID.Focus()
        Exit Sub
     End If

      'E: Code Check

    Dept = txtDepartment.Text.ToUpper()
    If Dept <> "TECH" And Dept <> "SCI" And Dept <> "ENG"
                    And Dept <> "BUS" Then
        MessageBox.Show("Enter Tech, Sci, Eng or Bus for dept.",
                Application.ProductName, MessageBoxButtons.OK,
                MessageBoxIcon.Information)
```

```
            txtDepartment.Focus()
            Exit Sub
        End If

    'F: Radio Button Selection

    If radMale.Checked = False And radFemale.Checked = False Then
        MessageBox.Show("Select a gender.",
                Application.ProductName, MessageBoxButtons.OK,
                MessageBoxIcon.Information)
            Exit Sub
    End If

    'G: ComboBox Selection

    If cboYear.SelectedIndex = -1 Then
        MessageBox.Show("Select a year.", Application.ProductName,
                MessageBoxButtons.OK, MessageBoxIcon.Information)
            cboYear.Focus()
            Exit Sub
    End If

    'Everything is valid, inform the user:

    MessageBox.Show("Student data is valid.",
                Application.ProductName, MessageBoxButtons.OK,
                MessageBoxIcon.Information)
End Sub
```

Part A: Existence Check

Part A in the code illustrates an existence check. An existence check is simply checking if the user has entered anything. If the user has not entered anything, the OK MessageBox is displayed with an appropriate message. Then the cursor is set to that TextBox. Finally, the statement Exit Sub is used to end the procedure execution. Notice that at this time, the Form will show up again and the user can enter a name.

 Exit Sub is a VB .NET statement that can be used inside a procedure to stop its execution. As soon as Exit Sub is executed, the program branches to the End Sub, hence the procedure execution ends.

Part B: Type Check

For this part, you can use the IsNumeric function or the TryParse method. If the goal is to check for a whole number, TryParse is the right choice. In order to use TryParse, you have to declare a variable to store the parsed value. In the code, variable Age is declared as Short, hence Short.TryParse is used to check the data entered for age. Remember that TryParse returns a False output if the first argument is not of proper type.

Part C: Range Check

Part C illustrates a range check. A programmer should always perform a type check before a range check to ensure that a numeric value has been entered. A range check is performed using logical operators in an If statement; it check whether the number is outside the valid range. Notice that if the data entered for Age was a whole number, the method TryParse in Part B, would store that value in variable Age.

 A programmer should always perform a type check before a range check to make sure that the program does not crash. These two checks should not be performed together using logical operators.

Part D: Pattern Check

Part D exemplifies a pattern check using the Like operator.

Part E: Code Check

Part E shows a code check. It is a code check that allows for an entry of specific text.

Part F: Radio Button Selection Check

Part F shows a selection check for RadioButtons. RadioButtons have a Boolean property called Checked. The Checked property is set to True if the RadioButton is selected and False if the RadioButton is not selected. In this If statement, we are checking if none of the Radio Buttons is selected; In that case, inform the user. Notice that the focus is not placed on either Radio Buttons, otherwise it would be selected.

 Using Logical Or instead of logical And when validating a selection in the RadioButtons. Notice that the following validation will always display the MessageBox, *because always one of the conditions will evaluate to true*

```
If radMale.Checked = False Or radFemale.Checked = False Then
    MessageBox.Show ("Select a gender. ", . . . )
```

Part G: ComboBox Selection Check

Part G illustrates a selection check for a ComboBox control.

 Storing the entered data in a variable before data validation is wrong. For example, the following code will result in runtime error on line 2, if the user enters "Apples" in txtPrice. In other words, the execution will not reach the If statement intended for data validation.

```
Dim Price As Decimal
Price = Decimal.Parse(txtPrice.Text)
If Decimal.TryParse(txtPrice.Text, Price) = False Then
    'Inform the user of invalid data
```

Not forming complete conditions when using logical And or logical Or. Note that the following range check for Integer variable Age is illegal, and results in a build error.

```
If  Age  <  0  Or  >  100  Then
        'Inform the user of invalid range
```

EXAMPLE 3

Let us redo Example 1 given at the beginning of this chapter and validate the data entered in TextBoxes for being numeric. In case of invalid data, inform the user using a MessageBox, set the focus to the TextBox with invalid data, stop the procedure execution, and allow the user to fix the problem. The following is the code for the click event procedure of the Add button with data validation included.

```vbnet
Private Sub btnAdd_Click (...) Handles btnAdd.Click
    'Declare Variables:
    Dim Num1 As Single
    Dim Num2 As Single
    Dim Sum As Single

    'Validate the data entered in txtNum1:
    If Single.TryParse(txtNum1.text, Num1) = False Then
        MessageBox.Show("Enter a numeric data.",
            Application.ProductName, MessageBoxButtons.OK,
            MessageBoxIcon.Information)
        txtNum1.focus()
        Exit Sub
    End If

    'Validate the data entered in txtNum2:
    If Single.TryParse(txtNum2.text, Num2) = False Then
        MessageBox.Show("Enter a numeric data.", _
            Application.ProductName, MessageBoxButtons.OK, _
            MessageBoxIcon.Information)
        txtNum2.focus()
        Exit Sub
    End If

    'Data is valid, go ahead compute the sum:
        Sum = Num1 + Num2
        lblSum.Text = Sum.ToString("N")
End Sub
```

5.6 Exception Handling in VB .NET

Data validation is usually performed for errors that the programmer might suspect such as entering a name instead of a number or forgetting to select a RadioButton, and so forth. Of course, a programmer cannot suspect all the errors that the program can generate, due to either user input or the nature of the programming language and compiler. For example, the result of a calculation might overflow the range of values that can be stored in a variable, the disk might be full, or the input data file might be corrupted. Such errors are referred to as exceptions, and should be handled using exception handling methods. For more information on exception handling, refer to Chapter 13.

Abbreviation Notice: From this point on in the book, when using a MessageBox to display an informative message, we will only include the message and show the other parameters using ellipsis (. . .). For example, the following statement.

```
MessageBox.Show("Enter a name.", Application.ProductName,
        MessageBoxButtons.OK, MessageBoxIcon.Information)
```

Will be replaced by:

```
MessageBox.Show("Enter a name.", . . .)
```

The reason is that these parameters are always the same in all the MessageBoxes that display an informative message, with an OK only Button. Be aware that you can not use this abbreviation when writing a program statement.

Review Questions

1. What is the best way to inform the user of something important during the program execution?

2. Write an If statement to perform an existence check for txtData.

3. How would you check for numeric data in txtData?

4. (T/F) You should store the input data in variables before validating the data.

5. (T/F) You should express the intensity of an error by placing the information, the exclamation, or the warning icon in the MessageBox.

6. What is the purpose of Exit Sub?

7. (T/F) It is possible to write the validation code using a nested If statement instead of using simple If statements and Exit Sub.

8. What will happen if there is no data validation code in the program, and the user enters his/her name instead of his/her salary in txtSalary? Assume that the salary amount should be used to calculate the income tax.

9. What is the outcome of the following segment of code? Assume that the user enters "ten" in txtData.
    ```
    Dim N As Integer
    If Integer.TryParse (txtData.Text, N) = False Then
        MessageBox.Show("Enter a whole number.", ...)
        txtData.Focus()
    End If
    lblOutput.Text = N.ToString()
        . . .
    ```

PROGRAMMING CHALLENGES

1. Redo problem #2 at the end of Chapter 4, by adding data validation to the code. In this project, accept only test scores that are whole numbers, and in range of 0 to 100. In case the user enters invalid data, the program should inform the user by displaying an informative message, and set the focus to the appropriate TextBox. This will allow the user to reenter the input and try again.

2. Redo problem #4 at the end of Chapter 4, by adding data validation to the code. In this project, the user enters three input data: two operands and one arithmetic operator in provided TextBoxes. Validate each operand for being a number, and the operator for being one of the arithmetic operators in VB .NET: $+$, $-$, $*$, $/$, $\backslash$, $\wedge$, Mod. Notice that the operator validation is a code check explained in this chapter. In case of invalid data, the program should inform the user by displaying and informative message, and set the focus to the TextBox with incorrect data. This will allow the user to reenter the input and try again.

3. Design a VB .NET project to help a university parking administrator to compute and display the cost a customer will incur, based on the price of the parking permit, the type of the customer, and the number of permits purchased. There are three types of customers: student, faculty, and staff. The price of a parking permit for students is $50.00, for staff $75.00, and for faculty is $100.00. Customers may purchase more than one parking permit for their family members. Assume that the customer purchases the same kind of permit for the family members.

    At run time, the clerk should enter the customer name, number of permits being purchased, and customer types: STA, FAC, or STU in the provided TextBoxes and click on a Button to have the amount due displayed.

    Validation rules are:

    *   Customer name must exist.

    *   Number of permits should be a number between 1 and 5, both inclusive.

    *   Customer type can be: FAC, STU, or STA, case insensitive.

    In case of invalid data, inform the user, and set the cursor to the TextBox.

    There should also be Buttons to clear the I/O boxes and to end the program execution.

CHAPTER 6

Modularity

LEARNING OBJECTIVES

After completing Chapter 6, students should be able to:

- ❑ Understand modularity
- ❑ Understand the concept of top-down design
- ❑ Understand the advantages of modularity
- ❑ Understand the drawbacks of modularity
- ❑ Implement modularity in VB .NET
- ❑ Construct general functions
- ❑ Construct general procedures
- ❑ Understand passing parameters
- ❑ Understand the difference between passing parameters ByVal and ByRef
- ❑ Understand the difference between using module-scope variables and passing parameters

6.1 Introduction

Modularity can be summarized in one phrase: Divide and Conquer. It is the heart of the Structured Programming Languages. Modularity uses the concept of top-down design. Top-down design means to look at a problem as a whole, break it down into smaller parts, develop a solution for each subpart, and finally, put all the pieces together to solve the big problem.

6.2 Why Modularize?

Can you imagine a Fortune 500 company that is run entirely by its chief executive? Such an idea is practically impossible. Normally, large corporations are divided into several divisions, each managed by an expert in that area. If the responsibilities of each division are clearly defined and the operations are properly planned, the entire company will run smoothly. In such organizations, the job of the CEO would be assigning tasks to different managers, coordinating the operations, and using the outcomes to make critical decisions. Writing large programs is similar to running a big organization. Programmers should analyze the given problem and divide it into logical subparts, with clear tasks assigned to them. Each subpart may be broken into smaller parts as well. Programmers should then write a segment of code (a module) to solve each subpart. Finally, all such modules written by several programmers are connected together to come up with an integrated solution for the given problem. This is called a top-down design.

Advantages of Modularity

- *Reduces complexity:* By breaking down a big problem into smaller subparts, the complexity of the problem gets partitioned among the subparts. Consequently, it will be easier to come up with a solution for each subpart.

- *Eliminates redundant code:* If a segment of code is repeated in several places in the program, the particular segment can be written as a module. Each segment of redundant code in the program will be then replaced by a simple call to this module.

- *Improves clarity:* By giving meaningful names to modules and calling them from event procedures, you can avoid clutter in the event procedures and consequently, the program becomes more readable.

- *Provides reusability:* Once you write a useful module, it can be reused in other programs as well. The whole module can be copied to a new programming project.

- *Easier to maintain:* It is much easier to understand and modify a program that is divided into smaller modules, than a huge program with long segments of code.

Disadvantages

- Breaking down the problem into parts that are not clearly defined can reduce the clarity of the program and defy the purpose.

- Calling modules to perform their task has an overhead. This means that the computer must remember from where each module is called, and be able to return the execution back to that location to finish the process. In programming terms, this is called the call stack. Therefore, by overusing the modules, the efficiency of the program can be compromised, i.e., the program might run slower.

6.3 Modularity in VB .NET

Modularity in VB .NET is accomplished by means of procedures, functions, and classes. In this chapter, we will restrict our focus to learning general procedures and functions and how to invoke them from or outside the event procedures within a program. VB .NET is inherently modularized by means of event procedures. We have already seen event procedures that get executed when the designated event takes place during program execution.

Besides event procedures, the programmer can write his/her own procedure or function to accomplish a specific task that is not directly related to an event. The purpose of this chapter is to learn how to write user-defined procedures and functions. We will start with explaining general procedures.

6.4 General Procedures

A general procedure is a segment of code that is written by the programmer to perform a certain task in the program. Unlike an event procedure, it is not directly associated with an event during the execution of the program; however, it can be called from an event procedure to do its job. A general procedure can be written anywhere in the code window between the Windows-generated code Public Class Form1 and End Class.

General Syntax

Like event procedures, the first line of a general procedure is Private Sub and the last line is End Sub. The keywords are shown in bold.

> **Private Sub** *ProcedureName (Parameter List)*
>
>   VB .NET Statement
>
>   . . .
>
> **End Sub**

ProcedureName: is a name that the programmer gives to the procedure. Naming a procedure follows the same rules as naming a variable. Give a meaningful name to the procedure, indicating its purpose.

Parameter List: A procedure may have zero or more input parameters. Each parameter is a pair consisting of a name and a data type. Each parameter is responsible for carrying an input information into the procedure to perform the intended task. In other words, the procedure communicates with outside world via its parameters. When writing a general procedure, give meaningful names to the parameters.

EXAMPLE 1

Write a general procedure to display a welcome message in a Label. Notice that this procedure does not have any input parameter; hence, it will always display the same message when it is called.

```
Private Sub DisplayGreetings()
      lblShow.Text = "Welcome to my program!"
End Sub
```

This procedure has to be called from another procedure or function to display the greeting message. The following statement will call this general procedure:

```
      Call DisplayGreetings()
```

EXAMPLE 2

Write a procedure to display a custom message in a Label. This procedure has a parameter of type String that receives the input message at the time of invocation. Therefore, the procedure will display the string passed to it when it is called.

```
Private Sub DisplayMessage (Message As String)
      lblShow.Text = Message
End Sub
```

This procedure has to be called from another procedure or function to display the input message. Let's call this procedure to display "Turn down the volume."

```
Call DisplayMessage ("Turn down the volume.")
```

EXAMPLE 3

Write a general procedure to clear all the input boxes on the Form. Assume that there are three TextBoxes on the Form: from top to bottom, txtName, txtQuantity, and txtPrice. This procedure does not have any input parameters. It simply clears the objects on the Form.

```
Private Sub ClearInput()
        txtName.Text = ""
        txtQuantity.Text = ""
        txtPrice.Text = ""
End Sub
```

This procedure has to be called from another procedure or function to clear the TextBoxes. To call this procedure:

```
Call ClearInput()
```

 Keyword Call is optional. We recommend including the keyword Call in order to increase the program's clarity.

- Calling the same procedures without using the Call keyword:

```
DisplayGreetings()

DisplayMessage("Increase the volume.")

ClearInput()
```

EXAMPLE 4

Write a general procedure, to display the input message using MessageBox.Show.

```
Private Sub DisplayMessageOK(Message As String)

    MessageBox.Show(Message, Application.ProductName,
            MessageBoxButtons.OK, MessageBoxIcon.Information)

End Sub
```

 It is helpful to have a general procedure like DisplayMessageOK in all of your VB .NET projects in order to display a custom message to the user by means of the MessageBox.

- Call DisplayMessageOK to inform the user of missing data, by displaying the message: "Enter your name."

```
Call DisplayMessageOK("Enter your name.")
```

6.5 Built-In Functions in VB .NET

VB .NET has a rich collection of built-in functions that are part of the language. Among them are string manipulation functions, math functions, financial functions, date and time functions, and so on. A function is a segment of code that performs certain task and returns one output. To use a function, you need to know function's name, the task it performs, the input data it requires, and the data type of the output it produces. To use a function, you do not need to know how the function performs its job. Some examples of built-in functions are IsNumeric(String), IsDate(String), Rnd(), and Int(4.16).

6.6 General Functions

If there is a built-in function for the task in hand, you should use it, because the built-in functions are usually more efficient than functions a programmer might write. If there is no built-in function, you will have to write a function to perform the task. Such functions are referred to as general functions. Think of a function as a closed box that takes zero or more input parameter(s), does some processing, and generates one result, which is referred to as the function's output.

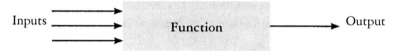

Below is the skeleton of a general function in the code window. The bold words are the keywords used in the function's definition.

General Syntax

```
Private Function FunctionName (Parameter List) As OutputDataType
    VB .NET Statement
    . . .
    Return expression
End Function
```

Let us explore each part of this code.

FunctionName: is the name you give to the function. The function's name should convey its purpose and is often a verb. It follows the same rules as naming variables.

OutputDataType: is the data type of the function's output. This data type is one of the existing data types in VB .NET.

Parameter List: The function communicates with outside the box through its parameter(s). For every input data required by the function, there should be one parameter. Each parameter is a pair, consisting of a name and a data type.

Return expression: The function sends out its output via the Return statement. The expression gets evaluated to some value and that value is sent/returned to the caller of the function. The expression can be a variable or an expression evaluating to a value of the same data type as the OutputDataType.

End Function: indicates the end of the function definition.

Body of the function is the VB .NET statement(s) written between Private Function and End Function.

 Without the Return statement, the function will not return any output.

To write a general function, you do not need to know the details of the entire project, but the following questions should be answered:

- Function's name
- Function's task description
- The input requirements to do the job

- The function's output
  - Determine the data type of the output

- The processing logic
  - The process of using the input data to produce the output.

EXAMPLE 5

Write a function to compute the commission of a salesperson based on the the following rules. Assume that the commission for the sales amount greater than or equal to $800 is 30%, for sales amount ≥ $300 and less than $800 is 15 %, and for sales amount less than $300 is 10 %.

After a little bit of thinking, one will realize that this function requires only one input data which is the amount of sale (data type Decimal). It computes and returns the commission as its output (data type Decimal). A meaningful name for this function would be ComputeCommission. Let us list different parts of this function:

- Function's name: ComputeCommission

- Function's task description:
  - Compute the commission for a given salesperson based-on the sales made

- Input requirements: Sales amount

- Function's output: the commission
  - Determine the data type of the output: Decimal

- The pseudocode for performing the task:
  1. If the sales amount is greater than or equal to 800, then the commission is 30% of the sales amount.
  2. Otherwise, if the sales amount is less than 800, but greater than or equal to 300, then the commission is 15% of the sales amount.
  3. Otherwise, the sales amount is less than 300, the commission is 10% of the sales amount.

Translate the pseudocode to VB .NET

```
Private Function ComputeCommission(SalesAmt As Decimal) As Decimal
    Dim Commission As Decimal
    If SalesAmt >= 800 Then
        Commission = SalesAmt * 0.30
    ElseIf SalesAmt >= 300 Then
        Commission = SalesAmt * 0.15
    Else
        Commission = SalesAmt * 0.10
    End If
    Return Commission
End Function
```

Invoking the Function

To use a function, you should invoke or call it by using its name followed by an open parenthesis and a list of input data it requires followed by a closed parenthesis. For example, to invoke the above function from the click event procedure of a Button, for a salesperson, who has sold $5000. To do this you would declare a variable to store the commission amount, and invoke the function as follows:

```
Dim Commission As Decimal
Commission = ComputeCommission(5000) ' invoke the function
```

Notice that at invocation time 5000 will be passed to the function's parameter, SalesAmt. The value passed to the function at invocation time can be a literal, i.e., 5000, or a variable with the sales amount stored in it. For example, assume that the sales amount is entered in a TextBox: txtSales. The code in the click event procedure of the Button will change accordingly:

```
Dim Sales As Decimal
Dim Commission As Decimal
Sales = Decimal.Parse (txtSales.Text)
Commission = ComputeCommission(Sales)
```

EXAMPLE 6

Design a VB .NET project to compute the weekly pay for a worker. Assume that the user enters the number of hours the worker has worked in a week and the hourly wage in the TextBoxes, and clicks on the Compute Button to have the weekly pay computed and displayed. Figure 6.1 shows the GUI designed for this project, and below is the code for the click event procedure of the Compute Button without using any functions.

In the click event procedure, the input data should be validated before it can be processed. Validate the hours and hourly wage for being valid numbers. Use TryParse to do type check.

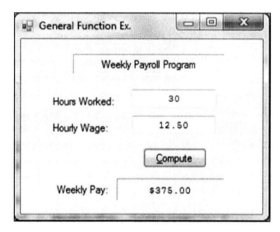

Figure 6.1 *Screen capture at runtime*

```
Private Sub btnCompute_Click(...) Handles btnCompute.Click
    Dim Hours As Double
    Dim Wage As Decimal
    Dim WeeklyPay As Decimal

    If Double.TryParse(txtHours.Text, Hours) = False Then
        MessageBox.Show("Enter a real number for hours.",...)
        txtHours.Focus()
        Exit Sub
    End If

    If Decimal.TryParse(txtWage.Text, Wage) = False Then
        MessageBox.Show("Enter a valid wage.",...)
        txtWage.Focus()
        Exit Sub
    End If

    WeeklyPay = Hours * Wage
    lblOutput.Text = WeeklyPay.ToString("c")
```

```
    txtHours.Text = ""
    txtWage.Text = ""
    txtHours.Focus()
End Sub
```

You can see that the code in this event procedure gets long and cluttered even for such a simple problem. It is a good idea to write a general function to validate the input data and remove the validation code out of the click event procedure.

 Write a general function to perform data validation on the input data.

To write a general function to validate the user's input, let us follow the steps outlined in Section 6.6, and think about the following:

- Function's name:
  ValidateData is a meaningful name.

- Function's job:
  Validate the data entered in TextBoxes.

- Identify the input requirements:
  None. The function can access the TextBoxes on the Form.

- Function's output:
  Boolean data type
  The function returns True, if all the input data is valid and False, if there is any invalid data.

- Processing logic:
  If the type of input entered in txtHours is not valid, then:
  - Inform the user
  - Set the focus to txtHours
  - Return False
  If the type of input entered in txtWage is not valid, then:
  - Inform the user
  - Set the focus to txtWage
  - Return False
  At this point, all user inputs are valid, therefore, Return True

Below is the translation of the pseudo-code to VB .NET code.

```
Private Function ValidateData() As Boolean
    Dim Hours As Double
    Dim Pay As Decimal

    If Double.TryParse(txtHours.Text, Hours) = False Then
        MessageBox.Show("Enter a real number for hours.",...)
        txtHours.Focus()
        Return False
    End If
```

```
     If Decimal.TryParse(txtWage.Text, Pay) = False Then
        MessageBox.Show("Enter a valid wage.", ...)
        txtWage.Focus()
        Return False
     End If

     Return True
End Function
```

 There can be several Return statements in a function, but only one of them gets executed. Return simply ends the function's execution and returns the output to the caller.

Obviously, this general function is only useful for validating the data entered in the TextBoxes on this Form, and cannot be used in another VB .NET project. But knowing the basic idea, one can write a similar function for any VB .NET project. Let us rewrite the code for the Click event procedure of the Compute Button and invoke this function to validate the input data. Since the general function returns a Boolean output, it can be invoked in an If statement. If the function's output is equal to False, the procedure execution should end, allowing the user fix the problem. One can end the procedure execution either by using Exit Sub or using an Else branch for the If statement.

The Click event procedure of the Compute button, using functions:

```
Private Sub btnCompute_Click(...) Handles btnCompute.Click
     Dim Hours As Double
     Dim Wage As Decimal
     Dim WeeklyPay As Decimal

    'Invoke the general function in an If statement:

     If ValidateData() = False Then
          Exit Sub
     End If

     Hours = Double.Parse(txtHours.Text)
     Wage = Decimal.Parse(txtWage.Text)

     WeeklyPay = Hours * Wage
     lblOutput.Text = WeeklyPay.ToString("c")

     txtHours.Text = ""
     txtWage.Text = ""
     txtHours.Focus()
End Sub
```

Further Modularization

Although the code inside the Click event procedure of the Compute Button is not lengthy, you may break it down even further and write a general procedure to clear the input data and set the focus to the top TextBox. A call to this procedure will replace the last three lines of code in the Click event procedure.

```
'General procedure to clear the input data and set the focus in the top box:

    Private Sub ClearInput()
        txtHours.Text = ""
        txtWage.Text = ""
        txtHours.Focus()
    End Sub

'Rewrite the click event procedure of the Compute button:

    Private Sub btnCompute_Click(...) Handles btnCompute.Click
        Dim Hours As Double
        Dim Wage As Decimal
        Dim WeeklyPay As Decimal

        If ValidateData() = False Then
            Exit Sub
        End If
        Hours = Double.Parse(txtHours.Text)
        Wage = Decimal.Parse(txtWage.Text)

        WeeklyPay = Hours * Wage
        lblOutput.Text = WeeklyPay.ToString("c")

        'Call the general procedure:

        Call ClearInput()
    End Sub
```

EXAMPLE 7

Design a VB .NET project to be used by a home mortgage company that gives loans to its customers to purchase a house. Allow the user to enter the amount of loan, annual interest rate in percentage (e.g. 7.8), and duration of the loan in months followed by a click on Compute Button. The program should then compute and display the monthly payment in the output Label (see the screen capture in Figure 6.2).

The formula for calculating the monthly payment:

$$\text{Payment} = \frac{\text{LoanAmount} * \text{Rate}}{1 - (1 + \text{Rate})^{-\text{months}}}$$

Figure 6.2 *Screen capture at runtime*

where Rate is the monthly interest rate (the annual rate/12), LoanAmount is the loan amount, and months is the duration of loan payment in months.

The Pseudocode of the Compute Button Is:

1.   Validate the entered data.

2.   Store the valid data in variables.

3.   Compute the monthly payment using the formula.

4.   Display the output.

5.   Disable the Button. The reason for disabling the Compute Button is to prevent the user from clicking on the button for the same set of data. This could cause a problem if you were counting the number of loans processed. In this example it does not make any difference.

Assume That the Validation Rules Are:

- Loan amount: Must be a number greater than 0.

- Annual interest rate: Must be a number greater than 0.

- Term of the loan: Must be a number, in range of 12 to 120 months (both inclusive)

- Cross reference validation: If amount of loan is less than $5000, the duration cannot be more than 48 months.

Modularize the Problem

If you code all these tasks in the Click event of the Button, it becomes very long and difficult to manage. Therefore, it is wise to break down this problem into several parts. Obvious breakdown would be as follows:

1.   Since there would be many uses of the MessageBox, let us write a general procedure that uses the MessageBox to display a specific message.

2.   Write a general function to do data validation.

3.   Write another general function to compute the monthly payment on a loan.

```
'1) General Procedure to display a message using the MessageBox.Show:

Private Sub MessageOK (Message As String)
    MessageBox.Show(Message, Application.ProductName,
        MessageBoxButtons.OK, MessageBoxIcon.Information)
End Sub

'2) General function to validate the input data:

Private Function ValidateData() As Boolean
    Dim Loan As Decimal
    Dim Rate As Single
    Dim Months As Short
    If Decimal.TryParse(txtLoan.Text, Loan) = False Then
        Call MessageOk("Enter a valid amount for loan.")
        txtLoan.Focus()
        Return False
    End If

    If Loan <= 0 Then
        Call MessageOk("Enter a positive amount for loan.")
        txtLoan.Focus()
        Return False
    End If
```

```
    If Single.TryParse(txtRate.Text, Rate)= False Then
        Call MessageOk("Enter a numeric data.")
        txtRate.Focus()
        Return False
    End If

    If Rate <= 0 Then
        Call MessageOk("Enter a positive value for rate.")
        txtRate.Focus()
        Return False
    End If

    If Short.TryParse(txtTerm.Text, Term) = False Then
        Call MessageOk("Enter a valid term.")
        txtTerm.Focus()
        Return False
    End If

    If Term < 12 Or Term > 120 Then
        Call MessageOk("Valid range is 12 to 120 months.")
        txtTerm.Focus()
        Return False
    End If

'Cross reference validation

    If Loan < 5000 And Term > 48 Then
        Call MessageOk("Choose a shorter term for this loan.")
        txtTerm.Focus()
        Return False
    End If

    Return True
End Function
```

To write the function to compute the monthly payment on a loan, look at the formula and think about the input requirements of this function, the output it generates, and the processing steps. Clearly the function requires three inputs to do its job. The produced output is the monthly payment. The processing involves using the input data in the given formula.

```
' 3) General function to compute the monthly payment on a loan:

Private Function ComputePayment(Loan As Decimal,
        AnnRate As Single, Term As Short) As Decimal
    Dim Pay As Decimal
    Dim MonthlyRate As Single
    Dim Denominator As Decimal

    MonthlyRate = (AnnRate / 12)/ 100
    Denominator = 1 - (1 + MonthlyRate) ^ -Term
    pay = (Loan * MonthlyRate) / Denominator
    Return Pay
```

```
End Function
```

'Now, we are ready to write the code for the click event procedure of the Compute Button. The
'Click event procedure will invoke the two general functions to do the data validation and calculate
'the monthly payment on the loan.

```
Private Sub btnCompute_Click(. . .) Handles btnCompute.Click
        Dim Loan As Decimal
        Dim Months As Short
        Dim Rate As Single
        Dim Payment As Decimal
```

'Invoke the general function to validate the data:

```
        If ValidateData() = False Then
            Exit Sub
        End If
        Loan = Decimal.Parse(txtLoan.Text)
        Rate = Single.Parse(txtRate.Text)
        Months = Short.Parse(txtTerm.Text)
```

'Invoke the general function to compute the monthly pay:

```
        Payment = ComputePayment(Loan, Rate, Months)
        lblPayment.Text = Payment.ToString("c")
```

'Disable the button:

```
        btnCompute.Enabled = False
End Sub
```

'Click event procedure of the Clear Button:

```
Private Sub btnClear_Click(...) Handles btnClear.Click
        txtLoan.Clear()
        txtRate.Clear()
        txtTerm.Clear()
        lblPayment.Text = ""
        txtLoan.Focus()
        btnCompute.Enabled = True
End Sub
```

6.7 Passing Parameters

There are two ways the data is passed to the parameters in a procedure or a function: By Value or By
Reference. The default in VB .NET is By Value. That is why in older versions of VB .NET or in express editions, the keyword ByVal is added (it is optional) in front of the parameter's name in a general procedure or
function that has one or more parameters. In programming terms, we say the parameter is pass-by-value or
pass-by-reference. Although most of the time, pass-by-value is all you need, it is worthwhile to understand
how these two methods differ.

Pass-By-Value

The keyword for this option is ByVal. It is the default in VB .NET. When a parameter has the keyword ByVal in front of its name, at invocation time, the value of the data passed to the parameter is copied in the parameter, and that copy is used in the code. Therefore, any changes made to the parameter is made to the copy and does not affect the variable that was passed to it at invocation time. The reason is that the variable passed to this parameter at invocation time resides in a different location in the computer's memory than the parameter it is being passed to.

Pass-By-Reference

The keyword for this option is ByRef. If you wish to make a parameter pass-by-reference, add the keyword ByRef in front of its name. When a parameter has the keyword ByRef in front of its name, at invocation time, the address of the variable gets passed to the parameter and the parameter references that variable in the computer's memory. In other words, during the execution, both the parameter and the variable passed to it reside at the same address in the computer's memory. Therefore, any change made to the parameter also changes the variable that was passed to it at invocation time. This method of passing parameters can be very useful in certain programming situations.

EXAMPLE 8

Write a procedure that takes two whole numbers as input and increments their value by 10. Let us write two procedures. One procedure has parameters that are pass-by-value and another one has parameters that are pass-by-reference. We will test these procedures by creating a simple project with a GUI that has a large Label to display the program output and one Button to do the processing.

```
'General Procedure, with pass-by-value parameters:
    Private Sub AddByValue(ByVal N1 As Integer, ByVal N2 As Integer)
        N1 = N1 + 10
        N2 = N2 + 10
    End Sub
'General Procedure, with pass-by-reference parameters:
    Private Sub AddByRef(ByRef N1 As Integer, ByRef N2 As Integer)
        N1 = N1 + 10
        N2 = N2 + 10
    End Sub
```

To compare these two methods of passing parameters in the Click event procedure of the Compare Button declare two Integer variables, and initialize them to some values. Then display the variables before and after calling each of these procedures. Figure 6.3 is the screen capture of this example at run time. Notice that the call to the procedure with pass-by-reference parameters, indeed increments the variables by 10.

Below is the entire code window for this example.

Figure 6.3 *Compare passing parameters*

```
Public Class Form1
    'General Procedure, parameters are pass-by-value:

    Private Sub AddByValue (ByVal N1 As Integer, ByVal N2 As Integer)
        N1 = N1 + 10
        N2 = N2 + 10
    End Sub

    'General Procedure, parameters are pass-by-reference:

    Private Sub AddByRef(ByRef N1 As Integer, ByRef N2 As Integer)
        N1 = N1 + 10
        N2 = N2 + 10
    End Sub

    'Compare the two procedures in the Click event of Compare button:

    Private Sub btnCompare_Click (...) Handles btnCompare.Click
        Dim Data1 As Integer
        Dim Data2 As Integer
        Data1 = 5
        Data2 = 5
        lblShow.Text = "Before calling AddByValue:"
        lblShow.Text = lblShow.Text & vbLf & "Data1=" & Data1.ToString &
            ", Data2 = " & Data2.ToString
        Call AddByValue (Data1, Data2)
        lblShow.Text  = lblShow.Text & vbLf & "After calling AddByValue:"
        lblShow.Text = lblShow.Text & vbLf & "Data1 = " &
            Data1.ToString & ", Data2 = " & Data2.ToString
        lblShow.Text = lblShow.Text & vbLf & "----------------"

    'Reset the variables to 5

        Data1 = 5
        Data2 = 5
        lblShow.Text = lblShow.Text & vbLf & "Before calling AddByRef:"
        lblShow.Text = lblShow.Text & vbLf & "Data1 = " &
            Data1.ToString & ", Data2 = " & Data2.ToString
```

```
        Call AddByRef (Data1, Data2)
        lblShow.Text = lblShow.Text & vbLf & "After calling AddByRef:"
        lblShow.Text = lblShow.Text & vbLf & " Data1 = " &
            Data1.ToString & ", Data2 = " & Data2.ToString
    End Sub
End Class
```

When to Use *ByVal* / *ByRef?*

Always use the default ByVal if the parameter is used merely as an input value to the fuction or procedure. This way the variable passed to the parameter will be protected from accidental changes within the procedure or function. If the purpose is to change the value of the variable passed to the parameter in a function or a procedure, use ByRef before the name of the parameter to make this change possible. Pass-by-reference, thus, makes it possible for a parameter to receive an input and generate an output, hence, play a dual role.

6.8 How to Choose between Function and Procedure

To decide between writing a general procedure or a general function, the programmer has to think about the task to be accomplished. If the task involves some calculation or processing that generates an output that has to be returned to the caller, write a general function. Otherwise, if the task involves some processing without returning any output, such as displaying results, or clearing the input boxes, a general procedure is preferred.

Review Questions:

1. List two advantages of modularity.

2. What is a general procedure?

3. Is the click event procedure of a Button a general procedure?

4. Name an intrinsic (built-in) function in VB .NET.

5. Assume that you are asked to write a module to compute the area of a circle. Would you write a general procedure or a general function?

6. What is the following segment of code?

```
Private Function Sum (ByVal a As Integer, ByVal b As Integer)
                                                    As Integer

    Dim Result As Integer
    Result = a + b
    Return Result
End Function
```

7. Call/Invoke the module given in the previous question from an event procedure with the following variables:

```
Dim N1, N2, SumUp As Integer
N1 = 203
N2 = 874
```

8. Write a general procedure to display instructions for making scrambled eggs.

PROGRAMMING CHALLENGES

1. Design a VB .NET project that works like a simple calculator that performs addition, subtraction, multiplication, and real division. There should be one Button per operator, with the operator displayed on the Button, i.e., on the Button for addition there should be a + character. At runtime, the user should enter two numbers, whole or real, in provided boxes, and click on a Button to perform the desired operation. The program should then display the result in the output Label. Write a general function to validate the entered data for being numeric. This function has to be invoked from the click event procedure of each Button that does one of the operations. Notice that in this project, using a general function for validation eliminates redundant code. There should be Buttons to clear the I/O boxes and end the program execution.

2. Aloha Corporation specializes in making cylinders from different materials. Design a VB .NET application to figure out the raw material cost of producing a cylinder. The cost of building a cylinder is calculated by price per square feet times the surface area. For each cylinder, the user should enter the radius of the base, the height, and the raw material (copper, aluminum, iron) in the provided boxes. The user should then click on a Button to have the price of building the cylinder calculated. The program should also display the total cost of all cylinders, and the number of cylinders processed. Provide Buttons to clear the I/O boxes, and end program execution. Assume that the price per square feet of copper is $3.90, iron is $2.00, and aluminum is $5.00. Program requirements are:

    Declare PI = 3.14159 as a named constant.

    Required functions and procedure:

    a)   A general function to validate input data. Validation rules are:
         - Radius should be a number greater than 0.
         - Height should be a number greater than or equal to 2 and less than or equal to 20 feet.
         - Material must be one of the metal names: copper, iron, aluminum. Perform a case insensitive check.

    b)   A general function to compute the surface area of a cylinder. The function should have two input parameters.

    c)   A general procedure to clear I/O boxes and set the focus to the top input box.

    d)   A general procedure that displays the given message using the MessageBox. This procedure should have one input parameter, which is the message to be displayed.

Repetition Structures

7.1 Why Use Loops?

Repetition structures, known as loops, offer a flexible yet convenient way to repeatedly process instructions in a program. Loops have many applications in computer programming. For example, when one searches for a certain product on eBay or when searching Google, the program uses a loop to search through many records and finds those with matching or similar keywords. Loops are also used in computer graphics programming, such as animation. Many frames are displayed within a loop showing an animation. Loops are also used when programming microprocessors and computing numerical series.

7.2 Introduction

There are three basic programming structures that are used in high-level programming languages. These structures are sequential, selection, and repetition. The sequential structure is a segment of code where the statements get executed in a sequence from top to bottom. The selection structure involves an If or a Select/Case statement, where the program execution branches to a different line, based on the outcome of a decision(s). The repetition structure, often referred to as a Loop, is used when a segment of the code needs to be executed repeatedly. Usually, a condition controls the continuation of the loop. There are different repetition structures available in VB .NET.

7.3 Terminology

There are certain terms that are used when working with loops. Here are some of the common terms that you should familiarize yourself with before reading any further.

- *Body of the loop:* Body of the loop is the segment of code that gets executed repeatedly.

- *Iteration|Cycle:* Each time the statements in the loop body get executed is referred to as one iteration, or cycle.

- *Loop condition:* There is usually a condition that controls the continuation or termination of a loop. For example, a loop may continue as long as the temperature is above 60 degrees.

- *Loop variable:* There is usually one variable that is used in forming the loop condition. This variable is referred to as the loop variable. It is possible to have more than one variable in the loop condition.

7.4 Different Kinds of Loops

In general, there are two categories of loops: pre-test loops and post-test loops. However, the pre-test loops are more commonly used loop structure by programmers to solve any problem that requires repetition.

Pre-test Loops

In a pre-test loop, the condition is evaluated at the beginning of the loop cycle. Therefore, the body of the loop will not get executed at all, if the condition does not evaluate to true the very first time.

Post-test Loops

In a post-test loop, the loop condition is evaluated at the end of the loop cycle. Therefore, the body of the loop will get executed the first time (and hence at least once), regardless of the condition. This is a major difference between a pre-test loop and a post-test loop. You may use a post-test loop if the problem description justifies the body of the loop be executed at least once.

Repetition Structures in VB .NET

- For. . .Next (pre-test loop)

- Do-While. . .Loop (pre-test loop)

- Do-Until. . . Loop (pre-test loop)

- Do. . .Loop-While (post-test loop)

- Do. . .Loop-Until (post-test loop)

- Do. . .Loop (unconditional loop)

The first three loop structures are important. Any problem that requires repetition can be coded using one of these loops. The other loop structures are provided for your information and are not used as often.

Actually, there is one more repetition structure: For Each. . .Next, which can be used when processing array elements. This loop structure will not be discussed in this chapter. If you would like to learn about the For Each. . .Next, refer to online resources.

7.5 For...Next Loop

The For loop is also known as a counting loop. It is an ideal loop structure when the number of iterations is known. The For loop is a powerful loop structure, in the sense that the initialization of the loop variable, the loop condition, and the updating of the loop variable are all embedded in the first line of the loop. There is always a loop variable that is used to form this loop. Below is the general syntax of the For loop.

General Syntax (keywords are in bold):

> **For** *loop_variable* = *initial_value* **To** *end_value* **Step** *step_value*
>   *Body of the loop*
> **Next** *loop_variable*

When a For loop begins, the loop_variable gets initialized to the initial_value. This initialization happens only once. The condition of the loop is specified by the range specified using the To keyword. The range of the values that the loop_variable can assume is from the initial_value to the end_value. The loop variable gets updated by the step_value, at the end of the cycle, upon execution of the Next statement. After the update, the execution goes back to the first line of the For loop. If the loop variable is within specified range, the body of the For loop gets executed one more time. The execution of the For loop stops when the loop_variable assumes a value beyond the end_value.

Key Points to Remember

- For loop is also known as counting loop
- For loop is a pre-test loop
- For loop is the preferred choice when the number of iterations is known
- The loop_variable gets updated by the step_value at the end of each cycle.
- The step_value can be a positive or a negative value
- Including the loop_variable after Next is optional
- If step_value is not specified in the first line, then the default step_value 1 will be assumed

EXAMPLE 1

Write a For loop to display "Hail Purdue" ten times in a Label.

This is an ideal problem to solve using a For loop, because it is a counting problem and the number of iterations is known. A computer program to solve this problem needs one variable that is used as a counter. The loop should iterate ten times, and each time "Hail Purdue" should be displayed in the Label. The most natural way of counting ten times is from 1 to 10. Therefore, the loop variable may start with the initial value of 1 and go up to the end value of 10, with the step value of 1. Below is the pseudocode for this solution.

Pseudocode

1. Declare a loop variable of type Integer
2. Start a For loop, with initial value of 1, end value of 10, and step_value of 1
   a. Display "Hail Purdue" in the Label
   b. Next: loop-variable gets incremented by 1
   c. Back to the beginning of the For loop to revaluate the condition.

Flowchart

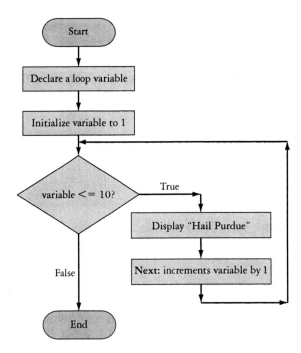

Translate to VB .NET Code

```
Dim Count As Integer
For Count = 1 To 10 Step 1
    lblShow.Text = lblShow.Text & "Hail Purdue" & vbLf
Next Count
```

EXAMPLE 2

Write a For loop to add up all the numbers from 1 to 100, i.e. 1 + 2 . . . 100.

This is also a good problem to solve using a For loop, because the number of iterations is known. To write a computer program for this problem, you need two variables: one variable to add up the numbers and a loop variable to assume the values 1, 2, . . ., 100. Hence, the loop variable should start with the initial value of 1, and go up to the end value of 100, with the step_value of 1. In the body of the loop, the loop variable should be added to the sum of the numbers. Let us look at the pseudocode followed by the flowchart of this logic.

Pseudocode

1. Declare two variables, one to add up the numbers, and a loop variable

2. Initialize the sum of numbers to 0

3. Start a For loop; loop variable starts with 1, goes up to 100, with steps of 1
    a. Add the loop variable to the sum of numbers
    b. Next: loop variable gets incremented by 1
        The loop continues as long as the loop variable is less than or equal to 100.

4. After the loop, display the sum in the Label.

Flowchart

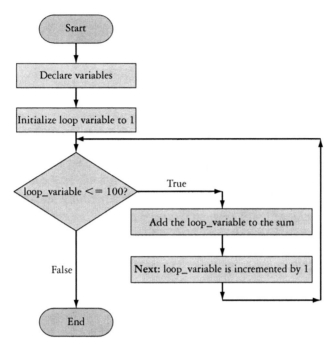

Translate to VB .NET Code

```
Dim Num As Integer
Dim Sum As Integer
Sum = 0
For Num = 1 To 100 Step 1
    Sum = Sum + Num
Next Num
lblShow.Text = Sum.ToString()
```

For Loop with Negative Step Value

Sometimes the logic of the problem requires a For loop with a negative step value. In such cases, the initial value must be greater than the end value for proper execution of the loop. In other words, the loop variable starts with the initial value and steps down to the end value.

For example, the following loop displays the numbers from 10 to 1 in a Label.

```
Dim Num As Integer
For Num = 10 To 1 Step -1
    lblOutput.Text = lblOutput.Text & Num.ToString() & vbLf
Next Num
```

For Loop with a Step Value other than 1

Step-value can be a number greater than 1, less than -1, or even a real number with fraction part, e.g. 0.25. In the latter case the loop variable's data type must be Single or Double.

For example, the following loop adds up all the even numbers from 0 to 200.

```
Dim Even As Integer
Dim Sum As Integer
For Even 0 To 200 Step 2
     Sum = Sum + Even
Next Even
lblOutput.Text = Sum.ToString()
```

7.6 Do-While...Loop

The Do-While is a pre-test loop. It is a good choice when the number of iterations is not known and the logic of the problem suggests that the loop should continue as long as a condition evaluates to True. To understand the logic of the Do-While loop, let us consider something realistic. For example, the night before the exam, a student thinks "I will keep studying, while the library is open"; or a person in a casino says "I will keep putting quarters in the slot machine, while I have quarters in my pocket"; There is usually a loop variable that is used to form the condition of the loop. Unlike the For loop, the initialization and updating of the loop variable is not a part of the syntax and should be coded explicitly. Below is the general syntax of the Do-While loop.

General Syntax (keywords are in bold):

```
Do While condition
  Body of the loop
Loop
```

The body of the loop gets executed while the condition evaluates to True. At the end of each cycle, the execution goes back to the first line and the condition is revaluated. If the condition evaluates to True, the loop goes through one more cycle. If the condition evaluates to False, the loop ends. Moreover, notice that the loop will not execute at all, if the condition evaluates to False at the very beginning of the loop.

Key Points to Remember

- Do-While is a pre-test loop

- The body of the loop is executed as long as the condition evaluates to True

- The loop variable must be explicitly updated within the body of the loop

EXAMPLE 3

Write a Do-While loop to add up all the numbers from 0 to 100, i.e. 0 + 1 + 2 + . . . 100

Although this is an ideal problem to code using a For loop, you can use a Do-While loop as well. As explained before, to write a computer program for this problem, you need two variables: one variable to add up the numbers and a loop variable to assume the values 0, 1, 2, . . ., 100. The variables should be initialized to 0 before the loop. Although VB .NET initializes all the numeric variables to 0, it is a good practice to explicitly initialize the variables to their initial values. The condition of the loop should be formed for the continuation of the loop. Therefore the condition should be while the loop variable is less than or equal to 100. In the body of the loop, the loop variable should be added to the sum of the numbers, and then incremented by 1 to assume the next value. Below is the pseudo-code for solving this problem using a Do-While loop.

Pseudocode

1. Declare two variables; a loop variable, and a variable to add up the numbers

2. Initialize both variables to 0

3. Start a Do-While loop with condition: loop variable <= *100*
    a. Add the loop variable to the sum of the numbers
    b. Increment the loop variable by 1
    c. Back to step 3, loop continues while the condition evaluates to True

4. After the loop, display the sum in the Label

Flowchart

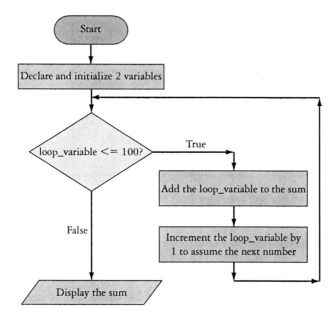

Translate to VB .NET Code

```
Dim Sum As Integer
Dim Num As Integer
Sum = 0
Num = 0
Do While Num <= 100
    Sum = Sum + Num
    Num = Num + 1
Loop
lblShow.Text = Sum.ToString()
```

7.7 Do-Until...Loop

Do-Until is another pre-test loop. The logic of Do-Until loop is the opposite of Do-While loop. The condition is for termination of the loop. In other words, the loop stops when the condition evaluates to True. To better understand the logic of the Do-Until, let us consider drinking a glass of iced water on a hot summer day. You might say "I will drink the water, until the glass is empty." You might consider a Do-Until loop, when the number of iterations is not known and the logic of the problem suggests that the loop should continue until the condition becomes True. There is usually a loop variable used to form the condition. Like a Do-While loop, the initialization and updating of the loop variable should be done explicitly. Below is the general syntax of a Do-Until loop.

General Syntax (keywords are in bold):

```
Do Until condition
     Body of the loop
Loop
```

Key Points to Remember

- Do-Until is a pre-test loop
- The body of the loop is executed until the condition evaluates to True
- Usually there is a loop variable that is used in the condition
- The loop variable should be explicitly updated in the loop

EXAMPLE 4

Write a Do-Until loop to add up all the odd numbers from 0 to 100, i.e. 1 + 3 + . . . 99

Although this is a good problem to code using a For loop, you can use a Do-Until loop as well. To write a computer program for this problem, you need two variables: one variable to add up the numbers and a loop variable to assume the values 1, 3, 5, . . . 99. The variables should be initialized before the loop. The condition of the loop should be for stopping the loop. Hence, the condition should be until the loop variable is greater than 100. In the body of the loop, the loop variable should be added to the sum of numbers, and then incremented by 2 to assume the next odd value. Below is a pseudocode of the Do-Until loop for solving this problem.

Flowchart

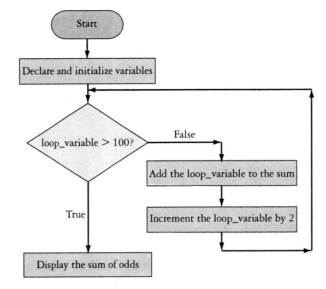

Pseudocode

1. Declare two variables

2. Initialize the loop variable to 1, the first odd number

3. Initialize the variable declared for the sum of numbers to 0

4. Start a Do-Until loop, with condition: loop variable > 100
   a. Add the loop variable to the sum of the numbers
   b. Increment the loop variable by 2
   c. Back to step 4, the loop will continue until the condition evaluates to True

5. After the loop, display the sum in the Label

Translate to VB .NET Code

```
Dim Sum As Integer
Dim Num As Integer
Sum = 0
Num = 1
Do Until Num > 100
    Sum = Sum + Num
    Num = Num + 2
Loop
lblShow.Text = Sum.ToString()
```

A Loop That Does Not Execute

A pretest loop will not execute at all if the loop condition does not hold at the very beginning of the loop. In a For loop with a positive step value, the loop will not execute if the initial value is greater than the end value, and vice versa.

Post-test Loops

In a post-test loop, the condition of the loop is checked at the end of each cycle. The body of a post-test loop gets executed at least once, regardless of the condition. Sometimes, the logic of the problem's solution fits well into a post-test loop. However, every solution that requires a loop can be coded using one of the pre-test loops covered in Sections 7.5 to 7.7.

7.8 Do...Loop-While

The statements surrounded with Do and Loop get executed at least once. The condition is examined at the end of each cycle. The loop continues while the condition evaluates to True.

General Syntax (keywords are in bold):

```
Do
  Body of the loop
Loop While condition
```

Key Points to Remember

- This is a posttest loop

- Body of the loop will be executed at least once, regardless of the condition

- The loop goes through one more cycle if the condition evaluates to True

- The loop variable should be explicitly updated in the body of the loop

EXAMPLE 5

Write a Do. . .Loop-While to add up all the numbers from 1 to 100, i.e. 1 + 2 + . . . 100.

As discussed in previous sections, a computer solution for this problem requires two variables: one variable to add up the numbers and another one to be used as a loop variable, which will assume the values 1, 2, . . . 100. Below is the pseudocode for this problem using a Do. . .Loop-While.

Flowchart

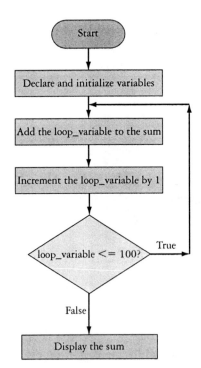

Pseudocode

1.   Declare two variables

2.   Initialize the loop variable to 1

3.   Initialize the variable for adding up the numbers to 0

4.   Start the loop, in each cycle:
      a.   Add the loop variable to the sum
      b.   Increment the loop variable by 1
      c.   The loop continues while the loop variable is less than or equal to 100

5.   After the loop, display the sum in the Label

Translate to VB .NET Code

```
Dim Num As Integer
Dim Sum As Integer
Sum = 0
Num = 1
Do
    Sum = Sum + Num
    Num = Num + 1
Loop While Num <= 100
lblOutput.Text = Sum.ToString()
```

7.9 Do...Loop-Until

The statements surrounded with the Do and Loop get executed at least once. The loop stops when the condition at the end of a cycle evaluates to True.

General Syntax (keywords are in bold):

```
Do
    Body of the loop
Loop Until condition
```

Key Points to Remember

- This is a post-test loop

- Body of the loop will be executed at least once, regardless of the condition

- The loop continues until the condition evaluates to True

- The loop variable should be explicitly updated within the body of the loop

EXAMPLE 6

Write a Do...Loop-Until to add up all the numbers from 1 to 100, i.e. 1 + 2 + ... 100.

Pseudocode

1. Declare two variables
2. Initialize the loop variable to 1
3. Initialize the variable for adding up the numbers to 0
4. Start the loop
   a. Add the loop variable to the sum
   b. Increment the loop variable by 1 (getting ready for the next cycle)
   c. The loop continues until the loop variable is greater than 100
5. After the loop, display the sum

Flowchart

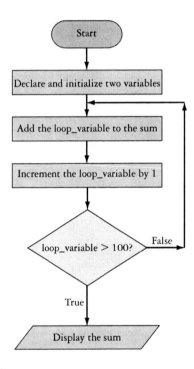

Translate to VB .NET Code

```
Dim Num As Integer
Dim Sum As Integer
Sum = 0
Num = 1
Do
    Sum = Sum + Num
    Num = Num + 1
Loop Until Num > 100
lblOutput.Text = Sum.ToString()
```

EXAMPLE 7

Write a loop to find the smallest whole number such that N^2 is greater than 1000.

This problem is a good candidate for a Do-Until Loop. The logic of the solution is as follows: You have to examine the square of every number starting with 1, 2, 3, . . . until the desired number is found. Inside the loop, raise the number to the power of 2, compare the square to 1000, stop the loop if the square is greater than 1000, otherwise continue the loop checking the next number. To write the code for this problem, you need two variables: A loop variable to assume the numbers 1, 2, 3, . . . and another variable to store the square of the loop variable.

Pseudocode

1. Declare two variables

2. Initialize the loop variable to the initial value of 0
    a. One may begin with an initial value of 10, since $10^2 = 100$ is not greater than 1,000.

3. Start the loop
    a. Increment the loop variable by 1
    b. Compute the square of the loop variable (raise it to the power of 2)
    c. Stop the loop once the power is greater than 1,000

4. After the loop, display the loop variable

Translate to VB .NET Code

```
Dim Num As Integer
Dim Power As Integer
Num = 0
Do
    Num = Num + 1
    Power = Num ^ 2
Loop Until Power > 1000
lblOutput.Text = Num.ToString()
```

7.10 Exit Do | Exit For

There are exit doors for theaters, stores, and restaurants. There are also emergency exits in buildings that are doors used for exit under special circumstances. Exit Do and Exit For statements are like emergency doors; they are used when the logic of the problem requires an exit from the loop before its normal termination.

- Exit For: Can be used in a For loop. It takes the execution out of the For loop.

- Exit Do: Can be used in any of the Do loops. It takes the execution out of the loop.

EXAMPLE 8

Find the smallest number between 100 and 200, that is divisible by 19.

To solve this problem, you have to examine each number, starting with 100 and going up to 200. If the number is divisible by 19, then stop the search, otherwise look at the next number. Obviously, the logic requires a loop and a loop variable that assumes values 100, 101, ... The pseudo-code of the solution is given below.

Pseudocode

1. Declare a loop variable
2. Start a For loop, with the loop variable assuming values from 100 to 200
    a. If the loop variable is divisible by 19 (use Mod operator), exit the loop
    b. Move to the next number
3. Outside the loop, display the number

Translate to VB .NET Code

```
Dim Num As Integer
For Num = 100 To 200 Step 1
     If Num Mod 19 = 0 Then
         Exit For
     End If
Next Num
lblOutput.Text = Num.ToString() & " Is divisible by 19."
```

Infinite Loop

An infinite loop is a loop that goes on forever. For this to happen, the condition of the loop should remain the same. In any of the Do loops, if you forget to update the loop variable in the body of the loop, the condition remains the same, and the loop will go on forever. Infinite loops have some applications, but generally they should be avoided.

7.11 Do...Loop

This is an unconditional loop. The loop continues forever, since there is no condition to control the continuation of the loop. Usually, an Exit Do statement is used to stop the loop based on some condition.

General Syntax (keywords are in bold):

```
Do
     Body of the loop
Loop
```

EXAMPLE 9

Write a loop to find the smallest number greater than 1000 that is divisible by 17.

To solve this problem, you have to check each number greater than 1000, one at a time, and see if it is divisible by 17. The loop should stop once such a number is found.

Pseudocode

1. Declare a loop variable

2. Initialize the loop variable to 1001

3. Start an unconditional Do Loop
   a. If the loop variable is divisible by 17
      Exit the Loop
   b. Increment the loop variable by 1
   c. Continue the loop

4. Outside the loop, display the loop variable

Translate to VB .NET Code

```
Dim N As Integer = 1001
Do
    If N Mod 17 = 0 Then
        Exit Do
    End If
    N = N + 1
Loop
lblOutput.Text = N.ToString() & " Is divisible by 17."
```

Off-By-One Error

This error means that the loop is iterated one extra, or one fewer times than expected. To avoid an Off-By-One error, be careful when forming the loop condition. For example, the following loop condition will process all the numbers from 1 to 99, excluding 100. Assume that Dim N As Integer = 1

```
Do While N < 100
    . . .
    N = N + 1
Loop
```

7.12 Nested Loops

A loop can be coded inside another loop to form nested loops. There can be many levels of nesting. Needless to say, there can be a selection structure coded inside a loop, a loop coded in a selection structure, and so on. Such nesting is possible as long as the inner structure is completely enclosed in the outer structure. Nested loops do have applications in programming. For example, nested loops are needed to display a table of values, to process the elements of a two-dimensional array, or to sort array elements using the Bubble Sort algorithm. Let us look at an example:

To better understand the concept of loops, try each example in a simple VB .NET project, set a break point, and observe the line by line execution of the loop by stepping into execution. Refer to Appendix A for setting break points.

EXAMPLE 10

Design a VB .NET project to display a multiplication table for numbers 1 to 10 on the screen. To do this, you need to display 10 rows, and in each row you have to display 10 values that correspond to 10 columns. The value in each column within a row is the product of the row number by the column number. The outer loop will go through the rows, and the inner loop will go through the columns. Notice that for each cycle of the outer loop, i.e., for each row, the inner loop goes through all the cycles, i.e., all the columns. Let us design a simple GUI for this project with one Button and one Label, and write the code in the click event procedure of the Button.

```
Private Sub btnDisplay_Click (. . .) Handles btnDisplay.Click
    Dim Row As Integer
    Dim Col As Integer
    Dim Pr As Integer        'Product of values
    For Row = 1 To 10 Step 1      'Outer loop
        For Col = 1 to 10 Step 1        'Inner loop
            Pr = Row * Col
            lblShow.Text = lblShow.Text & Pr.ToString & " "
        Next Col
        lblShow.Text = lblShow.Text & vbLf        'Line feed
    Next Row
End Sub
```

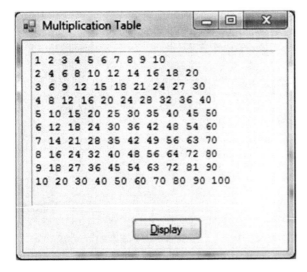

Figure 7.1 *Multiplication table*

Figure 7.1 is the screen capture of this project at runtime. The inner loop is responsible for displaying the values in each row. As you see the table is not quite tabular. To display the table in perfect tabular format, you have to use PadLeft and PadRight methods of the String class, and change the font of the Label to Courier New. Tabular display of output will be discussed in Chapter 8.

Review Questions:

1. What is the difference between the pre-test and post-test loops?

2. How many times will the following loop execute?
    ```
    Dim Ctr As Integer
    For Ctr = 1 To 10 Step 3
        ...
    Next Ctr
    ```
    a. 3
    b. 4
    c. 5
    d. None of above

3. What will be stored in variable Sum after the execution of the following loop?
    ```
    Dim Ctr As Integer
    Dim Sum As Integer = 0
    For Ctr = 0 To 20 Step 5
        Sum = Sum + Ctr
    Next Ctr
    ```
    a. 50
    b. 30
    c. Infinite loop!
    d. 40

4. What is the output of the following segment of code?
    ```
    Dim Ctr As Integer
    For Ctr = 1 To 10 Step 3
        ...
    Next Ctr
    lblShow.Text = Ctr.ToString
    ```
    a. 10
    b. 11
    c. 12
    d. 13
    e. 9

5. What is the outcome of the following loop?
    ```
    Dim Ctr As Integer = 1
    Do While Ctr <= 10
        lblShow.Text = lblShow.Text & Ctr.ToString & vbLf
    Loop
    ```
    a. Infinite loop
    b. Will not execute
    c. Results in run time error
    d. Displays: 1, 2, 3, . . ., 10 in the label

6. What is the outcome of the following loop?

```
Dim ctr As Integer = 10
Do While Ctr >= 0
    Ctr = Ctr - 1
Loop
lblShow.Text = Ctr.ToString
```

  a. Displays 10
  b. Displays 0
  c. Displays −1
  d. Results in error

7. What is the outcome of the following loop?

```
Dim N As Integer = 100
Do While N >= 10
    lblShow.Text = N.ToString
    N = N + 10
Loop
```

  a. An infinite loop
  b. Will not execute
  c. Displays 100, 90, 80, . . ., 10
  d. Displays 10

8. What is the outcome of the following loop?

```
Dim N As Integer = 100
Do Until N > 100
    lblShow.Text = N.ToString
    N = N + 1
Loop
```

  a. Displays numbers 1 to 100
  b. This is an infinite loop
  c. This loop will not execute
  d. Displays 100
  e. Displays 100 and 101

9. What is the outcome of the following loop?

```
Dim N As Integer = 0
Dim Sum As Integer = 0
Do Until N >= 100
    Sum = Sum + N
    N = N + 10
Loop
```

  a. Adds up 0 + 10 + 20 + . . .+ 100
  b. Adds up 0 + 10 + 20 + . . . + 90
  c. Adds up 0 + 10 + 20 + . . . + 100 + 110
  d. This is an infinite loop
  e. This loop will not execute

10. What is the outcome?
```
Dim N As Integer = 100
Dim Sum As Integer = 0
Do
     Sum = Sum + N
     N = N + 1
Loop While N < = 10
lblShow.Text = Sum.ToString
```
a. This is an infinite loop

b. 100

c. 101

d. This loop will not execute

PROGRAMMING CHALLENGES

1. Design a VB .NET project to allow the user enter a positive whole number in a TextBox, and click on a Button to have the program compute the sum of even numbers or the sum of odd numbers from 0 to the given number. (Add a Button for each task.) Validate the input number for being a positive whole number.

2. Design a VB .NET project to allow the user enter a whole number in a TextBox, and click on a Button to have the program determine whether the input number is a prime number or not. Make sure to validate the input data for being a whole number. If the number is negative, simply reverse its sign by a unary minus.

   Hint: A number is a prime if it is not divisible by any number smaller than itself except for 1. To determine if a number is divisible by another number use the Mod operator. Besides the loop variable, you may consider using a Boolean variable in your logic for this problem.

3. Design a VB .NET project to compute and display the monthly payment on a loan, for a range of the duration for the loan. This will help the user decide the duration of the loan. Allow the user to enter the amount of the loan, the annual interest rate (e.g., 6.25) the lower bound and upper bound for the duration of the loan (in months). Then the user must click on a Button to view the monthly payment for the range of terms between the lower bound and upper bound. The output should be displayed in a ListBox in two columns with column headers. The first column would be the duration in months, and the second column would be the monthly payment for the loan. The formula for computing the monthly payment on a loan is:

$$\text{Payment} = \frac{L * \text{Rate}/12}{1 - (1 + \text{Rate}/12)^{-m}}$$

   where:

       L: Amount of the loan
       m: Duration of the loan in months.
       Rate: Annual interest rate, ex: 0.0625

   There should be other Buttons on the Form to clear the I/O boxes, and end the program execution.

4. Design a VB .NET project to display the balance on a savings account that accumulates annually, based on a simple interest calculation. Assume that the interest earned is reinvested in the account at the end of each year. Allow the user to enter the initial amount of money being deposited, the annual interest rate e.g., 4.05, and the years of investment in provided boxes. The user can then click on a Button to have the balance at the end of each year displayed in two columns, with column headers. The output should be properly formatted. The first column would be the years 1, 2, . . . up to the year entered by user, and the second column would be the balance at the end of each year in the savings account.

   The balance at the end of the year is computed by:

$$\text{Balance} = \text{Amount} (1 + \text{Rate})$$

   Where Amount is the amount of money in the savings account at the beginning of the year, and the Rate is the annual interest rate (e.g., 0.0405). Notice that the balance at the end of each year should be used as the initial amount for the following year.

CHAPTER 8

Arrays

8.1 Introduction

Without using arrays, it is still possible to write programs to perform computations, process numeric data and so on. In some applications, one has to collect the data values, store them in the program, and be able to access each value later on. For example, consider an application designed for book keeping in a bookstore. It requires entering the name, ISBN, author's name and other data for each book, one at a time. The entered data should be stored in the computer's memory for certain processing required by the office. Without using arrays, you can write a program to get the data for one book, store it in variables, and do some processing. But once the next book's data is entered, it will be stored in the same variables, hence erasing the previously stored data. What is the solution? Is it possible to declare enough variables to store the data for all the books in the store? That would be similar to the old-fashioned paper-based bookkeeping; besides it would be practically impossible. Arrays, provide a solution for this kind of problem. By using arrays, many data values of the same data type can be stored in the computer's random access memory under one name. In other words, an array can be thought of as a variable that can store many data values of the same data type, instead of storing just one value. If you look up the word array in a dictionary, you will find that it refers to a group of similar objects that are arranged in an orderly fashion. Examples are array of numbers, array of houses, array of soldiers, and so on.

77	64	88	90	73

Array of numbers

© Corel.

Array of soldiers.

8.2 Definition

An array is a data structure that is used to store data values of the same data type in the computer's random access memory, RAM, under one name. Like a variable, to use an array, one has to declare it in the program.

8.3 Declaring a One-Dimensional Array

When declaring an array, the following information must be provided: Array's name, data type of array elements, and the number of values that can be stored in the array. The general syntax for declaration of arrays in VB .NET is as follows:

```
Dim|Private|Public ArrayName(LastIndex) As DataType
```

- Dim | Private | Public: Dim keyword is used when declaring an array with local scope, Private keyword is used when declaring an array with module scope, and Public keyword is used when declaring an array with project scope.
- ArrayName, is the name given to the array. To name an array, follow the same rules and standards specified to name variables (refer to chapter 2).
- DataType, is the data type of the values that can be stored in the array.
- LastIndex, is a whole number, greater than or equal to 0. The size of array, or the number of values that can be stored in an array, is equal to LastIndex + 1.

8.4 Index | Subscript

At the time of declaration, enough memory is allocated to store LastIndex + 1 values of the specified data type. For example, if DataType is Short, LastIndex + 1 consecutive memory locations, 2 bytes each will be allocated somewhere in computer's RAM. Each memory location is an array element. Array elements are assigned a whole number that is referred to as index or subscript. The index of the first element is always 0. The index of the last element is LastIndex. The elements in between are indexed sequentially as 1, 2, 3, and so on. Let us look at an example.

EXAMPLE 1

Declare an array to store the area codes of ten cities in Indiana. Assume that the area codes are three-digit whole numbers.

```
Dim Code(9) As Short
```

With the above declaration, ten consecutive memory locations, two bytes each will be allocated in the computer's RAM, and the memory locations will be assigned numbers from 0 to 9. The index of the first element is 0, the index of the last element is 9, and the indices of elements in between are 1, 2, ..., 8. One may picture the array Code in memory as follows:

0	1	2	3	4	5	6	7	8	9
0	0	0	0	0	0	0	0	0	0

All the elements of a numeric array are initialized to 0 at declaration time.

8.5 Accessing Array Elements

An array element can be used like a single variable of the same data type. To access an array element, use the name of the array followed by an open parenthesis, the index number, and a close parenthesis. For example, Code(0) will access the first element of array Code declared in the previous section. Array elements can be initialized at the time of declaration. This provides an easy way to declare and use small arrays. For example, the following declares array Data with 5 elements such that, 10 is stored in Data(0), 20 is stored in Data(1), 30 is stored in Data(2), 40 is stored in Data(3), and 50 is stored in Data(4).

```
Dim Data() As Short = {10, 20, 30, 40, 50}
```

Notice that the size of array should not be specified between () when declaring this kind of arrays.

EXAMPLE 2

Declare an array to store prices of 5 video games.

```
Dim Price(4) As Decimal
```

0	1	2	3	4
0	0	0	0	0

Perform the following operations on this array:

a. Store 12.50 in the first element of array.

```
Price(0) = 12.5
```

b. Store 89.95 at index 2 of this array.

```
Price(2) = 89.95
```

c. Given: Dim j As Integer = 3

Store 19.99 at index j of this array.

```
Price(j) = 19.99
```

d. Store 36 at the next index of this array.

```
Price (j+1) = 36
```

e. Assign the sum of values at indices 3 and 4 to the element at index 1.

```
Price(1) = Price(3) + Price(4)
```

f. Assign the value stored at the last element in array to the first element.

```
Price(0) = Price(4)
```

Array Price after above operations:

0	1	2	3	4
36	55.99	89.95	19.99	36

Subscript Out of Range Error:

An attempt to access a nonexisting index in an array, e.g. Price (6), results in a "Subscript out of Range" run-time error and the program execution halts.

8.6 Working with One-Dimensional Array

Arrays and loops go hand in hand. When working with arrays, one often needs to display the entire array, find the maximum or minimum value stored in the array, search for a certain value in the array, and so on. In such cases, a loop structure is needed.

EXAMPLE 3

Perform the following operations, in sequence.

a. Declare an array to store the test scores of 50 students. Assume that test scores are whole numbers.

```
Dim Score(49) As Integer
```

b. Fill this array with random test scores between 0 and 100.

```
Dim Index As Integer
For Index = 0 To 49 Step 1
    Score(Index) = Rnd() * 100
Next Index
```

c. Assume that array Score is filled with random numbers. Display all the scores in the output Label.

```
Dim Index As Integer
For Index = 0 To 49 Step 1
    lblShow.Text = lblShow.Text & Score(Index).ToString() & vbLf
Next Index
```

Rnd() is an intrinsic function in VB .NET. It returns a random real number between 0 and 1, including 0 but excluding 1. To generate a random number between 0 and 100, one has to scale up the output of the Rnd() function as follows: Rnd() * 100. By storing this real number in an integer array, it gets rounded up or rounded down to a whole number between 0 and 100 (both inclusive).

8.7 ListBox Control

The ListBox control can be found among the Common Controls in the ToolBox Window. A ListBox can be populated with all kinds of objects, such as numbers, strings, and so on. ListBox has several applications. One of the applications is presenting few choices to the user, and allowing the user to select one of them. It can also be used in place of the Label control, to display the program's output. Occasionally, a ListBox is preferred over a Label for displaying the output. The main advantage of the ListBox control is that a vertical scroll bar appears on its side, when the displayed output exceeds the size of the ListBox. Another advantage of the ListBox is that the user can click on the item displayed in the ListBox. Depending on the application, selecting an item in the ListBox may lead to some processing.

Important Properties

- **Name:** The Name property must be set at design time, when the ListBox is placed on a Form. The three-letter prefix for naming a ListBox is lst.

- **Items:** The Items property is a collection of values. It contains all the values displayed in the ListBox. A collection is a data structure, similar to an array, in the sense that the items in the collection are indexed as 0, 1, and so on. The index of the first item in the collection is 0, the index of the second item is 1 and so on. Unlike arrays, the values stored in a collection are of the generic data type Object, hence all kinds of values can be stored in it. The Items property may be filled with values at design time or at the run time using VB .NET code.

- **SelectedIndex:** This property exists at run time. Once the user selects an item in the ListBox, the index of the selected item is stored in the SelectedIndex Property. The SelectedIndex Property is equal to -1 when nothing is selected in the ListBox.

- **SelectedItem:** This property exists at runtime. Once the user selects an item in the ListBox at runtime, that item gets stored in the SelectedItem Property.

Important Methods

The following are the methods of the Items Property of the ListBox.

- **Add:** The Add method is used to add another item to a ListBox at runtime. It takes an object as an input argument. For example, the following statement adds "Math" to the list of the departments displayed in the ListBox named 1stOutput.

```
1stOutput.Items.Add("Math")
```

- **Clear:** The Clear method clears all the items displayed in a ListBox at runtime. For example, the following statement clears all the departments displayed in the lstOutput ListBox.

```
1stOutput.Items.Clear()
```

EXAMPLE 4

Design a VB .NET project to help the instructor of a class enter the students' quiz scores one at a time, display them on the screen, and compute the average score. Assume that there are 40 students in this class.

Let us follow the steps of the Programming Development Life Cycle (PDLC), introduced in Chapter 2:

Step 1: ANALYZE THE PROBLEM:

- Input needs:
  a. The user should enter the quiz score
- Output needs:
  a. Display all the scores and class average
- Processing needs:
  a. Enter the scores
  b. Display the scores
  c. Compute the average

Step 2: DESIGN THE GUI: The GUI for this problem requires a TextBox to enter quiz scores, a ListBox to display the output, and three Buttons to do the processing. The objects placed on the Form are named txtQuiz, lstOutput, btnEnter, btnDisplay, and btnAverage, as shown in Figure 8.1.

Step 3: DETERMINE WHICH CONTROLS RESPOND TO EVENTS: The three Buttons should respond to the click event and do the required tasks.

Step 4: DESIGN THE LOGIC OF THE EVENT PROCEDURES: In this example, we use pseudocode to explain the step-by-step solution of each event procedure. Using a flowchart is another way of showing the logic:

Since an array is needed in all the event procedures, it should be declared with module scope. Another reason for declaring the array with module scope is that, array should sustain the values stored in it during the program execution, hence it cannot be declared with local scope.

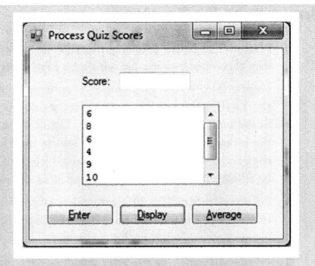

Figure 8.1 *Quiz Scores example at runtime*

Module Scope Declarations

```
Private Const cLast As Integer = 39

Private mScore(cLast) As Integer
```

 Declare the size of the array as a named constant. This makes it easier for the programmer to modify the size of the array in future, by making a single change in the code.

Pseudocode of the Click Event of the Enter Button

1. Validate the data entered in txtQuiz. Assume that the quiz score must be a whole number, greater than or equal to 0 and less than or equal to 10.

2. Store the valid score in the array at a proper index.

3. Clear the TextBox, txtQuiz.

4. Set the focus to txtQuiz for the next data entry.

> Q: At what index in the array should the quiz score be stored?
>
> A: Declare a variable with module scope, to keep track of the last index in array, where a value has been stored.

Declare an integer variable with module scope, to keep track of the next available index in the array.

```
Private mIndex As Integer = −1
```

At the beginning of the program execution, nothing has been entered, hence array is empty. Each time the user enters a score in txtQuiz and clicks on the Enter Button, the data must be stored in the array at the next available index, starting with index 0. In other words, the first score is stored at index 0, the next score is stored at index 1, and so on. Let us initialize mIndex to -1, to indicate an empty array. Each time the user enters a new score and clicks on the Enter Button, simply increment mIndex by 1 and store the entered data at that index in the array. Array is full when a value is stored at the last index in the array.

Pseudocode of the Click Event of the Display Button

1. Declare a loop variable to go through the array indices.

2. Clear the ListBox.

3. Write a For loop starting at index 0 to the last index where a data value is stored.
   a. In each cycle, display the quiz score stored in the array in the ListBox.

Pseudocode of the Click Event of the Average Button

1. Declare a loop variable, and a variable to add up the scores.

2. If array is empty (check if mIndex $= -1$), do nothing or Exit Sub.

3. Write a For loop starting at index 0, to the last index where a score is stored, i.e. mIndex.
   a. In each cycle, add the quiz score to the sum of scores.

4. Outside the loop, divide the sum of scores by the number of scores, which is mIndex plus one.

5. Display the average score in the ListBox.

Step 5: TRANSLATE THE PSEUDOCODES TO VB.NET CODE

```
Public Class Form1
Private Const cLast As Integer = 39
Private mScore(cLast) As Integer
Private mIndex As Integer = -1
Private Sub btnEnter_Click (. . .) Handles btnEnter.Click
    Dim Score As Integer
  'Validate the input:

    If Integer.TryParse(txtQuiz.Text, Score) = False Then
       MessageBox.Show("Enter a whole number.", . . .)
       txtQuiz.Focus()
    ElseIf Score < 0 or Score > 10 Then
       MessageBox.Show("Valid range is 0...10", . . .)
       txtQuiz.Focus()
    Else
     'Store the valid score in array:
       mIndex = mIndex + 1
       mScore(mIndex) = Score
       txtQuiz.Clear()
       txtQuiz.Focus()
    End If
End Sub
Private Sub btnDisplay_Click(. . .) Handles btnDisplay.Click
    Dim Ctr As Integer
    lstOutput.Items.Clear()
    For Ctr = 0 To mIndex Step 1
       lstOutput.Items.Add(mScore(Ctr))
    Next Ctr
End Sub
```

```
Private Sub btnAverage_Click(. . .) Handles btnAverage.Click
    Dim Sum As Integer
    Dim Average As Single
    Dim Ctr As Integer
    Sum = 0
    If mIndex = -1 Then 'Check for empty array
        Exit Sub
    End If
    'Add up the scores:
    For Ctr = 0 To mIndex
        Sum = Sum + mScore(Ctr)
    Next Ctr
    'Compute the average:
    Average = Sum/(mIndex + 1)
    lstOutput.Items.Add("Average = " & Average.ToString("n"))
End Sub
```

Empty Array: Array is empty, when the module scope variable, mIndex is equal to -1.

EXERCISE

As an exercise, design a VB .NET project to store the names of your friends. Let us assume that you have no more than 21 friends. The user should enter the names one at a time. There should also be a Button to display all the names in a ListBox.

8.8 Parallel Arrays

Parallel arrays are two or more one-dimensional arrays of the same size that are used to store different data values about an entity. Such arrays are processed in parallel. For example, to keep track of the names, test scores, and student IDs of the students in a class with 41 students, one has to declare three arrays:

```
Private Const cLast As Integer = 40
Private mName(cLast) As String
Private mID(cLast) As String
Private mScore(cLast) As Integer
```

	mName			mID			mScore
0	Alice		0	111-22-3333		0	92
1	Mark		1	333-44-5544		1	88
2	...		2	...		2	...
3			3			3	
40			40			40	

Each student's data is stored at the same index in three arrays. For example, different data regarding student "Alice" are stored at index 0 of three arrays. Different data about "Mark" are stored at index 1 of the parallel arrays, and so on.

EXAMPLE 5

Design a VB .NET project to process the midterm scores of the students in a class with 41 students. For each student, the instructor should enter a name and a test score. There should be a way in the program to display all the entered names and scores on the Form.

Let us follow the steps of the PDLC:

Step 1: ANALYZE THE PROBLEM

- Input needs:
  - a. The user should enter the student's name
  - b. The user should enter the test score

- Output needs:
  - a. Display all the students' names and scores

- Processing needs
  - a. Store the student's data in the program
  - b. Display the arrays' content

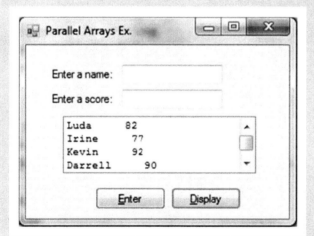

Figure 8.2 *Parallel arrays example at runtime*

Step 2: DESIGN THE GUI: According to step 1, the GUI for this project requires two TextBoxes to enter the name and score, a ListBox to display the program output, a Button to store the entered data in arrays, and another Button to display the array's content. The objects placed on the Form are named: txtName, txtScore, lstOutput, btnEnter, and btnDisplay (see Figure 8.2).

Step 3: DECIDE WHICH OBJECTS RESPOND TO EVENTS: Only Buttons should respond to the click event at runtime. To modularize the program further, we will write a general function to validate the entered data. This function will be invoked from the click event procedure of the Enter Button before processing the data.

Step 4: DESIGN THE LOGIC OF THE EVENT PROCEDURES:

Pseudocode of the Click Event of the Enter Button

1. Validate the input data:
   a. Validate the data entered in txtName for existence
   - Inform the user if there is no data, and set the focus to txtName
   b. Validate the data entered in txtScore for being a whole number
   - Inform the user if data not valid, and set the focus to txtScore

2. Store the valid data in the next available index in both arrays:
   a. Increment the module scope variable by 1
   b. Store data at that index in both arrays.

3. Check for full array, i.e. check if mIndex is equal to cLast. Disable the Enter Button if array is full

4. Clear both TextBoxes

5. Place the focus to txtName

Pseudocode for the Click Event of the Display Button

1. Start a For loop from index 0 to the last index where data has been stored.
   a. In each cycle, display the name and score of one student in the ListBox.

Data Structure

The data structure is where the program's data will be stored. To store the names and scores of all the students, two arrays are needed plus an integer counter to keep track of the last index (in both arrays) where a value is stored. Since both arrays and the integer variable are needed in the click event procedures of both Buttons, they should be declared with module scope. Another reason for declaring the data structure with module scope is that unlike the local variables, the module scope variables retain their values throughout the Form's execution, which in this case is the program's execution, since the program is composed of a single Form.

Step 5: TRANSLATE THE PSEUDOCODES TO VB .NET CODE.

```
Public Class Form1
'Module Scope Declarations:

 Private Const cLast As Integer = 40
 Private mName (cLast) As String
 Private mScore (cLast) As Integer
 Private mIndex As Integer = -1

 Private Sub btnEnter_Click(...) Handles btnEnter.Click
    If ValidateData() = False Then 'Validate Data
       Exit Sub
    End If
    'Store the valid data in both arrays:

    mIndex = mIndex + 1
    mName(mIndex) = txtName.Text
    mScore(mIndex) = Integer.Parse(txtScore.Text)
    'Check for full array:
    If mIndex = cLast Then
        btnEnter.Enabled = False
    End If
```

```
        'Get ready for the next data entry:
        txtName.Clear()
        txtScore.Clear()
        txtName.Focus()
    End Sub

    Private Sub btnDisplay_Click(...) Handles btnDisplay.Click
        Dim Ctr As Integer
        'Clear the listbox:
        lstShow.Items.Clear()

        For Ctr = 0 To mIndex Step 1
            lstShow.Items.Add(mName(Ctr) & Space(5) & mScore(Ctr).ToString)
        Next Ctr
    End Sub

    'General Function to validate the input data.
    Private Function ValidateData() As Boolean
        Dim Num As Short
        If txtName.Text = "" Then
            MessageBox.Show("Enter a name.", ...)
            txtName.Focus()
            Return False
        End If
        If Short.TryParse(txtScore.Text, Num) = False Then
            MessageBox.Show("Enter a whole number.", ...)
            txtScore.Focus()
            Return False
        End If

        Return True          'Do NOT forget!

    End Function
End Class
```

8.9 Displaying the Output in Tabular Format

In the previous example, the code in the Display Button spaces out the name and score of each student with five spaces; hence, the output does not appear in a tabular format, as shown in Figure 8.3. To display the program output in columns with fixed width, one may use the PadLeft and PadRight methods of the String class.

PadRight(n)

PadRight is a method of the String class. It can be used to left justify a string in n columns, where n is a positive whole number. If the string's length is less than n, it will be padded with spaces on the right-hand-side, creating a string with n characters. If the string's length is greater than n, then it overrides the specified width to display the entire string.

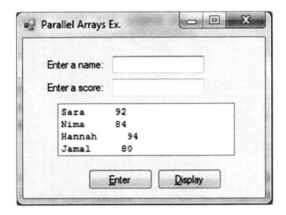

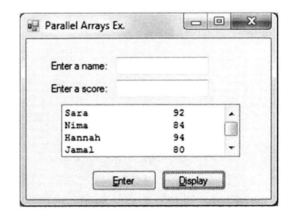

Figure 8.3 *Screen capture, non-aligned columns*

Figure 8.4 *Screen capture, with tabular format*

For example, consider the following statement:

```
lblShow.Text = "Hello".PadRight(10) & "Jimmy!"
```

It will display "Hello" in 10 columns, left justified, followed by "Jimmy!"

```
Hello-----Jimmy!
```

PadLeft(n)

PadLeft is a method of the String class. It does the opposite of the PadRight method. In other words, it can be used to right justify a string in *n* columns, padding the string from the left-hand-side with spaces.

For example, the following statement will display the name in 10 columns left justified and the score in 5 columns right justified:

```
lblShow.Text = "Shiva".PadRight(10) & "90".PadLeft(5)
```

Notice that name and score take 15 columns combined.

Font of the Output Box

The font of the output Label or ListBox should be changed to Courier New (a fixed-length font), in order to give each character the same width, resulting in a neat and tabular display.

 To Display the output in tabular format:
a. Change the font of the output box to Courier New
b. Use String methods PadRight and PadLeft to display the data in certain width.

```
'Revised code for Display Button:
Private Sub btnDisplay_Click(...) Handles btnDisplay.Click
    Dim Ctr As Integer
    'Clear the ListBox before displaying the output:
    1stShow.Items.Clear()
    For Ctr = 0 To mIndex Step 1
        1stShow.Items.Add(mName(Ctr).PadRight(15) &
            mScore(Ctr).ToString().PadLeft(5))
    Next Ctr
End Sub
```

Column Headers

Add the code for displaying the column headers, before the loop that displays the output. In our example, the following lines should be added before the loop in the click event of the Display Button.

```
1stShow.Items.Add("Name          Score")
1stShow.Items.Add("=====================")
```

EXERCISE

Design a VB .NET project to store the first name, last name, and the phone number of all your contacts in three parallel arrays. Assume that you have a maximum of 21 contacts. Provide Buttons in your application to display all the contacts in a ListBox and to end the program execution.

Review Questions:

1. What is the index of the first array element?

2. What is the index of the second array element?

3. Declare an array to store the names of students in a class of 120 students.

4. Store "Robin Hood" at index #4 of this array.

5. Declare an array to store salaries of 1,001 employees in a company.

6. Do the following:
    a. Declare a named constant of type integer = 20.
    b. Declare an array to store 21 test scores (whole number). Use the named constant at declaration.
    c. Assume that array is filled with some values, write a For loop to display all the scores in a ListBox.
    d. Write a segment of code to compute the class average.

7. What is the outcome of the following segment of code?

```
Dim Data(10) As Short
Dim Ctr As Short
For Ctr = 0 To 10 Step 1
    Data(Ctr) = Ctr
Next Ctr
```

PROGRAMMING CHALLENGES

1. Design a VB .NET project to store the test scores in a class of 21 students. The test scores which are whole numbers, should be stored in an array of proper size. Provide Buttons in the program to populate the array with random test scores in range of 0 to 100 [use the Rnd() function to populate the array], and compute the class average. You may add additional Buttons to find the maximum and minimum score stored in the array.

   Hint: In order to prevent the user from clicking on the compute average, maximum and minimum Buttons before populating the array, simply disable those Buttons at design time. The Buttons should be enabled once the user clicks the Button that populates the array.

2. Design a VB .NET project to store some information about the items sold in a store. Assume that for each item we want to store the name of the object and the unit price; also assume that there are no more than 101 objects in this store. Declare two parallel arrays of the proper size and data type to store the name and price of the objects. Let the user enter the name and the price of the objects one at a time followed by a click on a Button to store the data in the arrays. At any time the user may click on the Display Button to view the list of all the items along with their unit prices in an output box (ListBox would be appropriate) in a tabular format. Provide another Button to display some statistics about these items, such as the number of items entered in the program, and the average price of the objects sold in store. Use the same output box for displaying the statistics.

CHAPTER 9

Dynamic and Two-Dimensional Arrays

LEARNING OBJECTIVES

After completing Chapter 9, students should be able to:
- ❏ Understand and use dynamic arrays
- ❏ Understand and use two-dimensional arrays
- ❏ Understand the concept of the Sequential Search Algorithm
- ❏ Understand and implement the Bubble Sort Algorithm

9.1 Dynamic Arrays

A dynamic array is one that can be resized during the program execution. Unlike the static array, the size of a dynamic array is not specified at declaration time; hence, no memory gets allocated. It is sometimes difficult to decide the maximum number of values to be stored in an array. For example, the number of students in a class may change from one semester to the next, or the number of employees in a company may vary as the company grows or shrinks every year. In such cases, a dynamic array provides an efficient use of the computer's memory and allows the array to grow or shrink in size as needed. In VB .NET even a static array can be re-sized in the program.

9.2 Declaration

General Syntax

```
Dim | Private | Public ArrayName() As DataType
```

For example, the following statement declares a dynamic array to store an unknown number of names. This declaration informs the compiler of the name and data type of the dynamic array. No memory is allocated at declaration time.

```
Dim Name() As String
```

Keywords Dim, Private and Public are used to declare an array with local scope, module scope or global scope respectively.

9.3 Resizing a Dynamic Array

At declaration time, no memory is allocated for a dynamic array. In order to store values in a dynamic array, it has to be resized to allocate enough bytes in the computer's memory. There are two ways to resize a dynamic array:

a. **ReDim:** The keyword ReDim is used to resize a dynamic array to the desired size, while resetting the existing values in the array to their default values (0 for numeric arrays, and False for Boolean arrays). An array can be resized many times during the program execution to a bigger or a smaller size. The general syntax for using ReDim is:

```
ReDim ArrayName(n)
```

Where ArrayName is the name of the dynamic array, and n is a whole number greater than or equal to 0, specifying the last index in the resized array. After ReDim, the dynamic array will have $n + 1$ elements. n can be a numeric literal, or a variable. Notice that ReDim cannot be used to declare an array.

EXAMPLE 1

Consider the dynamic array Data of type Short.

```
Dim Data() As Short
```

Resize the array to store three values, 10, 11, and 12:

```
ReDim Data(2)
```

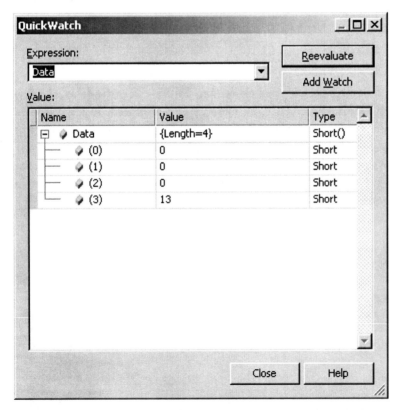

```
Data(0) = 10
Data(1) = 11
Data(2) = 12
```

Now, let us resize the array to store one more value, 13:

```
ReDim Data(3)
Data(3) = 13
```

Figure 9.1 shows the indices and values stored in array at runtime. Only the last value stored in array is present; all the previously stored values are reset to 0.

b. **ReDim Preserve:** The keywords ReDim Preserve are used to resize a dynamic array to the desired size, while preserving the existing values stored in the array. An array can be resized many times to a bigger or a smaller size. The syntax for using ReDim Preserve is very similar to the syntax for ReDim.

Figure 9.1 *Quick Watch is used to view the content of the dynamic array in ReDim example*

EXAMPLE 2

Consider the dynamic array Score declared to store an unknown number of test scores.

```
Dim Score() As Integer
```

Resize the array to store four values 90, 70, 65, and 100. One may use either ReDim or ReDim Preserve when resizing the dynamic array for the first time.

```
ReDim Score(3)
```

'or: ReDim Preserve Score (3)

```
Score(0) = 90
Score(1) = 70
Score(2) = 65
Score(3) = 100
```

Now let us resize the array to add one more score, while preserving the existing values:

```
ReDim Preserve Score(4)
Score(4) = 88
```

Figure 9.2 shows the indices and values stored in array Score after the second resizing at runtime.

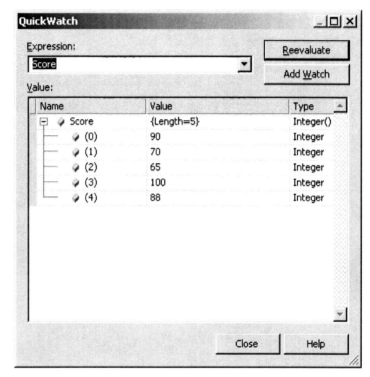

Figure 9.2 *Quick Watch is used to view the content of the dynamic array in ReDim Preserve example*

- ReDim ArrayName *(n)*: Resizes ArrayName to *n* + 1 elements, indexed 0 to *n*, clearing the existing values.
- ReDim Preserve ArrayName *(n)*: Resizes ArrayName to *n* + 1 elements, indexed 0 to *n*, preserving the existing values.
- *n* is a whole number ⩾ 0. It can be a literal or a variable.

 QuickWatch: To view the content of an array during the program execution, set a break point in the code. Right click on array's name, and select QuickWatch from dropped down menu.

How to Shrink a Dynamic Array

A dynamic array may be resized to a smaller size as well. However, it is impossible to get rid of the last element in array. For example, to delete all the elements of the dynamic array Score, you have to resize the array as follows:

```
ReDim Score(0)
```

This statement reduces the array to only one element at index 0. It also resets the value stored at index 0 after resizing to zero. Use ReDim Preserve to keep the value stored at index 0.

 VB .NET does not support the true notion of static arrays. In other words, any array can be resized using the keywords ReDim or ReDim Preserve. However, you have the option of declaring an array with no size and then resize it as needed, or declare it with a specific size and then resize it if needed.

EXAMPLE 3

Let us modify Example 5 presented in Chapter 8 as follows: Design a VB .NET project to process an unknown number of students in a class. For each student, the teacher enters student's name and test score followed by a click on the Enter Button. At any time, the teacher may click on the Display Button to view the list of students' names along with their test scores in the ListBox.

Let us follow the steps in the PDLC

The first two steps are the same as those explained in Example 5 in the previous chapter. The designed GUI is shown in Figure 9.3.

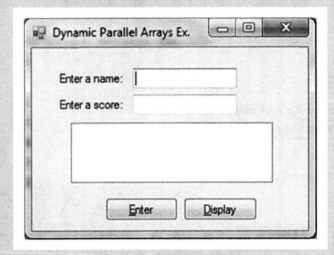

Figure 9.3 *Screen Capture at runtime*

Since the number of students in class is unknown, the data should be stored in two dynamic arrays with module scope. An integer counter with module scope must be used to keep track of the last index in arrays where data is stored.

Data Structure with Module Scope

```
Private mName() As String
Private mScore() As Integer
Private mIndex As Integer = -1
```

Step 3: DETERMINE WHICH OBJECTS RESPOND TO WHICH EVENTS

In this example, only the Buttons should respond to the click event. We will further modularize the program by writing a general function to validate the input data. This function should be invoked from the click event procedure of the Enter Button.

Step 4: DEVELOP THE LOGIC FOR EVENT PROCEDURES

Let us use pseudocode to explain the step-by-step solution for each event procedure.

The pseudocode for the click event procedure of the Enter Button:

1. Validate the input data by invoking the general function written for this task.

2. For valid data, increment mIndex by 1

3. Resize the dynamic arrays to store the entered data.

4. Store the valid data in both arrays, at mIndex

5. Clear the input boxes and set the focus to the top TextBox

The pseudocode for the click event procedure of the Display Button:

1. Clear the ListBox

2. Start a For loop to iterate through the array indices from 0 to mIndex
    a. Display data stored in both arrays at this index (the loop variable)

3. Continue the loop

Step 5: TRANSLATE THE LOGIC TO VB.NET CODE.

```vbnet
Public Class Form1
 Private mName() As String
 Private mScore() As Integer
 Private mIndex As Integer = -1
'Click event procedure of Button Enter:
 Private Sub btnEnter_Click(. . .) Handles btnEnter.Click
    If ValidateData() = False Then      'Invoke the function to validate data
       Exit Sub
    End If
    'Resize the dynamic arrays:

    mIndex = mIndex + 1
    ReDim Preserve mName(mIndex)
    ReDim Preserve mScore(mIndex)
    'Store the entered data in dynamic arrays:

    mName(mIndex) = txtName.Text
    mScore(mIndex) = Integer.Parse(txtScore.Text)
    'Get ready for the next data entry:

    txtName.Clear()
    txtScore.Clear()
    txtName.Focus()
 End Sub
'Click event procedure of btnDisplay:
 Private Sub btnDisplay_Click(. . .) Handles btnDisplay.Click
    Dim Ctr As Integer
    lstShow.Items.Clear() 'Clear the listbox
    For Ctr = 0 To mIndex Step 1
      lstShow.Items.Add(mName(Ctr).PadRight(15) &
        mScore(Ctr).ToString.PadLeft(5))
    Next Ctr
 End Sub
'General Function to validate the input data
 Private Function ValidateData() As Boolean
    Dim Score As Integer
    If txtName.Text = "" Then
```

```
            MessageBox.Show("Enter a name.",. . .)
            txtName.Focus()
            Return False
        End If
        If Integer.TryParse(txtScore.Text, Score) = False Then
            MessageBox.Show("Enter a whole number.", . . .)
            txtScore.Focus()
            Return False
        End If
        Return True        'Do not forget!
    End Function
    End Class
```

EXERCISE

Design a VB .NET project to store the first name, last name, and the phone number of all your friends in three dynamic parallel arrays. Assume that you do not know the exact number of your friends. Provide a Button to display all the contacts stored in the arrays in a ListBox in a neat and tabular format and a Button to end the program execution.

9.4 Two-Dimensional Arrays

Sometimes it makes sense to store the data values in a table with rows and columns. One example is to store the three test scores of students in a class of 40 students. The data can be stored in a table with 40 rows and 3 columns. Each row represents one student and each column represents all the test scores for one of the exams. Another example is storing the annual budget of all the states in America for the past 10 years. The data can be stored in a table with 51 rows and 10 columns. Each row represents one state and each column represents one year's budget for all the states. In a computer program, a table of values can be implemented using a two-dimensional array.

Declaration Syntax

```
Dim | Private | Public ArrayName (lastRow, LastCol) As DataType
```

- The keywords Dim, Private, or Public are used to declare an array with local scope, module scope, or global scope, respectively.

- ArrayName is the name of the array

- LastRow is the index of the last row in array

- LastCol is the index of the last column in array

- DataType is the data type of the values stored in array

EXAMPLE 4

This example has five parts:

a. Declare an array to store the annual sales of three branches of Kroger Supermarket in Indianapolis for the past five years:

```
Dim Sale(2, 4)As Decimal
```

	Year →				
Branch ↓	0	1	2	3	4
	0	0	0	0	0
	0	0	0	0	0
	0	0	0	0	0

Each row of array Sale represents one branch and each column represents one year. For example, the row at index 0 represents the first branch, the row at index 1 represents the second branch, and so on. Like numeric variables, all the array elements are initialized to 0 at declaration time.

b. Assume that the second branch has sold $35,000 during the fifth year. Store this value in array Sale:

```
Sale(1, 4) = 35000
```

c. Assume that all the branches have sold $50,000 during the second year. Write a loop to assign this value to all the array elements in Column #1:

```
Dim Row As Integer
For Row = 0 To 2 Step 1
    Sale(Row, 1) = 50000
Next Row
```

d. Compute the total sales made by the first branch in five years. To do this, write a loop to add up all the values in the first row:

```
Dim Year As Integer
Dim TotalSale As Decimal = 0
For Year = 0 To 4 Step 1
    TotalSale = TotalSale + Sale(0, Year)
Next Year
```

e. Display all the values stored in array Sale in a ListBox in a tabular format. To do this, a nested loop is required. The outer loop represents branches, and the inner loop represents years.

```
Dim Row, Col As Integer
Dim OneRow As String

For Row = 0 To 2 Step 1      'Outer loop
    OneRow = ""
    For Col = 0 To 4 Step 1      'Inner loop
        OneRow =OneRow & Sale(Row, Col).ToString("c").PadLeft(10)
    Next Col
    lstOutput.Items.Add(OneRow)
Next Row
```

 VB .NET allows declaring arrays with up to 32 dimensions. Private ArrayName (dim1, dim2, dim3, . . .)

9.5 More on Arrays

Length Property:

In VB .NET, Array is a class and has useful properties and methods. The Length property, provides the number of elements in the array: ArrayName.Length

Sort Method:

Array class has a Sort method; it sorts the array in ascending order: Array.Sort(ArrayName)

Reverse Method:

Array class has a Reverse method; it sorts the array in descending order: Array.Reverse(ArrayName)

EXAMPLE 5

Example 5: Consider the array Data declared below.

```
Dim Data(20) As Double
```

a.   Fill the array with random numbers in range of 0 to 100:

```
Dim Index As Integer
For Index = 0 To Data.Length - 1    'Data.Length is 21
    Data(Index) = Rnd() * 100
Next Index
```

b.   Sort the array in ascending order:

```
Array.Sort(Data)
```

9.6 Searching and Sorting

Often when working with arrays, it is necessary to search an array for a specific value or sort the array in certain order. There are several searching algorithms available to search an array for a given value. In this chapter, we examine the sequential search and bubble sort algorithms.

9.7 Sequential Search

The sequential search is the easiest and the most common search algorithm. In fact, it is the only way to search for a certain value in an unsorted array. The logic of a sequential search is similar to looking through a pile of mixed-up papers for a certain document. The natural way to search is to start at the beginning of the pile, and examine papers one by one until the desired document is found or the end of the pile is reached.

Sequential Search Algorithm

It is helpful to use a Boolean variable in the code, to signal the success or failure of a search. Sequential search can be used to find a unique value in a list, or more than one value that are in the same category.

Sequential search for easter eggs!

1. Searching for a unique value:
   a. Declare a Boolean variable to indicate the success or failure of the search, name it Flag.
   b. Initialize the Flag to False, assuming that there is no such value in the array.
   c. Start a For loop from index 0 to the last index in the array where data has been stored.
      i. Compare the search Key to the array element.
      ii. If they are equal, change the Flag to True, and end the loop.
      iii. Otherwise, continue the loop.
   d. After the loop examine the boolean variable. If Flag is equal to False, the search has failed, otherwise display the search results.

2. Searching for all the values matching the search criteria. For example, one might search for all the students with the last name "Doe" or all the students who received a score greater than 90, and so on.
   a. Declare a Flag to indicate the success or failure of the search.
   b. Initialize the Flag to False, assuming that there is no such value in the array.
   c. Start a For loop from index 0 to the last index in array where data has been stored.
      i. Compare the search Key to the array element. If there is a match, change the Flag to True.
      ii. Continue the loop.
   d. After the loop, check the Flag. If it is equal to false, the search has failed.

EXAMPLE 6

Assume that array SSNO is filled with social security numbers of students in a class. Write a segment of code to search for a given social security number, e.g., "111-22-3333", in this array.

```
Private SSNO(100) As String
'Segment of code to search for a unique value in array:
Dim Ctr As Integer
Dim Flag As Boolean
Flag = False
For Ctr 0 To 100 Step 1
    If SSNO(Ctr) = "111-22-3333" Then
        Flag = True
        Exit For
    End If
Next Ctr

If Flag = False Then
    MessageBox.Show("Search Failed!", . . .)
Else
    MessageBox.Show("Item was found at index:" & Ctr.ToString, . . .)
End If
```

 An alternate way to check a Boolean variable for being equal to True:
`If Flag Then`   Is the same as: `If Flag = True Then`

 An alternate way to check a Boolean variable for being equal to False:
`If Not Flag Then`   Is the same as: `If Flag = False Then`

9.8 Bubble Sort

There are several sorting algorithms available in computer programming for sorting arrays in ascending or descending order. The Bubble Sort is one of the most common sorting algorithms. The logic is based on going through the array elements several times. In each pass, one should compare the two consecutive elements in the array, and swap them if they are not in proper (ascending or descending) order. To sort an array of n elements, one has to go through the array elements at most $n - 1$ times. Let us use this algorithm to sort a small array in ascending order.

EXAMPLE 7

Consider array Data declared below. Use the Bubble Sort algorithm to sort array Data in ascending order. Below are the values stored in the array after each pass. Notice that the biggest value is moved to the end of the array after each pass.

```
Private Data() = {88, 66, 50, 46, 34, 10}
```

	0	1	2	3	4	5
After Pass #1:	66	50	46	34	10	88
After Pass #2:	50	46	34	10	66	88
After Pass #3:	46	34	10	50	66	88
After Pass #4:	34	10	46	50	66	88
After Pass #5:	10	34	46	50	66	88

Notice that the array in this example is originally in descending order. It takes five passes to sort array in ascending order. Notice that in each pass, the next biggest value moves to the end of array. It is possible for an array to be sorted after the first pass. For example, it takes only one pass to sort the following array in ascending order:

```
Private Value() = {90, 10, 20, 30, 40, 50, 60, 70, 80}
```

Bubble Sort Algorithm: To sort a numeric array of $n + 1$ elements:

1. Outer Loop: Start a loop that iterates n times.
   a. Inner Loop: Start a loop from index 0 to index $n-1$
      i. Compare the two consecutive array elements
      ii. If they are not in proper order, i.e., ascending:
         • Swap the values
      iii. Move on to the next pair of elements.

      Continue the inner loop

   Continue the outer loop

To translate this algorithm to VB .NET code, let us write a general procedure that takes an integer array and its size as input and sorts the array.

```
'General procedure to sort a given array in ascending order
    Private Sub BubbleSort (A() As Integer, LastIndex As Integer)
        Dim Pass As Integer      'Outer loop counter
        Dim Index As Integer     'Inner loop counter
        Dim Temp As Integer      'Variable used in swapping

        For Pass = 1 To LastIndex Step 1      'Outer loop
            For Index = 0 To LastIndex - 1     'Inner loop
                If A(Index) > A(Index + 1) Then      'Swap the values
                    Temp = A(Index)
                    A(Index) = A(Index + 1)
                    A(Index + 1) = Temp
                End If
            Next Index
        Next Pass
    End Sub
```

Note: The code can be made more efficient in two ways:

1. The inner loop does not have to go until the end of the array in each pass. Since in each pass, the largest value sinks to the end of the array, the inner loop may go up to one less index in each pass.

2. A lot of times the array gets sorted after a few passes, and there is no need for the outer loop to complete all its cycles. The array is sorted when no values are swapped in the inner loop. This can be detected by using a Boolean variable. Below is the more efficient version of the code:

```
    Private Sub EffBubbleSort (A() As Integer, LastIndex As Integer)
        Dim Pass As Integer      'Outer loop counter
        Dim Index As Integer     'Inner loop counter
        Dim Temp As Integer      'Variable used in swapping
        Dim Last As Integer      'Where to stop the inner loop
        Dim SwapFlag As Boolean      'Detect if there was a swap
        Last = LastIndex - 1
        SwapFlag = True
        'Change the outer loop to a Do-While loop:
        Do While (Pass <= Last And SwapFlag = True)
            SwapFlag = False
            For Index = 0 To Last Step 1      'Inner loop
                If A(Index) > A(Index + 1) Then      'Swap values
                    Temp = A(Index)
                    A(Index) = A(Index + 1)
                    A(Index + 1) = Temp
                    SwapFlag = True      'There was a swap
                End If
            Next Index
            Last = Last - 1      'Inner loop iterates one less cycle each time
            Pass = Pass + 1      'Update the outer loop variable
        Loop
    End Sub
```

You can call this general procedure from another procedure or function. Assume that there is an Integer array mData in a VB .NET project. Assume that the last index in the array with data values stored in it is mIndex. The following code will call the general procedure to sort this array in ascending order:

```
Call BubbleSort (mData, mIndex)
```

Review Questions:

1. What is a dynamic array?

2. What is the lowest index in a dynamic array?

3. Declare a dynamic array to store social security numbers of students at "Purdue University".

4. Resize the array to store 5,001 data values.

5. Given the following declaration for array Data, what will be the arrangements of values in the array after the first pass of the Bubble Sort? Assume that array is being sorted in ascending order.

```
Private Data () As Short = {6, 23, 90, 50, 44, 17, 96, 33}
```

6. Explain the difference between ReDim and ReDim Preserve

PROGRAMMING CHALLENGES

1. Design a VB .NET project to store the test scores in a class of unknown number of students. The test scores, which are whole numbers, should be stored in a dynamic array that is of Integer data type. Allow the user to enter the scores one at a time, followed by a click on a Button to store the grade in the array. Add Buttons to compute the class average, the maximum score, and the minimum test score.

2. Design a VB. NET project to store some data about the items sold in a store. Assume that for each item we want to store the name of the object and the unit price; also assume that there is an unknown number of objects in this store. Declare two parallel arrays of proper data types to store the name and price of the objects. Let the user enter the name and the price of the objects one at a time followed by a click on a Button to store the data in the arrays. At any time the user may click on the Display Button to view the list of all the items along with their unit prices in an output box (ListBox would be appropriate) in a tabular format. Provide another Button to display some statistics about these items, such as the number of items entered in the program, and the average price of the objects sold in store. Use the same output box for displaying the statistics.

3. Design a VB .NET project to store some data about the employees who are taking part in a golf tournament in a company. The number of employees who will sign up for this event is not known. For each employee, the user should enter the first name, last name, the email address, and a phone number followed by a click on a Button to store data in the program. Declare four dynamic arrays to store this data. Provide another Button to display the list of employees (last name, first name, email, and phone #) in a tabular format in a ListBox. Also add a Button to search for an employee based on the last name entered in the TextBox. The Search Button should display all the employees that have that last name along with their other information; inform the user if there is no employee with that name. There should be other Buttons to clear the I/O boxes, and end the program execution. **Validation Rules:** Validate the first name, and last name for existence, the email should contain a @ and a · character, and the phone number should follow this pattern ###-###-####.

   Hint: Use the Like operator to validate the email address and the phone number.

CHAPTER 10

User-Defined Data Types

LEARNING OBJECTIVES

After completing Chapter 10, students should be able to:

☐ Define structures

☐ Implement and understand an array of structure

☐ Use the InputBox function

10.1 Structure

Most programming languages have a way of defining an abstract data type. An abstract data type is a user-defined data type (UDT) that is introduced by a programmer to facilitate programming task by making the problem clearer and easier to manage. In VB .NET, a programmer may use structures to declare abstract data types. A structure is an aggregated data type that is composed of several preexisting data types. So far we have only worked with built-in data types such as Integer, Double, and etc. Structure provide a way to define a data type to pull together related data about a certain entity. For example, to store different pieces of data about an employee in a program, several variables should be declared, one for each piece of data. A structure allows the programmer to declare an abstract data type, consisting of several members, to store the entire data about an employee in one variable.

Declaration Syntax (keywords are in bold)

```
Private|Public Structure StructureName
    Dim Member-1 As DataType-1
    Dim Member-2 As DataType-2
    . . .
    Dim Member-i As DataType-i
End Structure
```

- A structure cannot be declared with local scope within a procedure or function. Use keyword Private or Public to declare a structure with module or global scope respectively.

- Structure is the keyword used for defining the user defined data type.

- StructureName is the name of the user-defined data type. It follows the same naming rules as variables.

- Member-i is the name of the ith data member in the structure. A data member can be a variable, an array, another structure, or even a function. Normally, a data member is a variable of an existing data type. The data members must have a unique name within the structure.

- DataType-i is the data type of the ith member in the structure.

- End Structure ends the definition of the structure.

 A structure can *not* be declared locally inside a procedure or a function. It must be declared either with module scope or project scope.

10.2 Structure Variable

Once a structure is introduced, one may declare variables and arrays of the structure data type, the same way variables and arrays of built-in data types are declared. Let us look at an example:

EXAMPLE 1

Declare a structure to hold the following data about your favorite college basketball team: the team's name, number of wins, number of losses, and whether the team is ranked or not.

```
Private Structure mTeamRecord
    Dim Name As String
    Dim WinCount As Integer
    Dim LossCount As Integer
    Dim Ranked As Boolean
End Structure
```

a. Declare a variable of this structure type, named MyTeam.

```
Dim MyTeam As mTeamRecord
```

b. Declare an array of structure, to store sixteen NCAA teams.

```
Private mSweetSixteen(15) As mTeamRecord
```

c. Declare a dynamic array to store unknown number of teams.

```
Private mTeam() As mTeamRecord
```

10.3 Accessing the Data Members

To access the data members of a structure variable, use the dot (.) operator:

```
StructureVariable.MemberName
```

EXAMPLE 2

Given the structure and variables declared in Example 1, perform the following:

a. Store the team name "Purdue", 16 wins, 8 losses, and ranked in variable MyTeam.

```
MyTeam.Name = "Purdue"
MyTeam.WinCount = 16
MyTeam.LossCount = 8
MyTeam.Ranked = True
```

b. Store the team name "North Carolina", 12 wins, 7 losses, and not ranked at index 3 of array mSweetSixteen.

```
mSweetSixteen(3).Name = "North Carolina"
mSweetSixteen(3).WinCount = 12
mSweetSixteen(3).LossCount = 7
mSweetSixteen(3).Ranked = False
```

c. Resize the dynamic array mTeam to store the team name "UCLA," 26 wins, 5 losses, and team ranked.

```
ReDim mTeam(0)
mTeam(0).Name = "UCLA"
mTeam(0).WinCount = 26
mTeam(0).LossCount = 5
mTeam(0).Ranked = True
```

10.4 Assigning One Structure Variable to Another

Structure variables of the same data type may be assigned to one another. For example, consider the structure defined in Example 1. Let us declare two structure variables, named Team1, and Team2:

```
Dim Team1, Team2 As mTeamRecord
```

Let us store some values are stored in Team1.

```
Team1.Name = "Purdue"
Team1.WinCount = 12
Team1.LossCount = 5
Team1.Ranked = True
```

To store exactly the same values in variable Team2, one way is to assign each member of Team1 to the corresponding member in Team2 as follows:

```
Team2.Name = Team1.Name
Team2.WinCount = Team1.WinCount
Team2.LossCount = Team1.LossCount
Team2.Ranked = Team1.Ranked
```

However, VB .NET and most programming languages allow the entire structure variable to be assigned to another structure variable of the same data type. In other words, instead of member by member copying, one may simply assign variable Team1 to Team2 and achieve the same result.

```
Team2 = Team1
```

EXAMPLE 3

Design a VB .NET project to store the information of unknown number of college basketball teams who play in the NCAA season. For each team, the user enters the team's name, the number of wins, the number of losses, and checks the CheckBox if the team is ranked, followed by a click on a Button to store the data in a dynamic array of structure. There should be other Buttons on the Form to display all the teams in a ListBox, and to search for a team in the array. Also, write the code to populate the input boxes with the team's data if the user clicks on the team's name in the ListBox at runtime.

Let us go through the Program Development Life Cycle (PDLC):

Step 1: ANALYZE THE PROBLEM:

a.   Input needs:

- Team's name
- Number of wins
- Number of losses
- Is the team ranked?

b.   Output needs:

- Display all the teams on the Form

c.   Processing needs:

- Store each team's data in the program
- Search for a team
- Display all the teams

Step 2: DESIGN THE GUI BASED ON THE PROBLEM ANALYSIS:

a.   For input needs, there should be three TextBoxes to enter the team's name, number of wins, and number of losses. A CheckBox is an ideal control to get the user's input on whether the team

Figure 10.1 *GUI designed for NCAA project*

is ranked or not. The user checks the CheckBox, if the team is ranked. For output needs, a ListBox is a good choice to display all the teams entered in the program. For processing needs, there should be three Buttons. The objects on the Form are named txtName, txtWins, txtLosses, chkRank, lstShow, btnEnter, btnDisplay, and btnSearch. The outcome is shown in Figure 10.1.

Step 3: DETERMINE WHICH OBJECTS SHOULD RESPOND TO WHICH EVENTS: Each Button should respond to the click event at runtime to do its required task. The ListBox object should respond to the SelectedIndexChanged event which is triggered when one of the teams in the ListBox is selected, or clicked. To further modularize the program we will write a general function to validate the input data. This function should be invoked from the click event procedure of the Enter Button.

Step 4: DEVELOP THE LOGIC FOR EACH EVENT PROCEDURE.

Pseudocode for the Click event of the Enter Button:

- Validate the data, by invoking the general function

- Store the valid data in array of structure

- Clear the entered data

- Set the focus to the top TextBox

Pseudocode for the Click event of the Display Button:

- Clear the ListBox

- Add a column header for displaying the output

- Write a For loop to go through all the teams stored in the array

- In each iteration, display one team's data in the ListBox

Pseudocode for the Click event of the Search Button:

- Use an InputBox function to get the name of the team to search for (refer to Section 10.5 on InputBox) It is also possible to ask the user to enter the team's name in the provided TextBox.

- Use the sequential search algorithm to search for this team in the array

- If the team is found, display its data in the input TextBoxes and in the CheckBox

- Inform the user if the search has failed

Pseudocode for SelectedIndexChanged event of the ListBox:

This event takes place when the user clicks on an item in the ListBox, during the program's execution.

- Get the index of the selected team in the ListBox (that is the SelectedIndex property)

- The item in the ListBox is stored at SelectedIndex-1 in the array (because the first line in the ListBox is column header). Display the array element at that index in the input boxes on the Form.

Pseudocode of the general function

- Validate the team name for existence. If it does not exist,
  - Inform the user
  - Set the focus to the TextBox
  - Return False

- Validate the number of wins for being a whole number, if it is not,
  - Inform the user
  - Set the focus to the TextBox
  - Return False

- Make sure the number of wins is greater than or equal to 0, if it is not,
  - Inform the user
  - Set the focus to the TextBox
  - Return False

- Validate the number of losses for being a whole number, if it is not,
  - Inform the user
  - Set the focus to the TextBox
  - Return False

- Make sure the number of losses is greater than or equal to 0, if it is not,
  - Inform the user
  - Set the focus to the TextBox
  - Return False

- Everything is valid, return True.

 SelectedIndexChanged is an event of the ListBox control. It takes place when one of the items in the ListBox is selected or clicked at runtime.

Data Structure

Before writing any code, you must make decisions about the data structure and determine where the data should be stored. To store an unknown number of teams in a program requires dynamic array(s). You can declare four dynamic arrays to store different information about the teams, or you can store all the teams, in a dynamic array of structure. The latter is the preferred choice by most programmers.

```
Private Structure mTeamRecord
    Dim TeamName As String
    Dim WinCount As Integer
    Dim LossCount As Integer
    Dim Ranked As Boolean
End Structure
Private mTeam() As mTeamRecord
Private mIndex As Integer = -1
```

STEP 5. TRANSLATE THE PSEUDOCODES TO VB .NET CODE.

```
Private Sub btnEnter_Click(. . .) Handles btnEnter.Click
    If ValidateData() = False then
        Exit Sub
    End If

    'Resize the array and store the valid data at mIndex:

    mIndex = mIndex + 1
    ReDim Preserve mTeam(mIndex)
    mTeam(mIndex).TeamName = txtName.text
    mTeam(mIndex).WinCount = Integer.Parse(txtWins.Text)
    mTeam(mIndex).LossCount = Integer.Parse(txtLosses.Text)
    If chkRank.Checked = True Then
        mTeam(mIndex).Ranked = True
    Else
        mTeam(mIndex).Ranked = False
    End If

    'Get ready for the next data entry:

    txtName.Clear()
    txtWins.Clear()
    txtLosses.Clear()
    chkRank.Checked = False
    txtName.Focus()
End Sub
```

```
Private Sub btnDisplay_Click(. . .) Handles btnDisplay.Click
    Dim Count As Integer
    Dim Line As String
    lstShow.Items.Clear()        'Clear the listbox
    lstShow.Items.Add ("Name      Wins     Losses     Ranked?")
    For Count = 0 To mIndex Step 1
        Line = mTeam(Count).TeamName.PadRight(15) &
            mTeam(Count).WinCount.ToString().PadLeft(5) &
            mTeam(Count).LossCount.ToString().PadLeft(5) &
            mTeam(Count).Ranked.ToString().PadLeft(10)
        lstShow.Items.Add(Line)
    Next Count
End Sub

Private Sub btnSearch_Click(. . .) Handles btnSearch.Click
    Dim Team As String
    Dim Found As Boolean      'To determine the search outcome
    Dim Count As Integer      'Loop variable
    Team = InputBox("Enter the team's name.")
    If Team = "" Then
      MessageBox.Show("A name is required", . . .)
      Exit Sub
    End If
    Found = False      'Assume the team is not in the array
    For Count = 0 To mIndex Step 1
        If mTeam(Count).TeamName = Team Then
           Found = True
           Exit For      'Stop the search
        End If
    Next Count
    If Found = True Then      'Display the team found at index: Count
        txtName.Text = mTeam(Count).TeamName
        txtWins.Text = mTeam(Count).WinCount.ToString()
        txtLosses.Text = mTeam(Count).LossCount.ToString()
        chkRank.Checked = mTeam(Count).Ranked
    Else
      MessageBox.Show("Search Failed.", . . .)
    End If
End Sub
```

'SelectedIndexChanged event procedure of the ListBox:

```
Private Sub lstShow_SelectedIndexChanged(. . .) Handles
          lstShow.SelectedIndexChanged
    Dim Index As Integer
```

'Due to column header, index of the selected team in array, will be SelectedIndex - 1

```
    Index = lstShow.SelectedIndex - 1
    txtName.Text = mTeam(Index).TeamName
    txtWins.Text = mTeam(Index).WinCount.ToString()
```

```
      txtLosses.Text = mTeam(Index).LossCount.ToString()
      chkRank.Checked = mTeam(Index).Ranked
End Sub
```

'General Function to validate the input date:

```
Private Function ValidateData() As Boolean
    Dim Wins As Integer
    Dim Losses As Integer
    If txtName.Text = "" Then
        MessageBox.Show ("Enter a name.", . . .)
        txtName.Focus()
        Return False
    End If
    If Integer.TryParse (txtWins.Text, Wins) = False Then
        MessageBox.Show ("Enter a whole number for wins.", . . .)
        txtWins.Focus()
        Return False
    End If
    If Wins < 0 Then
        MessageBox.Show ("Enter a number >= 0.", . . .)
        txtWins.Focus()
        Return False
    End If
    If Integer.TryParse (txtLosses.Text, Losses) = False Then
        MessageBox.Show ("Enter a whole number.", . . .)
        txtLosses.Focus()
        Return False
    End If
    If Losses < 0 Then
        MessageBox.Show ("Enter a whole number >= 0", . . .)
        txtLosses.Focus()
        Return False
    End If
```

'Everything is valid:

```
    Return True
End Function
```

 Since the Checked property of the CheckBox is Boolean, to store it in the Ranked member of the structure which is also Boolean, the If-Else statement can be replaced by:
`mTeam(mIndex).Ranked = chkRank.Checked`

Figure 10.2 shows the screen capture at runtime, after few teams are entered and Display Button is clicked.

Figure 10.3 shows the screen capture of the InputBox that opens up on the screen when the user clicks on the Search Button at runtime.

Figure 10.4 shows the screen capture when searching for Texas at runtime.

Figure 10.5 shows the screen capture when the user clicks on UCLA in the ListBox at runtime.

Figure 10.2 *Screen capture at runtime*

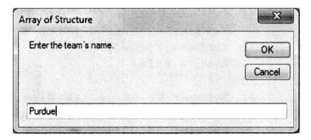

Figure 10.3 *InputBox is used to input the team's name*

Figure 10.4 *Search results for Purdue*

Figure 10.5 *Clicking on a team in the ListBox*

10.5 InputBox Function

Sometimes, it is necessary to ask the user to enter data for which there is no TextBox on the Form. The InputBox function is used to get additional data from the user at runtime. The function takes one to three parameters, and returns a string as its output. In our example, there is a TextBox to enter the team's name to search for, but an InputBox function is used to show this feature of the language.

General Syntax

```
InputBox(par1, par2, par3)
```

Where:

Par1, is a the custom message that gets displayed in the InputBox.

Par2, is the caption that is displayed in the title bar of the InputBox.

Par3, provides a default value, for the required input.

The InputBox function can be used with one, two, or three parameters.

The Way the InputBox Works

When the InputBox function is invoked, a dialog Form shows up on the screen with the custom message (the first parameter) displayed on it. The user should enter the required data in the provided TextBox, followed by a click on the Ok Button. At this point the dialog Form closes, and the function returns the text entered in the TextBox as an output. If the user clicks on the Cancel Button, the dialog box closes, and an empty string will be returned as the function's output.

EXAMPLE 4

This example has three parts.

a.   Use an InputBox function to get the name of the school. See Figure 10.6.

```
Dim School As String
School = InputBox("Enter the school name:")
```

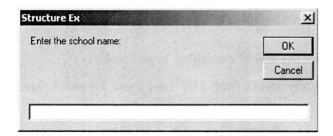

Figure 10.6 *Simple version of the InputBox*

b.   Use an InputBox to get the school name. Change the title bar to Schools. Refer to Figure 10.7.

```
Dim School As String
School = InputBox("Enter the school name:", "Schools")
```

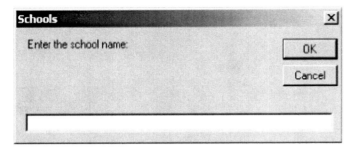

Figure 10.7 *Adding a title bar*

    c.   Use an InputBox to get the school name. Use "Purdue" as the default name for school. See Figure 10.8.

```
Dim School As String
School = InputBox("Enter the school name:", "Schools", "Purdue")
```

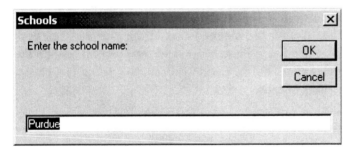

Figure 10.8 *Use purdue as default school*

In this case the user may click on the Ok Button to accept the default input, or override the default value with another name.

Review Questions:

1.   In a VB .NET project how would you inform the user of something important?

2.   In a VB .NET program, how would you ask the user to enter additional input for which there is no TextBox on the Form?

3.   Declare a structure to store information about a college football team. A team has the following data: college name, team's name, coach's name, and number of players.

4.   Declare a variable *Team* of this structure data type.

5.   Store: "Purdue", "Boilermaker", "Darrell Hazell", and 46 in variable *Team*.

6.   Declare an array of structure to store data about ten college football teams.

7.   Store the data stored in *Team* in the first element of this array.

8.   Store: "Michigan," "Wolverines", "Brady Hoke", and 32 at index 4 of this array.

PROGRAMMING CHALLENGES

1. Design a VB .NET project to store the following data about students in a class. The data includes student's last name, first name, ID, and GPA. Allow the user to enter data for each student followed by a click on a Button to store the data in a dynamic array of structure. Add Buttons to display all the students in a ListBox, compute the average GPA, and end the program execution. Write a general function to validate the input data before processing. Validation rules are: last name and first name must exist, ID must be like ###-##-####, and GPA must be a number in range of 0 to 4.

    Provide another Button to search for a student based on an ID. Use an InputBox function to prompt the user to enter the student-ID to search for.

2. Design a VB .NET project to store useful data about an unknown number of objects sold in a store. Assume that for each object we want to store the name, # of those objects in store, and the unit price. Let the user enter the name, the count and the unit price of each object followed by a click on a Button to store the data in a dynamic array of structure. At any time the user may click on the Display Button to view the list of all the objects along with their count and unit price in an output box (ListBox would be appropriate) in a tabular format. Provide another Button to display some statistics about these objects in the cleared ListBox. The statistics should include: number of objects entered in the program, the total worth of objects in store [sum of items * unit_price] and the average unit price of the objects. Use the same output box for displaying the statistics.

3. Design a VB .NET project to store some data about the employees who are taking part in a golf tournament in the company. The number of employees who will sign up for this event is not known. For each employee, the user should enter a first name, a last name, an email address, and a phone number followed by a click on the Button to store data in a dynamic array of structure. Provide another Button to display the list of employees (last name, first name, email, and phone #) in a tabular format in a ListBox. Also add a Button to search for an employee based on the last name. When the user clicks on the search Button use an InputBox function to get the last name. The program should display all the employees that have that last name along with their information. There should be other Buttons to clear the I/O boxes and end the program execution. **Validation Rules:** Validate the first name, and last name for existence, the email should contain a @ and a . character (use like operator for pattern check), and the phone number should follow the pattern (###)-###-####.

CHAPTER 11

Multiform Projects

LEARNING OBJECTIVES

After completing Chapter 11, students should be able to:
- ❑ Add additional Forms to the project
- ❑ Navigate between Forms
- ❑ Understand the difference between Modal and Modeless Forms
- ❑ Understand and use project scope variables

11.1 Introduction

It is very common to have a Windows application with multiple Forms. Additional Forms are used for various reasons. For example, a splash Form may be displayed while the main Form is being loaded into the memory to give some feedback to the user; a Form may be used to display the instructions about using an application; or it can be used to display the program's output, and etc. Each additional Form has its own graphical user interface (GUI) and the code window. Each Form is an object of the Form class, which has properties and methods that facilitate navigation among forms during the program execution. In this chapter, we explain how to add additional Forms to a project, and how to navigate between them.

11.2 Adding a Form to a VB .NET Project

It is easy to add another form to a VB .NET project. Open the VB .NET project. In the Integrated Development Environment (IDE), click on the Project on the menu bar, and select Add Windows Form from the dropped down menu. A dialog box will open up on the screen. In the dialog box, select Windows Forms in the left panel, and Windows Form in the right panel as shown in Figure 11.1. At the bottom of the dialog box, there is a TextBox with a default name for the new Form. Give a meaningful name to the Form, such as frmDisplay. Click on the Add Button to close the dialog box and add the new Form to the project. The new Form's name and icon will appear in the Solution Explorer window, and a blank Form will be displayed on the screen. Now, you can design a GUI for this Form and write code in its code window. Click on the Save All disk icon in the tool bar to save the changes made to the project. To navigate between the Forms at design time, you can double click on the Form icon in the Solution Explorer

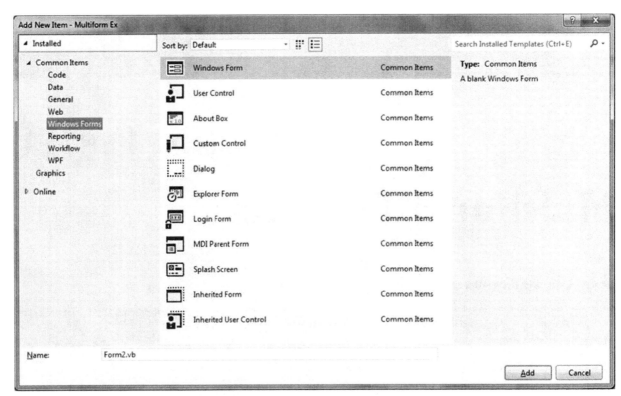

Figure 11.1 *Dialog Box opened when adding a Windows Form*

window, or click on the tabs Form1.vb [Design] or frmDisplay.vb [Design] that appear at the top of the screen, under the tool bar. To navigate between the Forms at runtime, you have to write code using Form object's methods. In the next section, we will explain some useful methods and events of the Form object.

Form's Name Property and Form File Name

As mentioned earlier, each Form is a class, and like all classes it has properties and methods. The name of the class is the same as the Name property of the Form. For example, consider the VB .NET project in the previous section with two Forms. Let us change the Name property of the first Form from Form1 to frmMain, and its Text property to Main Form in the Properties window.

Let us study the code window of this Form. There are only two lines in the code window. The first line Public Class frmMain specifies the beginning of the frmMain class, and the second line, End Class, specifies the end of frmMain class. All the code related to this Form will be written between these two lines.

```
Public Class frmMain

End Class
```

Now, have a look at the Solution Explorer window shown in Figure 11.2. Notice that, although the Name property of the Form has been changed to frmMain, the name of the file on the disk remains Form1.vb. For consistency reasons, it is recommended to make the file name same as the class name. To change the file name, right click on Form1.vb in the Solution Explorer window, choose Rename from the dropped down menu, and change the file name to frmMain.vb. This way the name of the file on the disk will be changed to frmMain.vb which can be viewed in Windows Explorer. It is worthwhile to mention that in VB .NET 2012, if you change the Form's file name in the Solution Explorer window, the Name property of the Form, and as a result the class name will automatically change to the same name.

Figure 11.2 *In Solution Explorer, filename is Form1.vb*

11.3 Important Methods of the Form Object

Show() Method

The Show method is used to display a Form on the screen as a modeless Form. A modeless Form is a form that the user can click out of during the program execution, without closing the Form. In other words, the user may click in and out of a modeless Form without any limitation. For example, to open a second Form named frmDisplay from the main Form, the following code should be written in the click event procedure of a Button on the main Form.

```
Dim F2 As New frmDisplay
F2.Show()
```

This declaration creates an instance of frmDisplay in the computer's memory and makes F2 reference this instance. Note that the name of the object variable does not have to be F2, it can be any name given by the programmer.

ShowDialog() Method

The ShowDialog method is used to display a Form on the screen as a modal Form. A modal Form is a form that the user has to close before being able to click outside of the Form. The following code will open the Form named frmDisplay as a modal Form.

```
Dim F2 As New frmDisplay
F2.ShowDialog()
```

Again, this declaration creates an instance of frmDisplay in the computer's memory; F2 is a reference to this instance.

Always, open additional Forms in a VB .NET project as modal Forms. There are some instances where a modeless Form has to be opened.

Close() Method

The Close method is used to unload a Form from the memory, hence close it. To close a Form, simply write the following code in the click event procedure of the Button used for closing the Form. Me, in this code, refers to the current Form:

```
Me.Close()
```

11.4 Important Events of the Form Object

Form Load Event

The Form Load event takes place when the Form gets loaded into the memory. Each VB .NET project has a start-up Form, which is typically the first Form that was created in the project. At the beginning of the program execution, The start-up Form gets loaded into the memory. This triggers the Form load event of the start-up Form. Technically speaking, any of the Forms in the project may be designated as the start-up Form. To change the start-up Form of a project, right click on the project's name in the Solution Explorer window, select Properties; a dialog box will be opened. In the Properties window, select the name of the start-up Form from the provided list. Any initial processing in the project can be coded in the Form Load event procedure of the start-up Form. In other words, to accomplish any task at the beginning of the program execution, write the required code in the Form Load event procedure of the start-up Form. Such processing includes, but is not limited to loading data from an input file into the program, connecting to a database, initializing module scope or global variables, and so on.

Activated Event

The Form Activated event takes place when the Form gets the focus and becomes an active Form. The Activated event takes place right after the Form Load event. One of the applications of this event procedure is to write the code for setting focus to a certain object when the Form becomes active.

Form Closing Event

The Form Closing event takes place right before the Form gets unloaded from the memory. You can write the finishing tasks of a project in the Form Closing event procedure of the main Form. The finishing tasks include, but are not limited to, saving the data to a text file, closing a database connection, and so on. The Form Closing event takes place when the user clicks on the x icon on the top right corner of the Form, or when the Form gets unloaded by execution of the Me.Close() statement in the program.

Most Windows applications confirm with the user before ending the program execution. In a VB .NET project, the programmer may use a MessageBox to get the user's confirmation in the Form Closing event procedure. The MessageBox should pose a question to the user, and provide two Buttons Yes and No for the user to choose from. The output of the MessageBox function corresponds to the Button that was clicked by the user to answer the question and close the dialog Form. If the user clicks on the Button Yes, then the MessageBox closes followed by closing of the Form. If the user clicks on the Button No, the closing event can be cancelled by using the "e" parameter of this event procedure as follows: e.Cancel = True. Let us look at an example:

Write the code in the Form Closing event procedure of the main Form in a VB .NET project to get the user's approval for ending the program execution. The program should cancel the closing event, if the user answers No to the question.

```
Private Sub frmMain_FormClosing(sender As Object, e As
                FormClosingEventArgs) Handles MyBase.FormClosing

    If MessageBox.Show("Are you ready to end?",
          Application.ProductName, MessageBoxButtons.YesNo,
          MessageBoxIcon.Question) = Windows.Forms.DialogResult.No Then
              e.Cancel = True

    End If
End Sub
```

11.5 Creating the Skeleton of the Event Procedures in the Code Window

The Form Load event is the default event of the Form object, therefore by double clicking on a blank space on the Form, the skeleton of the Form Load event procedure gets created in the Code Window. Likewise, the click event is the default event of the Button. Therefore, by double clicking on a Button, the skeleton of the Click event procedure of the Button gets created. Alternatively, the skeleton of any event procedure (including the afore said ones) can be created with two options. One way is to go to the code window of the Form, and choose appropriate selections from the left and right drop down boxes on the top of code window. For instance, to create skeleton of the FormClosing event for a particular Form, you can choose the Form Events in the drop-down box on the top left-hand side and choose the name of the event from the drop down box on the right-hand-side. The skeleton of that event procedure will be created in the code window. Another way is to go to the Form design window, and select the object (e.g., Form). In the Properties window, click on the lightening icon. The list of all the events for that object will appear. Select the event name you want. The skeleton of that event procedure will be created in the code window. Figure 11.3 is a screen capture for selecting a Form event using the first option.

Figure 11.3 *Creating the skeleton of the FormClosing event procedure*

11.6 Global Variables

In order to use a variable, a named constant, a general procedure, or a general function in more than one Form in a multiform VB .NET project, the programmer has to declare the variable, constant, procedure, or function with project scope, which is also referred to as global scope. Project scope identifiers must be declared in a Code Module with keyword Public. The scope of a global identifier is the entire project; this means that the global identifiers can be used in the code window of all the Forms in the project.

Code Module

Code Module is an additional file that is added to a VB .NET project. The file is saved on the disk with .vb extension. A code module consists of only a code window and is without a GUI. A large project may have several modules to group together global variables, constants, functions, and so on. To add a modules to a project, click on the Project on the menu bar and select Add Module from the sub menu. A dialog box shows up. Select Code under the Common Items in the left panel, and Module in the right panel. There is a TextBox at the bottom of the dialog box with a default name for the module. You may replace it with a meaningful name, or use the default name Module1.vb. Finally, click on the Add Button to close the dialog box. Figure 11.4 is the screen capture of this phase.

Figure 11.4 *Adding a Code module to the project*

After clicking on the Add Button, the Code Module window opens up, as shown in Figure 11.5.

Declaring a Global Identifier

- Global identifiers can be declared in a Standard Code Module.
- The keyword Public must be used to declare a global identifier.
- Precede the name of a global identifier with lowercase *g*.
- Precede the name of a global named constant with lowercase *gc*.
- As always, give a meaningful name to a global identifier.

Figure 11.5 *Code Module*

Let us declare a named constant with global scope to store a sales tax of 7%.

```
Module Module1
      Public Const gcSalesTax As Double = 0.07
End Module
```

EXAMPLE 1

Design a **VB .NET** project with two **Forms**. On the main **Form**, allow the user to click on a **Button** in order to view the name of your favorite flower on the second **Form**. There is minimal code required for this project.

Figure 11.6 shows the GUI designed for the main Form. It consists of a big Label that simply displays "Main Form" in a large font, and a Button that shows the second Form when clicked. Table 11.1 shows the detailed information on the GUI objects used for this Form.

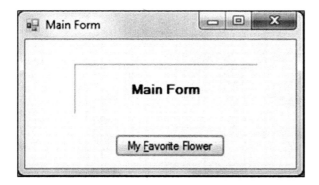

Figure 11.6 *Main Form*

TABLE 11.1 Main Form GUI Objects and Properties

OBJECT	PROPERTY	VALUE
Form	Name	frmMain
	Text	Main Form
	StartPosition	CenterScreen
Label	Name	lblTitle
	Text	Main Form
	Font	Size = 10
		Style = Bold
	TextAlign	MiddleCenter
Button	Name	btnShow
	Text	My &Favorite Flower

The code window of the Main Form:

```
Public Class frmMain
    Private Sub btnShow_Click(. . .) Handles btnShow.Click

        Dim Form2 As New frmSecond
        Form2.ShowDialog()
    End Sub
End Class
```

Figure 11.7 *Second Form*

The second Form is shown in Figure 11.7. It consists of a PictureBox object, to display an image of your favorite flower; a Label, to display the name of the flower and a Button to close the Form. Table 11.2 shows the detailed information on the GUI objects used for this Form. Make sure to change the SizeMode property of the PictureBox to StretchImage, in order to properly fit the picture in the PictureBox. On this Form, only the Button responds to the Click event. Properties of the objects are set at design time.

The Code Window of the Second Form:

```
Public Class frmShow
    Private Sub btnClose_Click(...) Handles btnClose.Click
        Me.Close()
    End Sub
End Class
```

TABLE 11.2 Second Form's GUI Objects and their Properties

OBJECT	PROPERTY	VALUE
Form	Name	frmSecond
	Text	Second Form
	StartPosition	CenterParent
	FormBorderStyle	FixedDialog
	MinimizeBox	False
	MaximizeBox	False
PictureBox	Name	PicFlower
	Image . . .	System.Drawing.Bitmap
	Click on . . . to download an image	
	SizeMode	StrechImage
Label	Name	lblInfo
	Text	Tulips – Source of the image
	BorderStyle	None
Button	Name	btnClose
	Text	&Close

EXAMPLE 2

Design a VB .NET project with two Forms to process the quiz scores in a class of unknown number of students. Allow the user to enter the quiz scores one at a time on the main Form, and display the statistics on the second Form. When the second Form shows up, it should display the number of scores entered and the quiz average.

Let us follow the Program Development Life Cycle (PDLC):

Step 1: ANALYZE THE PROBLEM

The Main Form:

    1. Input requirement(s): Quiz score

    2. Output requirement(s): None

    3. Processing requirements:
        a.   Process the quiz score
        b.   Display the second Form
        c.   End the program execution.

The Second Form:

    1. Input requirement(s): None

    2. Output requirement(s): Quiz Statistics

    3. Processing requirement(s):
        a.   Display statistics
        b.   Close the Form

Step 2: DESIGN THE GUI FOR EACH FORM

Based on the analysis in Step 1, the main Form should have a TextBox for data entry and three Buttons for processing as shown in figure 11.8. Let us name the objects frmMain, txtScore, btnEnter, btnExit, and btnShow. The second Form should have a Label to display the statistics and a Button to close the Form. Let us name these objects frmStats, lblshow and btnClose. The GUI for this Form is shown in figure 11.9.

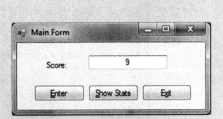

Figure 11.8 *Main Form*   **Figure 11.9** *Second Form*

Data Structure

The solution for this example can be completed with or without using an array. Let us consider a solution that uses a dynamic array. Since the array is needed in both Forms, it should be declared in a Standard Code Module, with Project (global) scope. The following are the global declarations in the Code Module that should be added to the project.

```
Module GlobalDeclarations
    Public gScore() As Integer
    Public gIndex As Integer = -1
End Module
```

Step 3: DETERMINE WHICH OBJECTS RESPOND TO WHICH EVENTS:

On the main Form, the Buttons should respond to the click events to do their required tasks. On the second Form, the Form object should respond to the Load event and display the statistics about the quiz scores, and the Button should respond to the click event.

Step 4: DEVELOP LOGICAL SOLUTION FOR EACH EVENT PROCEDURE:

Pseudocode of the Enter Button:

1. Validate the entered data for being a whole number between 0 to 10
   a. Do not process the score if it is not valid

2. Resize the dynamic array

3. Store the score in the array

4. Clear the TextBox

5. Set the focus to the TextBox

Pseudocode of the Show Stat Button:

1. Don't do anything if array is empty

2. Otherwise, show the second Form as a modal Form

Pseudocode of the Form Load Event of the Second Form:

As soon as the second Form is loaded on the screen, the required statistics should be displayed in the provided Label. To accomplish this, the code should be written in the Form Load event procedure of the second Form.

1. Start a loop to go through array elements
   a. In each iteration add the quiz score to the sum of scores

2. After the loop, divide the sum by (gIndex + 1) to compute the quiz average

3. Display the number of students who took the quiz (gIndex + 1)

4. Display the computed quiz average

Pseudocode of the Close Button:

Close the Form.

Step 5: TRANSLATE THE LOGIC INTO VB .NET CODE:

The code window of the Main Form:

```
Public Class frmMain
  'Click event procedure of the Enter Button:
    Private Sub btnEnter_Click(...) Handles btnEnter.Click
      Dim Score As Integer
      If Integer.TryParse(txtScore.Text, Score) = False Then
        MessageBox.Show("Enter a whole number.", ...)
        txtScore.Focus()
        Exit Sub
      End If
      'Validate the range of the input data:
        If Score < 0 Or Score > 10 Then
        MessageBox.Show("range is 0 .. 10", ...)
        txtScore.Focus()
        Exit Sub
      End If

      'Resize the array:
      gIndex = gIndex + 1
      ReDim Preserve gScore(gIndex)

      'Store data in the array:
      gScore(gIndex) = Score
```

```
        'Get ready for the next data entry:
        txtScore.Text = ""
        txtScore.Focus()
    End Sub
'Click event procedure of the Show Stat Button:
    Private Sub btnStat_Click(...) Handles btnStat.Click
        Dim Form2 As New frmStats
        If gIndex = -1 Then    'Check for empty array
            Exit Sub
        End If
        Form2.ShowDialog()
    End Sub
End Class
```

The code window of the Second Form:

```
Public Class frmStats
    Private Sub btnClose_Click(...) Handles btnClose.Click
        Me.Close()
    End Sub
'Form Load event of the second Form:

    Private Sub frmStats_Load(sender As Object, e As EventArgs)
            Handles MyBase.Load
        Dim Sum As Integer
        Dim Average As Double
        Dim NumberOfEntries As Integer
        Dim Index As Integer    'Loop counter

        Sum = 0
        For Index = 0 To gIndex Step 1
            Sum = Sum + gScore(Index)
        Next Index

        NumberOfEntries = gIndex + 1
        Average = Sum/NumberOfEntries

        lblShow.Text = NumberOfEntries.ToString() &
            " Students took the quiz." & vbLf
        lblShow.Text = lblShow.Text & "Average score  = " &
            Average.ToString("N")
    End Sub
End Class
```

Review Questions

1. Name two applications of multiform projects.

2. What is a modal Form?

3. What is a modeless Form?

4. When does the Form Load event take place?

5. When does the Form Closing event take place?

6. What is the keyword for declaring global variables?

7. (T / F) A VB project may have several code modules.

PROGRAMMING CHALLENGES

1. Design a VB project to process test scores in a class with unknown number of students. On the main Form allow in which the user inputs the following: a) the student name and b) the student test score. Validation rules are: Name is required; test score is a number greater than or equal to zero, but less than or equal to 100. On the second Form, display some statistics about the entered data. The main Form should have a Statistics Button. When that Button is clicked, it should display the second Form. On the second Form upon display, the following should be displayed to the user: a) the maximum test score; b) the minimum test score; c) the average test score; d) the number of students entered.

2. Design a VB project to process data in a car dealership. On the main Form, the user inputs the following: a) customer name; b) the type of car the customer purchased (sedan, SUV, coupe); and c) price of the car. When the Add Button is clicked, the input data should be stored in a global dynamic array of Structure, or several parallel dynamic arrays, and the customer name should be added to the provided ListBox on the main Form. The user should then be able to select an item from the ListBox and click the Update Button. When that Update Button is clicked, a second dialog Form should open up, displaying the data for the selected item in provided boxes. The user then has the ability to change the data in the second Form and click OK to save the changes in the array(s) and go back to the main Form. The user may also click on a Cancel Button to close the Form without making any changes. Once the main Form is shown, the ListBox in the main Form should be refreshed with the updated data. Validation rules are: Name must exist, type of car can only be (sedan, SUV, coupe), price of a car must be a number greater than zero.

   Hint: Use the SelectedIndex property of the ListBox, and that should reflect the item's index in the global array.

Files

LEARNING OBJECTIVES

After completing Chapter 12, students should be able to:

- ❑ List and understand the difference between three kinds of files
- ❑ Understand how to implement sequential access files in VB .NET
- ❑ Save data generated in the program to a text file
- ❑ Read data from a text file into the program

12.1 Introduction

Data generated in a computer program is typically stored in the computer's Random Access Memory (RAM) during the program execution. The data stored in RAM gets destroyed once a program's execution ends. It is essential to find a way to save the data generated in a program for future access; this is also referred to as persisting. For example, in a program where the user enters the records of hundreds of students, there should be a way to save the data permanently for future reference. In the old days, this was usually performed by storing the data in physical files. In today's computer-driven society, this job can be accomplished by using digital files. A computer program may use files to persist data, by storing it on "secondary storage devices" such as jump drives (USB), hard drives, CDs, etc. Files are commonly used in business and industry to save the data. However, nowadays more and more programmers use databases to save data for better performance, transaction control, and security advantages. For more information on databases, refer to chapter 14 and online resources.

Be aware that during the program execution, variables, data structures, arrays, etc. are created in the computer's RAM, while files are stored on a secondary storage device. In general, the speed of accessing files is slower than accessing the data in computer's RAM.

12.2 Input | Output File

Input file: The file that provides the input data for the program is referred to as the input file. The data is transferred from the file that is stored on a secondary storage device into the program into array(s), variable(s), etc.

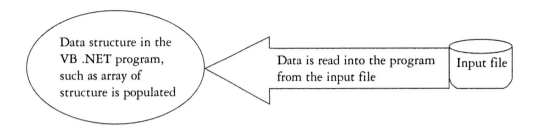

Output file: The file that the data generated in a program is saved to is referred to as the output file. The data is transferred from the program to the file on a secondary storage device.

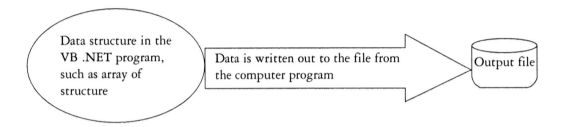

12.3 Categories of Files

There are many categories of files. Some of the file categories have a standard extension specific to that kind of file, such as .doc for Microsoft Word Documents, .exe for executable files, .xls for Microsoft Excel files, and so on. However, when working with data files in a computer program, there are three types of files, which are discussed below.

Sequential Access File

The sequential access file, often referred to as a text file, is the most common and easiest kind of file to work with. The data stored in a sequential access file can be accessed sequentially, starting from the beginning of the file. For example, to read something in the middle of the file, you have to go through all the previously stored data, until the desired location in the file is reached. Accessing data in a sequential access file is similar to accessing music stored on a cassette tape. The content of a sequential access file can be viewed using any text editor such as Notepad. Since sequential access files are the most common files used in business and industry, in this chapter, we will only discuss this type of file in detail.

Random Access File

The data stored in a random access file can be accessed sequentially or in random order. A random access file enables the programmer to read or write anywhere in the file. Accessing the data in a random access file is similar to accessing the music stored on a CD. You can access any data stored in the file by directly going to that location in the file.

Binary File

Binary files are a special kind of files where the data is compressed and is intended for computer use only. The data stored in a binary file cannot be viewed using Notepad, in other words if you open a binary file with a text editor, the content will be bunches of characters that make no sense. All the compiled programs (object files), executable programs, image files, and music files are binary files.

12.4 VB .NET Classes and Methods

A Brief Introduction to Object-Oriented Programming

VB .NET is a true object-oriented language, the same as Java and C++.

The foundation of an objected-oriented language is based on Classes and Objects.

What Is a Class?

A class is an abstract data type that encapsulates the data and behavior together. The data is referred to as property, and the behavior is referred to as a method. Think of a class as a blueprint that defines a group of objects that have common properties and behaviors (methods). To use an analogy from nature, a Person class can be a blueprint to be used to define many instances of people. Each object of this class has its own properties such as name, height, weight, gender, race, age, etc. All the objects of the Person class have common behaviors (methods), such as walk, run, sleep, eat, etc.

What Is an Object?

An object is an instance of a class that has specific properties. In other words, an object is a variable of a class data type. In general, you have to instantiate an object of a class, before utilizing the methods and properties of the class. However, there is an exception to this rule. For some classes, you can directly use their methods and properties without creating an object of the class type. One example, that is an exception to this rule is the System.IO.File class.

Brief Overview of the .NET and Its Class Library

The .NET framework includes two components: the Common Language Runtime (CLR) and the .NET Framework Class Library. The discussion of the CLR is beyond the scope of this book.

The .NET Framework Class Library is a collection of reusable types, classes, and interfaces, like a huge toolbox to help a programmer develop VB .NET applications. It describes the foundation set of objects available to developers in all the Visual Studio .NET languages. For ease of use, these entities (types, classes, interfaces) are grouped together into a hierarchical set of namespaces. All the namespaces in the .NET Framework developed by Microsoft begin with the root class System. Derived from the System is the IO namespace, and derived from IO is the File namespace and so on. Use a dot (.) operator to access the different levels of class hierarchy, starting with the root class. For example, to refer to the File class, you need to use System.IO.File.

Figure 12.1 is a brief view of namespaces in .NET Framework.

Framework Class Library

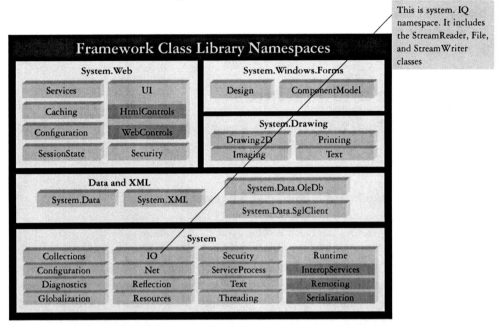

Figure 12.1 .NET Framework Class Library Namespaces (Courtesy: InformIT.com)

TABLE 12.1 The following table lists a few important System namespaces in .NET

Namespace	Definition	Sample Classes
System.IO	Implements the classes used for input/output with data streams and files.	File, StreamReader, StreamWriter, FileStream, etc.
System.Windows.Forms	Provides classes that implement all controls used in Windows applications.	ComboBox, Button, CheckBox, Form, etc.

Methods Used When Working with Sequential Access Files

TABLE 12.2 Methods of System.IO.File

Method	Description	Parameter
OpenText (to read)	Opens an existing sequential access file for reading data into a program. VB .NET generates a run-time error if the file does not exist.	String Ex: "data.txt"
CreateText (to write)	Opens a sequential access file for saving data from a VB .NET program. It creates a new file if no file with the given name exists; otherwise, opens the existing file, and erases its content before writing new data to the file.	String Ex: "data.txt"

TABLE 12.2 (Continued)

Method	Description	Parameter
AppendText (to write)	Opens a sequential access file for saving data from the VB .NET program. If the file exists, the old content is kept and new data is written to the end of the file; if the file does not exist, a new file is created for writing.	String Ex: "data.txt"
Exists	Determines whether a file exists on the disk. It returns True if the file exists and returns False otherwise.	String Ex: "data.txt"

TABLE 12.3 Methods of System.IO.StreamReader

Method	Description	Parameter
ReadLine ( )	Reads one line from the sequential access file. As an output, it returns a string, which is the read line.	None
Peek ( )	Detects the end of the input file. It returns-1 if the end of the file is reached.	None
Close ( )	Closes the input file associated with the StreamReader object.	None

TABLE 12.4 Methods of System.IO.StreamWriter

Method	Description	Parameter
Write ( )	Writes data to a sequential access file. It positions the file pointer at the end of the last character it writes to the output file.	String
WriteLine ( )	Writes data to a sequential access file and inserts a line terminator character at the end of the line. It positions the file pointer at the beginning of the next line in the file.	String
Close ( )	Closes the output file associated with the StreamWriter object.	None

12.5 Writing Data to the Sequential Access File

To save data generated in a VB .NET program to a text file, you must declare an object of the System. IO.StreamWriter class, and then open the file for writing:

1. Declare an object of System.IO.StreamWriter class. Let us name the object OutputDataStream.

   ```
   Dim OutputDataStream As System.IO.StreamWriter
   ```

2. Open a text file for writing. Use the CreateText method of System.IO.File class.

   ```
   OutputDataStream = System.IO.File.CreateText(FileName)
   ```

   where the FileName is the name of the file. It can be a string literal (e.g., "output.txt"), or a string variable that contains the name of the file. The FileName may include the entire path of the file on the disk. This statement opens the file and makes the OutputDataStream reference the file on the disk.

When the FileName does not include the file's path, the program locates the file in the bin folder of the project, where the executable file (.exe) resides.

3. Write to the file using the Write or WriteLine method of the StreamWriter class.

```
OutputDataStream.Write("Life is full of surprises.")
```

The Write method writes the input string to the file and leaves the write cursor at the end of the line in the file.

```
OutputDataStream.WriteLine("Do not take it too seriously!")
```

The WriteLine method writes the input string to the file and moves the write cursor to the next line in the file.

4. Close the file. Use the Close method of the StreamWriter class to close the file. Always close the file after you are done saving to the file.

```
OutputDataStream.Close()
```

 FileName is not case sensitive. i.e., data.txt is the same as Data.txt

EXAMPLE 1

Assume that there is a VB .NET project that processes test scores for a group of students. Assume that the Mean, Max, and Min are three variables that the average score, the maximum score, and the minimum score are stored in them. Write a segment of code to save these variable to a text file called statistics.txt in the bin folder of the VB .NET project.

```
'Save the variables Mean, Max and Min to a text file:
'1) Declare an object variable of StreamWriter class:
    Dim OutStream As System.IO.StreamWriter
'2) Open a text file in the bin folder:
    OutStream = System.IO.File.CreateText ("statistics.txt")
'3) Write the variables to the file, in separate lines:
    OutStream.WriteLine ("Class Statistics: ")
    OutStream.WriteLine ("=====================")
    OutStream.WriteLine ("Mean = " & Mean.Tostring())
    OutStream.WriteLine("Maximum Score = "& Max.ToString())
    OutStream.WriteLine("Minimum Score = "& Min.ToString())
'4) Close the file:
    OutStream.Close()
```

 When opening a text file for writing with the CreateText method, if the file does not exist, it gets created; otherwise, its content gets erased.

 When opening a text file for writing with the AppendText method, if the file does not exist, it gets created; otherwise, it gets opened with the existing content intact. The new data will be written to the end of the file.

12.6 Reading Data from a Sequential Access File

Normally, the input file is a file that is created by the previous run of the same *VB* .NET program, by another application, or by simply typing the data into the text file, using a program like Notepad. More work is required when reading data from a text file into the program than simply writing to the file. Before opening the file for reading, you have to make sure that it exists on the disk. Attempting to open a nonexistent file for reading purposes, will generate a runtime error. Additionally, when reading from a file, you must check for the end of the file. Attempting to read past the end of the file generates a runtime error.

 When opening a file to read from, the file MUST exist, otherwise a runtime error will occur.

Steps for Reading from a Sequential Access File

1. Declare an object variable of System.IO.StreamReader class. Let us name the object InputDataStream.

    ```
    Dim InputDataStream As System.IO.StreamReader
    ```

2. Invoke the Exists method of the System.IO.File to verify that the file exists on the disk. Assume the input file name is data.txt. Do not attempt to open the file, if it does not exist.

    ```
    If System.IO.File.Exists("data.txt") = False Then
          Messagebox.Show("The input file does not exit.", ...)
          Exit Sub
    End If
    ```

3. Open the existing file to read from, using the OpenText method of the System.IO.File class. This statement will tie the file on the disk to the object variable InputDataStream.

    ```
    InputDataStream = System.IO.File.OpenText("data.txt")
    ```

4. Use the Peek method of the StreamReader class to detect the end of the file. The Peek method returns −1 when the end of the file is reached. Normally, a loop is required to read all the lines in the file. A Do-Until loop is ideal for this purpose.

    ```
    Do Until InputDataStream.Peek() = -1
       'Read a line from the file
    Loop
    ```

5. Use the ReadLine method of the System.IO.StreamReader class, to read a line from the file. Normally a line of the file is read into a string variable.

    ```
    Dim Line As String
    Do Until InputDataStream.Peek() = -1
          Line = InputDataStream.ReadLine()
          ...
    Loop
    ```

    Depending on the project, the line that was read may be displayed in a ListBox, or parsed into pieces of data it holds. For example, each line of the file may consist of the name, ID, and salary of an employee.

6. Close the file. Use the Close method of the StreamReader class to close the file. Always close the file after you are done reading from it.
    ```
    InputDataStream.Close()
    ```

EXAMPLE 2

Assume that there is a sequential access file named "student.txt". Each line of the file has data regarding one student, which consists of a student's name, GPA, and gender separated by a tab character. Write a segment of code to read the data from this file into the program, extract the pieces of data from the read line, and store them in a dynamic array of structure. Usually, reading from the input file is done in the Form Load event procedure of the main Form.

Assume the lines in the file are arranged as follows:

Peter   3.2   M

Julia   4   F

....

The flowchart for reading from the file into the program is shown in Figure 12.2.

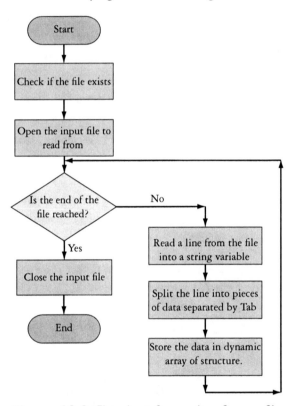

Figure 12.2 *Flowchart for reading from a file*

The Data Structure:

```
Private Structure mStudentRecord
     Dim Name As String
     Dim GPA As Single
     Dim Gender As String
End Structure
```

'Dynamic array of structure

```
Private mStudents() As mStudentRecord
```

'keep track of the last index in array

```
Private mIndex As Integer = -1
```

Form Load Event

- Form Load event takes place when the Form gets loaded into the memory. Upon the program execution, the main Form gets loaded into the memory; hence the Form Load event takes place.
- Write the initial processing of the program in the Form Load event procedure.
- Read the data from an input file into the program, in the Form Load event procedure.
- To create the skeleton of this event procedure, double click on an empty spot on the Form.

```
'Translate the flowchart to VB .NET code:
Private Sub frmMain_Load(...) Handles MyBase.Load
    Dim InputDataStream As System.IO.StreamReader
    Dim Line As String
    Dim Parts() As String      'Used to split the read line into separate fields
    'Check for file existence
    If System.IO.File.Exists("Student.txt") = False Then
        Exit Sub
    End If

    InputDataStream = System.IO.File.OpenText("Student.txt")
    'Read from the file, until the end of the file is reached.
    'To understand the Split method, refer to the text that follows this example.

    Do Until InputDataStream.Peek() = -1
        Line = InputDataStream.ReadLine()
        'Split the line into pieces:
        Parts = Line.Split(vbTab)
        'Resize the dynamic array:
        mIndex = mIndex + 1
        ReDim Preserve mStudents(mIndex)
        'Store pieces of data in the dynamic array of structure:
        mStudents(mIndex).Name = Parts(0)
        mStudents(mIndex).GPA = Single.Parse(Parts(1))
        mStudents(mIndex).Gender = Parts(2)
    Loop
    InputDataStream.Close()
End Sub
```

Split Method

- Split is a method of the String class. It takes a string as input argument.
- It splits a string into substrings that are separated by a certain delimiter character, such as a space, comma, tab, etc.
- The Split method invoked on a string, returns an array of string.

General Syntax:

```
Dim StringArray() As String
StringArray = StringVariableName.Split(delimiter-character)
```

StringArray will be resized to enough elements to store all the substrings within the StringVariableName that are separated by the delimiter character.

Example:

```
Dim Data As String = "Peter     3.5     M"  'Assume the tab character is the delimiter
Dim StrArray() As String
StrArray = Data.Split(vbTab)
```

After the above statements are executed, StrArray will be resized to three elements with the following values stored in them:

StrArray(0) = "Peter",   StrArray(1) = "3.5",   StrArray(2) = "M"

Note that, vbTab is a VB constant that represents a tab character.

Imports System

To avoid including System.IO each time referencing the subsequent classes, simply use the Imports statement at the beginning of the code window, before the line: Public Class Form1:

```
Imports System.IO
Public Class Form1
```

After including the Imports statement in the code window, the StreamWriter object may be declared as follows:

```
Dim OutputDataStream As StreamWriter
```

12.7 Case Study

Develop a VB .NET program to maintain the students' academic records by using a sequential access file. The student consists of name, GPA, and gender. When the program execution begins, the program should read from the input file into the program and store the data in a dynamic array of structure. Provide TextBoxes for the user to enter new students' name, GPA, and gender. At the end of the program execution, all the data should be saved to the same text file.

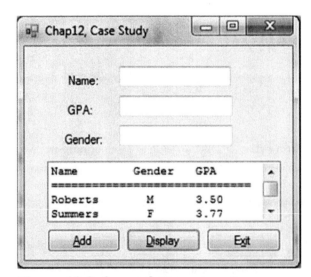

Figure 12.3 *Screen Capture at runtime*

After analyzing the problem, the Graphical User Interface (GUI) shown in Figure 12.3 was created.

Assume that the input file named "Student.txt" is placed in the bin > Debug folder of the VB .NET project. Each record (line) in the file consists of a name, GPA, and gender separated by a tab character. The following is an example of a record in the file:

Rice   3.50   M

The Data Structure:

```
Private Structure mStudentRecord
    Dim Name As String
    Dim GPA As Single
    Dim Gender As String
End Structure

    'Dynamic array of structure

Private mStudents() As mStudentRecord

Private mIndex As Integer = -1
```

The data is to be read into the program in the Form Load event procedure of the main Form, and stored in a dynamic array of structure. Any additional student data will be added to the same dynamic array of structure. At the end of the program execution, the data stored in the dynamic array is to be saved to the same text file in the FormClosing event procedure of the Form. Below is the entire code for this example.

FormClosing Event

- FormClosing event takes place right before the Form gets unloaded from the memory.
- This event takes place when Me.Close gets executed, or when the user clicks on the *x* icon on the top right corner of the Form.
- Save the data stored in the program to the file in the FormClosing event procedure.
- To create the skeleton of this event procedure: select the Form in design mode; click on the lightening icon in the Properties window to view all the Form's events; then click on the FormClosing event.

```
Imports System.IO
Public Class frmMain

    'Data Structure:
Private Structure mStudentRecord
    Dim Name As String
    Dim GPA As Single
    Dim Gender As String
End Structure
Private mStudents() As mStudentRecord
Private mIndex As Integer = -1

    'Read data into the program in the Form_Load event
Private Sub frmMain_Load(...) Handles MyBase.Load
    Dim InputDataStream As StreamReader
    Dim Line As String
    Dim Parts() As String
    If Not File.Exists("students.txt") Then
        Exit Sub
    End If
```

```
    InputDataStream = File.OpenText("students.txt")
    Do Until InputDataStream.Peek() = -1
        Line = InputDataStream.ReadLine()
        Parts = Line.Split(vbTab)
        mIndex = mIndex + 1
        ReDim Preserve mStudents(mIndex)
        mStudents(mIndex).Name = Parts(0)
        mStudents(mIndex).GPA = Single.Parse(Parts(1))
        mStudents(mIndex).Gender = Parts(2)
    Loop
    InputDataStream.Close()
End Sub

    'Save data to the file in FormClosing event:
Private Sub frmMain_FormClosing(...) Handles Me.FormClosing
    Dim Ctr As Integer
    Dim OutputDataStream As StreamWriter
    'Confirm with user:
    If MessageBox.Show("End the Program?",
            Application.ProductName,
            MessageBoxButtons.YesNo,
            MessageBoxIcon.Question) =
            Windows.Forms.DialogResult.No Then
            e.Cancel = True
            Exit Sub
    End If

    'Save data to the file:
    OutputDataStream = File.CreateText("students.txt")
    For Ctr = 0 To mIndex Step 1
        OutputDataStream.WriteLine(mStudents(Ctr).Name
        & vbTab &  mStudents(Ctr).GPA.ToString()
        & vbTab &  mStudents(Ctr).Gender)
    Next Ctr
    OutputDataStream.Close()
End Sub

    'Click event procedure of the Add Button:
Private Sub btnAdd_Click(...) Handles btnAdd.Click
    If ValidateData() = False Then
        Exit Sub
    End If
    mIndex = mIndex + 1
    ReDim Preserve mStudents(mIndex)
    mStudents(mIndex).Name = txtName.Text
    mStudents(mIndex).GPA = Single.Parse(txtGPA.Text)
    mStudents(mIndex).Gender = txtGender.Text
    txtName.Clear()
    txtGPA.Clear()
    txtGender.Clear()
End Sub
```

```
'Click event procedure of the Display Button:
Private Sub btnDisplay_Click(...) Handles btnDisplay.Click
    Dim Ctr As Integer
    lstShow.Items.Clear()
    'Display the column headers:
    lstShow.Items.Add("Name          Gender    GPA")
    lstShow.Items.Add("==============================")

    'Display array content to the ListBox:
    For Ctr = 0 To mIndex Step 1
        lstShow.Items.Add(mStudents(Ctr).Name.PadRight(10) &
            mStudents(Ctr).Gender.PadLeft(5) &
            mStudents(Ctr).GPA.ToString("N").PadLeft(10))
    Next Ctr
End Sub

'General function to validate the user's input.
Private Function ValidateData() As Boolean
    Dim Gpa As Single
    If txtName.Text = "" Then
        MessageBox.Show("Name is required.", ...)
        txtName.Focus()
        Return False
    End If
    If Single.TryParse(txtGPA.Text, Gpa) = False Then
        MessageBox.Show("Enter a valid GPA.", ...)
        txtGPA.Focus()
        Return False
    End If
    If txtGender.Text.ToUpper() <> "M" And
        txtGender.Text.ToUpper() <> "F" Then
        MessageBox.Show("Enter gender as M or F.", ...)
        txtGender.Focus()
        Return False
    End If
    Return True
End Function
'Click event of the Exit Button:
Private Sub btnExit_Click(...) Handles btnExit.Click
    Me.Close()
End Sub
End Class
```

 Cancelling the FormClosing event
- Use the MessageBox to ask the user whether to end the program or not.
- If the user's answer was no, cancel the closing event of the Form by using the **e** parameter of this event procedure as follows: e.Cancel=True

 When processing files, it is important to handle any exception that might occur. Exception handling is covered in Chapter 13.

Review Questions:

1. (T / F) When opening a file for writing purposes, the file must exist.

2. (T / F) When opening a file for reading purposes, the file must exist.

3. (T / F) When opening a file for appending purposes, the file must exist.

4. Which method should be used to check for existence of the file on the disk?

5. Which method should be used to detect the end of the file?

6. You are to save the data generated in the program to a file in the .... procedure.

7. You are to read data from the input file into the program in the .... procedure.

PROGRAMMING CHALLENGES

1. Design a program that keeps track of the students and their respective grades for one exam. When the program is closed, the data should be saved to a file. When the program loads, the data should be loaded from the file and displayed in a ListBox. The file should be Tab delimited, and the contents should look something like this:

    Abe   76

    John   78

    ....

    Validation rules are: Name must exist, and score must be a number in range of 0 to 100, both inclusive.

2. Design a program for a boat rental shop. Customers can rent one of three items (jet skis, paddleboats or speedboats). In order to be able to process a rent, a customer must be over eighteen. The data used for input requirements includes: a) customer name, b) customer age, c) rental price, d) rental date. When the program is closed the data should be saved to a file. When the program is opened, the data should be loaded into an array of structure. The user should be able to add more rental boat information to the array. The file should be Tab delimited, and the content should be similar to this:

Bob	18	20	Jet Ski	12/12/2004
Laura	20	50	Speed Boat	12/12/2006

    ....

    Validation rules: Name must exist, age must be a number greater than or equal to eighteen to process, type of boat must be selected (or entered), cost must be a number greater than zero, data must be a valid date

    Hint: You might want to use a DateTimePicker control to select a date.

CHAPTER 13

Exception Handling

LEARNING OBJECTIVES

After completing Chapter 13, students should be able to:

- ❏ Understand the importance of exception handling
- ❏ Implement exception handling in VB .NET
- ❏ List the important properties of the exception object
- ❏ Understand the exception call stack

13.1 Introduction

Let us start this chapter with the following hypothetical statement—"The best applications are those that never fail." Till this day, the authors of this book have yet to experience an application that never failed on them. A computer might lose power or a network connection, there might be a failure in a computer's memory, sharing violations amongst multiple users . . . and the list goes on. Almost all applications in this world will fail at some point, but the important thing for programmers is to minimize those failures. It is virtually impossible to think of every possible case where an application would fail, because the possibilities are numerous.

So far we have discussed data validation as a way of checking for user input errors that can cause applications to crash. There are errors, however, that are caused by the nature of the programming languages and compilers. Data can be lost in files and databases causing data integrity issues if these errors are not dealt with.

Programmers often differentiate between the terms errors and exceptions. Errors are expected situations in applications. For example, if a user tries to read a file and the file doesn't exist, a runtime error occurs, and the operating system will throw an exception. However, since this is an expected situation, a good application developer should not leave it up to the operating system to catch that error. A good application developer should test for that specific error and make sure the file exists before attempting to read it.

Exceptions, on the contrary, deal with runtime errors that are hard to predict. The loss of network connectivity can be an example of that, if a programmer is writing a program that deals with connecting to another computer.

Microsoft has implemented an exception handling model in Visual Studio .NET that has proven to be successful over the past years. Such exception handling exists in all the .NET languages, including Visual C++ and C#, by means of Try - Catch statement.

13.2 Try-Catch Statement

In its simplest form, exception handling can be preformed with a Try-Catch statement. This statement has two blocks, Try and Catch. The VB .NET statements that might generate an exception should be written under the Try keyword. These statements will always get executed. If an exception occurs during the execution of any of the statements in the Try block, the program execution branches to the Catch block, and the statements in the Catch block will get executed, otherwise, the Catch block will be skipped. End Try ends this statement.

General Syntax

```
Try
    'VB code that might generate an exception.
    . . .

Catch
    'The exception is caught here.
    MessageBox.Show ("An error occurred.", . . .)

End Try
```

EXAMPLE 1

Assume that in a VB .NET application the purpose is to retrieve the user's input from the TextBox and display the number raised to the power of 10 in the Label. Assume that the objects on the Form are: txtData, lblOutput, and btnProcess. See the Graphical User Interface (GUI) shown in Figure 13.1.

The following is the code for the click event procedure of btnProcess:

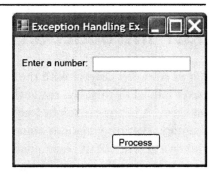

Figure 13.1
Exception handling GUI

```
Private Sub btnProcess_Click (...) Handles btnProcess.Click
    Dim Num As Short
    Dim Result As Short
    Num = Short.Parse(txtData.Text)
    Result = Num ^ 10
    lblOutput.Text = Result.ToString()
End Sub
```

This code might generate several runtime errors. For example, if the user enters 2.6 in txtData, the statement Short.Parse (txtData.Text) will generate a runtime error, because Short.Parse cannot parse a real number into a Short. The dialog box generated by the .NET Framework will be displayed as shown in Figure 13.2, informing the user of an unhandled exception.

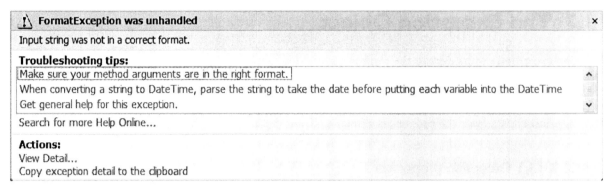

Figure 13.2 *Unhandled format exception*

Also, if the user enters 3 in txtData, 3 ^ 10 results in 59,049 which is too big for a variable of type Short. Therefore, statement Result = Num ^ 10 will generate a runtime error, and the dialog box in Figure 13.3 will be displayed on screen.

To be safe, it is suggested to write the code in a Try block, and catch the possible exceptions in the Catch block, as shown in the following segment of the code. Figure 13.4 shows the outcome of the program execution, when 5 is entered in txtData and the exception is handled in the Catch block.

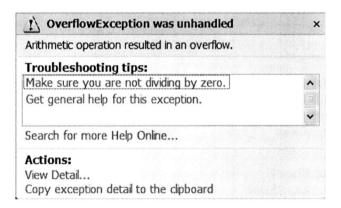

Figure 13.3 *Unhandled overflow exception*

```
Private Sub btnProcess_Click(...) Handles btnProcess.
Click
    Try
        Dim Num As Short
        Dim Result As Short
        Num = Short.Parse(txtData.Text)
        Result = Num ^ 10
        lblOutput.Text = Result.ToString()
    Catch
        MessageBox.Show("Error Occurred!", Application.
            ProductName,
            MessageBoxButtons.OK, MessageBoxIcon.
            Information)
    End Try
End Sub
```

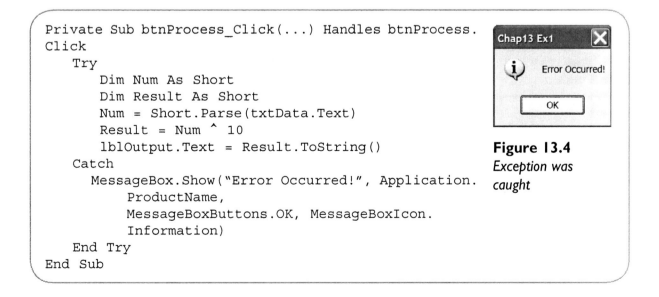

Figure 13.4
Exception was caught

13.3 The Exception Object

When an exception occurs during the program execution, an exception object gets created by VB .NET. The exception object has several properties that can be used to identify the exact nature of the runtime error.

All exception classes have the properties shown in Table 13.1.

TABLE 13.1 Exception properties

HelpLink	The HelpLink property contains the Uniform Resource Name (URN) or Uniform Resource Locater (URL) of the help file associated with this exception. This can be useful in directing the user to more information about the exception.
Message	The Message property is very important. It is a string that provides the description of the runtime error that can be displayed to the user.
Source	This property shows the application that caused the exception. This property can be useful when writing code for large applications.
StackTrace	The StackTrace is explained later in this chapter. This property shows the sequence of procedure calls that lead to the part of the code where the exception took place.

EXAMPLE 2

Revise Example 1 using the Message property of the exception object to display the exact nature of the runtime error.

```
Private Sub btnProcess_Click(...) Handles btnProcess.Click
    Try

        Dim Num As Short
        Dim Result As Short
        Num = Short.Parse(txtData.Text)
        Result = Num ^ 10
        lblOutput.Text = Result.ToString()
    Catch Ex As Exception
        MessageBox.Show(Ex.Message, Application.ProductName,
            MessageBoxButtons.OK, MessageBoxIcon.Information)
    End Try
End Sub
```

Figure 13.5 shows the outcome of the revised program, when 3 is entered in txtData. Notice that this time the MessageBox in the Catch block displays an informative message regarding the nature of the runtime error.

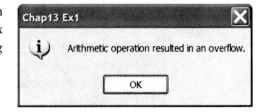

Figure 13.5 *Using the exception object in program*

13.4 Try-Catch-Finally Statement

The Try-Catch statement may have a Finally block at the end. This block of code will always get executed. The Try and Catch blocks are required, but the Finally block is optional. The Finally block should be included in applications where it is needed, like closing a file that has been opened in a Try block.

General Syntax

```
Try
    'VB Statements that might generate an exception
    ...
Catch
    'This part is executed only if the code under Try throws an exception
Finally
    'This part will always get executed
End Try
```

13.5 Using Multiple Catch Blocks

When using a Try block, more than one exception can be generated. To catch specific exceptions, multiple Catch blocks can be used. It is usually a good idea to catch a specific exception and show an appropriate message to the user. For example, if the user wished to catch an arithmetic exception and any other exception, the code would be:

```
Private Sub btnProcess_Click(...) Handles btnProcess.Click
    Dim Num As Integer = 0
    Dim Div As Integer = 0
    Try

        Div = 100 / Num    'This statement should produce an error.

    Catch DEx As System.ArithmeticException
    'Note below the message in the MessageBox has our own message. This is good because
    'we can tell the user exactly what the error is. Also, add DEx.Message to show system's
    'diagnosis:

        MessagBox.show("Error in division."
            & DEx.Message, Application.ProductName,
            MessageBoxButtons.OK, MessageBoxIcon.Information)

    Catch Ex As Exception
    'To be safe catch any other exception that might occur.

        MessageBox.Show(Ex.Message, Application.ProductName,
            MessageBoxButtons.OK, MessageBoxIcon.Information)
    End Try
End Sub
```

This code may include as many Catch blocks as a programmer needs. The two main types of exceptions a programmer can catch in VB .NET are System Exceptions, and Application Exceptions. Table 13.2 shows a list of commonly used exceptions in VB .NET. The first exception is a System. Arithmetic Exception. If a programmer wanted to catch all the arithmetic exceptions, including the DivideByZeroException, then the base class System.ArithmeticException should be used. Therefore, exception handling can be as specific or as general as the programmer makes it to be.

 The rule of thumb is that at least general exception handling code should be present in every general procedure, function, and event procedure.

TABLE 13.2 Common VB .NET exceptions

- System.ArithmeticException—This is the base class for exceptions that occur during arithmetic operations, such as System.DivideByZeroException and System.OverflowException.

- System.ArrayTypeMismatchException—ArrayTypeMismatchException is thrown when an incompatible object is attempted to store into an array.

- System.DivideByZeroException—This exception is thrown when an attempt to divide a number by zero.

- System.IndexOutOfRangeException—IndexOutOfRangeException is thrown when attempted to access an array element using an index that is less than zero or outside the bounds of the array.

- System.InvalidCastException—InvalidCastException is thrown when an explicit type conversion from a base type or interface to a derived type fails at runtime.

- System.NullReferenceException—This exception is thrown when an object is accessed but it is null.

- System.OutOfMemoryException—OutOfMemoryException is thrown if the "new" operation (creating new object) fails due to insufficient memory.

- System.OverflowException—OverflowException is thrown when an arithmetic operation overflows.

- System.StackOverflowException—StackOverflowException is thrown when the execution stack is exhausted by having too many pending method calls, most probably due to infinite loop.

- ArgumentException—This exception is thrown when one of the arguments provided to a method is not valid.

The above common exceptions were retrieved from Microsoft's msdn website, from http://msdn2.microsoft.com/en-us/library/aa664610(VS.71).aspx

13.6 Understanding the Exception Call Stack

In previous chapters we illustrated the use of general procedures and functions. These functions and procedures were usually called from a click event procedure. If a programmer writes a procedure or function that generates an exception, should the programmer write exception handling in each specific procedure or function? What about writing the exception handling inside the event procedure that calls this procedure or function?

Consider Figure 13.6 that depicts the following scenario. The code in the click event procedure of a Button in a main Form, invokes a general function. If the function generates an exception, it will be thrown back to the Button's click event procedure in the main Form. At that point, if the Button's click event procedure contains exception handling code, the exception will be handled and a proper message will be displayed by the program, otherwise, the application will crash.

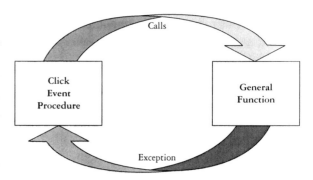

Figure 13.6 *Exception Call Stack*

EXAMPLE 3

Consider the following click event procedure of a Button, and the code for a general function that will always generates an exception:

```
Private Sub btnWhatever_Click(...)Handles btnWhatever.Click
    Try
        Dim Div As Integer
        'Invoke a function:
        Div = DevideByZero()
        lblOutput.Text = Div.ToString()
    Catch Ex As Exception
        MessageBox.Show(Ex.Message, Application.ProductName,
            MessageBoxButtons.OK, MessageBoxIcon.Information)
    End Try
End Sub
```

The code for a general function that throws an exception:

```
Private Function DivideByZero() As Integer
    Dim Num As Integer = 0
    Dim Result As Integer = 0

    'This will produce an exception.

    Result = 100/Num
    Return Result
End Function
```

The division in function DivideByZero, will always generate a runtime error. This exception will be raised in the function, but it will be caught in the Catch block in the Button's click event procedure, displaying the message that was generated by the System and stored in the Message property of the Exception object. This is shown in figure 13.7. An error is basically raised up the stack, until it is caught by a Catch block. This could also work if another procedure was called from the function, or even another function is called from the function—at the end the error will be caught in the Catch block in the Button's click event procedure. To better understand the call stack, type above example in a VB project, and set break points in the procedure and the function. Then, run the program and observe the flow of the execution step by step.

If a programmer keeps catching errors as they move up the stack, some data might be lost about the exception. An appropriate message should be displayed to the user explaining what the error is, and why it could have occurred for usability reasons. This is why handling exceptions in each procedure and function can be important as well. Throwing and creating your own exceptions will not be discussed in this chapter, but these topics are readily available on numerous websites.

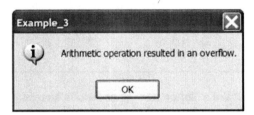

Figure 13.7 *Exception caught in the Button*

Review Questions:

1. What is the difference between exception handling and data validation?

2. Give two examples of exceptions.

3. What is a Try block used for?

4. What is a Catch block used for?

5. When would a Finally block be useful?

6. (T/F) A programmer can have more than one Catch block.

7. Why is it useful to use more than one Catch block?

8. (T/F) A programmer can code his/her own exceptions.

9. Which exception object's property is used to display a description about the generated error?

10. What are the two major exception classes in .NET?

PROGRAMMING CHALLENGES

1. Redo problem 1 at the end of chapter 12. In this version, add code to handle possible exceptions when reading from a file into the program, and saving data to a file. To do this, you should place the code for reading from a file in the FormLoad event procedure, and writing to a file in the FormClosing event procedure in the Try block of the Try / Catch statements. In general, when working with files, there is always a chance to encounter an exception such as drive not ready, disk is full, therefore implementing exception handling is crucial when working with files.

2. Redo problem 2 at the end of chapter 12. This time add exception handling code to the code written in the FormLoad event procedure and the FormClosing event procedure, and the Click event of the Enter Button.

CHAPTER 14

Introduction to Databases

After completing Chapter 14, students should be able to:

- ☐ Understand what a database is
- ☐ List and understand the meaning of rows, columns, fields, and records
- ☐ Understand how to create MS Access databases
- ☐ Understand the difference between the Data Connection, a Data Adapter, and a Dataset
- ☐ Create a simple database-driven program

14.1 Introduction

If you have ever used a corporate website to purchase something, like a laptop or a book, it is highly unlikely that these websites are using text files to store data about their customers, products, and services. A database is a very important technological concept and tool that helps in mitigating the hassles of dealing with large amounts of data.

This chapter aims at introducing the student to databases. One can think of a database as a repository of data in which data can be easily queried from, added, updated, and deleted. There are numerous Relational Database Management Systems (RDBMS), like Oracle, Microsoft SQL server, MySQL, and Microsoft Access just to name a few. Information technology–dependent companies use databases to keep track of their data.

Databases are important to store and organize data. In the prior chapter, we used text files to store data, but it becomes difficult to query text files for large amounts of data. Databases also help in minimizing the amount of redundant data, which can help in decreasing the amount of consumed disk space. This chapter will not go into details of database analysis, design, and programming methodologies, but aims at giving the student a brief introduction to databases.

14.2 What Is a Database?

As already mentioned, a database can be a repository in which data can be easily accessed, added, updated, and deleted. A database is made up of one or more tables. A table is an entity that represents data about something, or someone. For example, a table called tblBooks can be included in the database to store data on books.

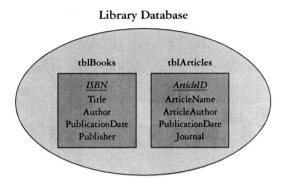

Figure 14.1 *Database Representation*

A table is made of rows and columns. Rows can also be referred to as records. Each record represents data about one object, e.g., book. A record is composed of several fields. These fields are things like book's title, book's author, date of publication, ISBN number, etc. Refer to Table 14.1 for a view of the table structure. A database can contain more than one table. For example, a simple library database can contain two different tables, one that keeps track of the books and the other that keeps track of journal articles. This might be better understood if you refer to Figure 14.1. Note, in tblBooks and tblArticles, the first field is underlined and italicized. This is used to indicate that that field is a primary key. A primary key is a unique identifier for a certain entity. For example, ISBN numbers are internationally recognized unique identifiers for books. No two books should have the same ISBN numbers. This makes the process of querying the database possible and more efficient.

It is important to note that the tables in a database can be related. For example, in a situation where a company is selling a product, a customer can place more than one order. This relationship is denoted as a one-to-many relationship. Advanced database design will not be discussed in this chapter, but we would just like the reader to be aware of the fact that tables in a database can have relationships. In order to query databases, a standardized language known as Structured Query Language (SQL) is widely used by many database systems. We will not get into the details of SQL, but for advanced database programming, it is important to understand how to use SQL.

Data in databases is organized in tables. Each table has rows, which represent the records, and columns, which represent the fields. This is illustrated in Table 14.1 pertaining to the tblBooks shown in Figure 14.1.

TABLE 14.1 Table structure

Record

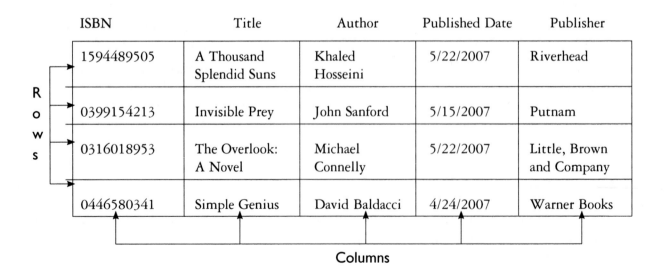

	ISBN	Title	Author	Published Date	Publisher
R o w s	1594489505	A Thousand Splendid Suns	Khaled Hosseini	5/22/2007	Riverhead
	0399154213	Invisible Prey	John Sanford	5/15/2007	Putnam
	0316018953	The Overlook: A Novel	Michael Connelly	5/22/2007	Little, Brown and Company
	0446580341	Simple Genius	David Baldacci	4/24/2007	Warner Books

Columns

14.3 Access as a RDBMS Example

Microsoft Access is a Relational Database Management System (RDBMS) that comes with the Microsoft Office suite of products. In this section, we will demonstrate how to use Microsoft Access to create a simple database of books kept in a library. The following is step by step instructions for creating an Access database:

Start MS Access, and create a blank database, name it "Library.mdb," and store it in C:\ as shown in Figure 14.2, then click the Create Button. Note: If you are using a newer version of MS Access (2010), the database files are no longer mdb files, they are now accdb files. Therefore, the file name would be "Library. accdb" when you are done creating the database.

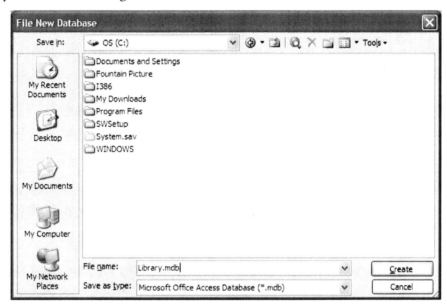

Figure 14.2 *Creating an Access Database*

Once the database file is created, click on "Create table in Design view" as shown in Figure 14.3.

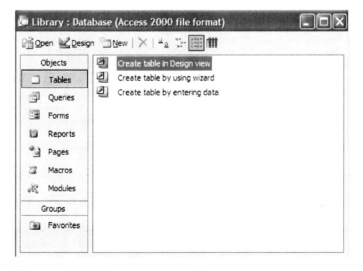

Figure 14.3 *Create a new table*

The next step is to create a table in the database. We will call the table, tblBooks. The table's fields should be made up of the "ISBN," "Title," "Author," "Publication Year," and "Publisher" with their respective data types as shown in Figure 14.4.

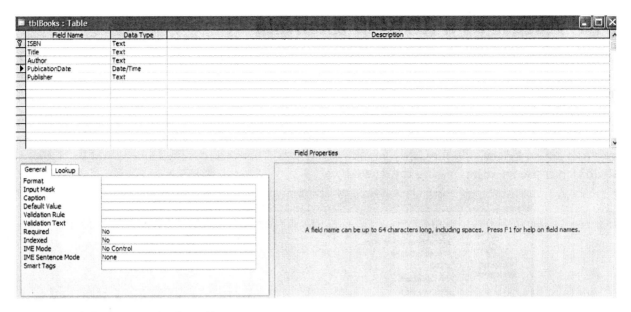

Figure 14.4 *Creating Books table*

Note, in Figure 14.4 the ISBN has a key next to it. The ISBN is known as a primary key, which, as discussed before, is a unique identifier. This means that no two books can have the same ISBN. Making the field a primary key is simple, all you have to do is to right click on the space to the left of the field and choose Primary Key from the pop-up menu as shown in Figure 14.5.

After the primary key is set, close that form and save the table as tblBooks. To do this, close the form shown in Figure 14.4, and a MessageBox as shown in Figure 14.6 will be displayed. Click Yes and save the Table with the name tblBooks as shown in Figure 14.7. Once the table is saved, it will be listed under Tables as shown in Figure 14.8.

Figure 14.5 *Making a field a primary key*

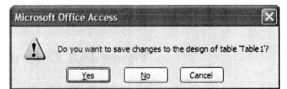

Figure 14.6 *Save MessageBox*

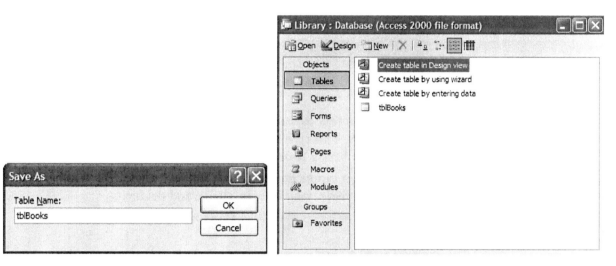

Figure 14.7 *Save Dialog*   **Figure 14.8** *Tables*

The next step is to enter the data into the database. To do that, double click on tblBooks and you will get a screen similar to the one shown in Figure 14.9. Now simply type the data into their respective columns. Once the data is entered, it will look similar to Figure 14.10.

	ISBN	Title	Author	PublicationDate	Publisher
▶					

Figure 14.9 *Empty Database*

Record

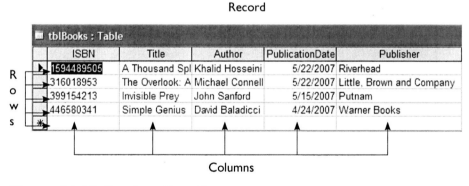

Columns

Figure 14.10 *Database Data View*

The library database created in this example is a simple database. Companies usually have databases with many tables and large volumes of data. This small example was used to introduce the reader to simple database terminology.

14.4 VB .NET and MS Access Data Types

A programmer should always be aware of the various field data types that can be stored in a database system. This is imperative because programming languages have their own set of data types when compared to a RDBMS. Table 14.2 illustrates the field data types available in MS Access. Table 14.3 maps those data types to the data types available in VB .NET.

TABLE 14.2 MS Access data types

Field Data Type	Description
Text	Any text limited to 255 characters. Can be text, numbers, or any other character.
Memo	This is similar to the Text data type, but can be lengthier. It can contain up to 1.2 billion characters. This type is important for things such as comments or anything that might have a large amount of text.
Number	The number data type can be numeric, both real and whole. The number type can be set to byte, integer, long integer, single, and double.
Date/Time	This field can store both date and time. Dates are stored in the format MM/DD/YYYY.
Currency	This is used for fields that contain money values. It is better to use this because it does not perform rounding.
AutoNumber	These are sequential numbers that are automatically generated by the database engine. The numbers starts with 1.
Yes/No	Can hold a Yes/No value.
OLE Object	This field can store objects that were created using OLE.

TABLE 14.3 VB .NET versus MS Access data types

MS Access Data Type	VB .NET Data Type
Text	String
Memo	String
Number (byte)	Byte
Number (integer)	Integer
Number (long integer)	Long
Number (single)	Single
Number (double)	Double
Date/Time	Date
Currency	Decimal
AutoNumber	Long
Yes/No	Boolean

14.5 Brief Introduction to ADO .NET

ADO .NET stands for ActiveX Data Objects, and could be thought of as a database programming technology that allows a VB .NET application to connect to a variety of databases. ADO .NET is intensive, and in this chapter we will use a VB .NET–driven wizard in order to utilize ADO .NET. In order to connect a VB .NET application to a database, the following steps have to be performed:

- A database connection has to be established to the Data Source.

- A Data Adapter has to be utilized to perform the transfer of data between the data source and the VB .NET application.

- A DataSet has to be created. A DataSet is a set of data retrieved from the data source, which resides in the VB .NET application's memory, i.e., RAM.

Data Source

A Data Source can be one of many things. In the example that will be discussed in the next section, the Data Source is a Microsoft .mdb file, which is an MS Access database. The Data Source could also be an Excel spreadsheet, or any other type of database system supported by ADO .NET. A Data Source can reside as a file on the computer with a .mdb extension, as shown in the example. However, a Data Source can also reside on another computer, which in most cases would be a database server.

Data Adapter

A Data Adapter is a .NET object that provides methods for retrieving data from the Data Source. It also has methods that allow the programmer to update the data in the Data Source after the application has made changes in the DataSet.

DataSet

A DataSet, as has been mentioned earlier, is the data that is retrieved from the Data Source residing in the application's memory. An application does not work with data that resides in the Data Source; it first retrieves data from the Data Source, creating the DataSet in the memory, then manipulates the data in the DataSet. This way all the changes are made to the DataSet, and the programmer may choose to update those changes in the Data Source. The relationship between all these objects is shown in Figure 14.11.

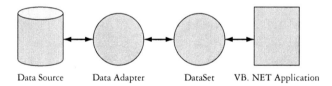

Data Source   Data Adapter   DataSet   VB. NET Application

Figure 14.11 *Relationship amongst ADO .NET objects*

14.6 Connecting to MS Access Database in VB .NET

In this part of the chapter, we will go through a small example that illustrates a quick way of establishing a connection to a .mdb file, MS Access database. We will use the MS Access database that was created in the first part of the chapter. To establish a connection to that database, the first step is to start a new VB .NET project. Once this is done, click on the Data Sources tab next to the Solution Explorer tab as shown in Figure 14.12. Then click on Add New Data Source . . . and the screen depicted in Figure 14.13 is shown.

Choose Database and click Next. Once Next is clicked, the image given in Figure 14.14 is shown.

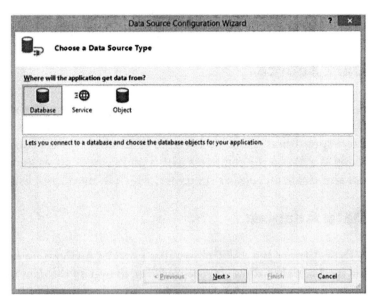

Figure 14.12 *Adding Data Source* **Figure 14.13** *Data Source Configuration*

Figure 14.14 *Creating a Connection*

The next step is to click on the New Connection Button. The screen given in Figure 14.15 is shown. Now click on the Change Button and change the Data Source to Microsoft Access Database File as shown in Figure 14.16. Click the OK Button.

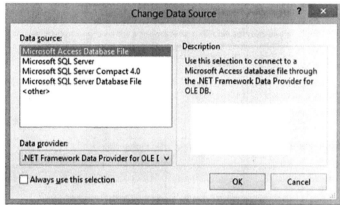

Figure 14.15 *Changing the Data Source*   **Figure 14.16** *Selecting MS Access Data Source*

Once the OK Button is clicked, choose the database file that was created in the earlier part of the chapter called Library.accdb by clicking on the Browse Button, and the result should be similar to Figure 14.17.

It is always a good idea to test the connection to the database. Therefore, click the Test Connection Button as shown in Figure 14.17; if the connection works, you will get a message as shown in Figure 14.18.

Once this is done and you have successfully connected to the database, click the OK Button, and then Next. You will get the long message shown in Figure 14.19. Click NO and you will get the screen shown in Figure 14.20. Now click Next and it's time to create the DataSet as shown in Figure 14.21. Click the + to the left of Tables, and check some or all the fields in tblBooks as shown in Figure 14.21.

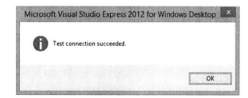

Figure 14.17 *Browsing for database file*   **Figure 14.18** *Connection success message*

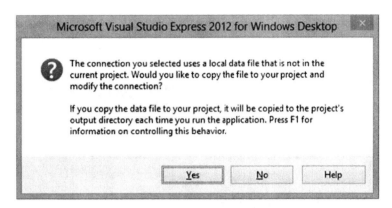

Figure 14.19 *Click NO, to close this dialog box*

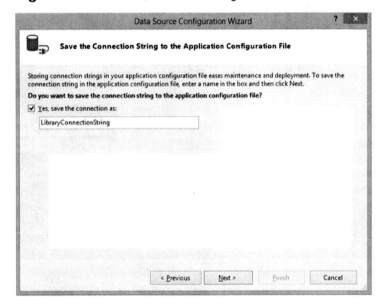

Figure 14.20 *Connection String*

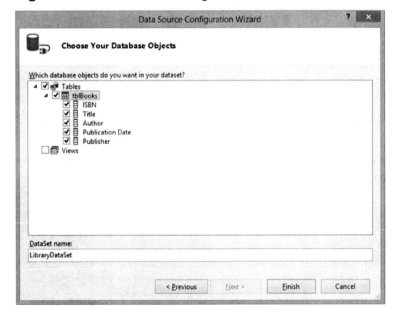

Figure 14.21 *Creating a DataSet*

Now click on the Finish Button. After you have done this it will show tblBooks in the Data Sources window as shown in Figure 14.22. Notice abl icon next to the ISBN, it means that ISBN is a TextBox, and the icon to the left of PublicationDate means that it is a DateTimePicker. After this you can simply drag and drop ISBN and other fields onto the Form in the design view. Figure 14.23 illustrates what will happen if you drag and drop all of them onto the Form.

Note in Figure 14.23, the DataSet and Data Adapter are automatically added to the lower part of the screen. Also note the ToolBar that automatically gets generated at the top of the Form. If you now compile and run the program, the controls are automatically bound to the DataSet retrieved from the DataSource, which in this case is the MS Library.accdb file. Figure 14.24 shows the screen capture during the run time.

Figure 14.22 *Data Sources Window*

Note that the user can navigate through the records using the ToolBar at the top of the Form. You can also Add (+), Delete (X), and Save records by using their respective icons on the Form.

In this exercise, you were able to create a simple database-driven application by using a Wizard type technique without writing any code. We used this example to illustrate the use of Data Sources, DataSets, and Data Adapters. In large applications, ADO .NET is programmatically used. Programmers actually have to implement all the database code in the code window of an application; our intention was to simply introduce the reader to databases. If you wish to familiarize yourself with advanced database programming topics, simply look up the online sources on ADO .NET.

Figure 14.23 *Accessing the Data in DataSet*

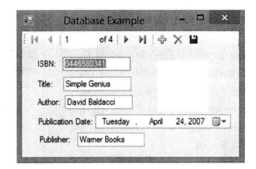

Figure 14.24 *Traversing the DataSet at Runtime*

Review Questions:

1. What is a database?

2. What is a database composed of?

3. What is a primary key?

4. (T/F) Can a database contain more than one table?

5. What is MS Access data type comparable to the Decimal data type in VB .NET?

6. What makes up a Row?

7. What makes up a Column?

8. What is a DataSet?

9. What is a Data Adapter?

10. Give two examples of a Data Source.

PROGRAMMING CHALLENGES

1. By following the example shown in Chapter 14, create a database with the following columns/ fields—make sure to name the Table (tblStudents).

    a. StudentID (*Primary Key*)

    b. StudentName

    c. StudentTestScore

    d. StudentAge

    Make the StudentID the primary key for tblStudents.

    Enter some fictitious data into the generated MS Access database.

2. Using the Wizard create a connection to the MS Access database. then test the connection. Configure the DataSource and create the DataSet. Finally drag that data to the Form in VB .NET. Play around with the navigation Toolbar. Try adding, updating and deleting records form the database using the VB .NET project.

Appendix A

Debugging

LEARNING OBJECTIVES

After completing Appendix A, students should be able to:

❑ Understand the importance of debugging

❑ Understand the process of debugging

❑ Implement debugging techniques in VB .NET

A.1 Introduction

The mistakes in a computer program, are referred to as errors or bugs. Debugging means getting rid of the errors in a program. This is a very important part of software development that should not be underestimated. The concept of a computer bug dates back to 1945 when an actual moth was found in one of the most primitive computers. Once the problem was fixed and the moth was removed, it was said that the person "debugged" the machine.

A good programmer should be able to efficiently debug a flawed program, making the program run more reliably. How to debug a program efficiently mainly depends on two things, (1) the tools available to debug an application, and (2) the debugging skills of a programmer.

For example, if one were using a programming language and writing code in Notepad, it would be difficult to debug the code since Notepad does not have a built-in debugger. On the other hand, the VB .NET's Integrated Development Environment (IDE) has a built-in debugging tool, i.e., a debugger. It is a programming tool that helps the developers detect syntax errors while typing the code, and also allows monitoring each step of the program execution.

A.2 Four Steps to Debugging

1. Find out that the bug exists in a program

2. Figure out what is causing the error

3. Figure out how to fix the error

4. Fix the error, and test the new code

The error in a program can either be found through program testing, or it could be discovered by accident as users use the software. The most difficult part is to find out the cause of the bug. Once the cause is found, fixing the bug can also be a challenge, depending on its nature and complexity. In programming there are different types of bugs, or errors, which are listed in Chapter 3. Some of the errors discussed are:

1. Compile Error: A compile error, also known as build error or syntax error, occurs during the compilation of the program, when the rules of the language are violated.

2. Runtime Error: This error occurs when the computer is not able to execute a program statement, e.g., division by zero.

3. Logic Error: This error occurs as a result of miscalculation in a program, e.g., using an incorrect formula for calculating the circumference of a circle.

A.3 Debugging in VB .NET

Debugging in VB .NET is easier than other programming languages because the debugging tools that come with the .NET IDE are very useful and comprehensive. It is easy to detect compile errors because the IDE automatically underlines any violations to the programming language as the code is being typed in. However, it is difficult to detect runtime errors and logic errors without the intensive use or testing of an application.

Let us go through an example of debugging in Visual Studio .NET 2012. The DEBUG menu shown in Figure A.1 is used when debugging a program. Note: Some of these debugging items are also available in the ToolBar and can only be activated once the start debugging program button is clicked.

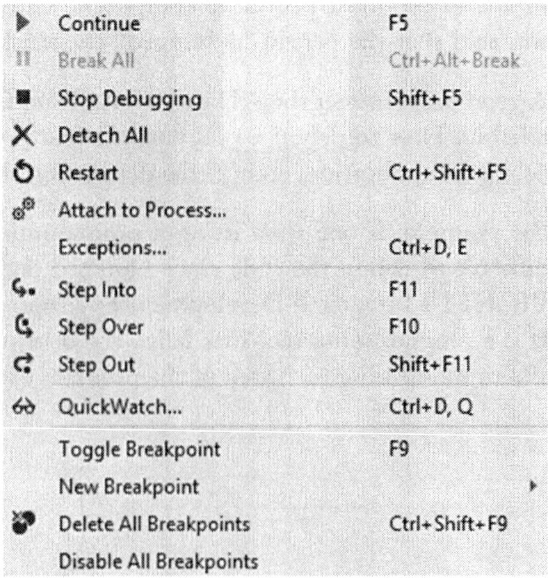

Before we discuss the functionality of the ToolBar icons, it is important to understand the concept of a Break Point. A Break Point is a marker that is placed in the code that makes the program execution break (pause) on that line, and allows the programmer to view the content of the variable(s) at runtime by hovering the mouse over each variable. To place a Break Point, simply move the mouse cursor to the left-hand side of the code and click with the left mouse button on the grey-shaded area. A red Break Point is then shown on the screen, as shown in Figure A.2. You can set several Break Points in the program to make the

	Continue	F5
II	Break All	Ctrl+Alt+Break
■	Stop Debugging	Shift+F5
X	Detach All	
○	Restart	Ctrl+Shift+F5
☞	Attach to Process...	
	Exceptions...	Ctrl+D, E
↳	Step Into	F11
↳	Step Over	F10
↱	Step Out	Shift+F11
66	QuickWatch...	Ctrl+D, Q
	Toggle Breakpoint	F9
	New Breakpoint	▶
☞	Delete All Breakpoints	Ctrl+Shift+F9
	Disable All Breakpoints	

Figure A.1 *Debugging ToolBar icons*

program execution pause at different lines. To get rid of a Break Point, simply click again on the Break Point in the left margin with the left mouse button.

Let us consider the click event procedure of a Button, btnProcess, in a VB .NET project. The code in this event procedure will get executed when the Button is clicked during the program execution. Figure A.2 is the screen capture of this segment of code at design time, with a Break Point placed in front of the If statement.

```
        End Sub


        Private Sub btnProcess_Click(sender As Object, e As EventArgs) Handles btnProcess.Click
            ' Declare Variables
            Dim State As String

            'Validate if something is selected
            If cboStates.SelectedIndex = -1 Then
                MessageBox.Show("Select a state.", Application.ProductName, MessageBoxButtons.OK,
                            MessageBoxIcon.Information)
                Exit Sub
            End If

            'If it is selected, assign the value in the combobox to the variable
            State = cboStates.Text

            'Display selected output into a label
            lblOutput.Text = State
        End Sub
End Class
```

Figure A.2 *Setting a Break Point*

Once the Break Point is set, the programmer can run the program by clicking on the Start Debugging icon in the ToolBar. Note that the line of code will only be executed when the Process Button is clicked. Once the Process Button is clicked, the screen, as given in Figure A.3, is shown to the programmer.

```
        Private Sub btnProcess_Click(sender As Object, e As EventArgs) Handles btnProcess.Click
            ' Declare Variables
            Dim State As String

            'Validate if something is selected
            If cboStates.SelectedIndex = -1 Then
                MessageBox.Show("Select a state.", Application.ProductName, MessageBoxButtons.OK,
                            MessageBoxIcon.Information)
                Exit Sub
            End If

            'If it is selected, assign the value in the combobox to the variable
            State = cboStates.Text

            'Display selected output into a label
            lblOutput.Text = State
        End Sub
```

Figure A.3 *Program execution pauses at the line with Break Point*

Note how the red highlighted line turns into yellow when the program execution pauses at that line. To step into the execution, or to go through the program execution one line at a time, click on the Step Into icon on the ToolBar as shown in Figure A.1, or press the F10 key on the keyboard. Notice how the yellow highlight moves to the next line of code that will be executed next, as shown in Figure A.4. If the Step Out icon or Start Debugging icon is clicked, the rest of the code will continue to execute. If the Stop Debugging Button is clicked, the IDE will stop debugging and will go back into the design mode.

```vb
Private Sub btnProcess_Click(sender As Object, e As EventArgs) Handles btnProcess.Click
    ' Declare Variables
    Dim State As String

    'Validate if something is selected
    If cboStates.SelectedIndex = -1 Then
        MessageBox.Show("Select a state.", Application.ProductName, MessageBoxButtons.OK,
                        MessageBoxIcon.Information)
        Exit Sub
    End If

    'If it is selected, assign the value in the combobox to the variable
    State = cboStates.Text

    'Display selected output into a label
    lblOutput.Text = State
End Sub
```

Figure A.4 *Stepping into Program execution by pressing F10 key*

While the code window is in debugging mode, the IDE gives the programmer the ability to hover the mouse over variables and objects to see the data they contain. For example, as shown in Figure A.5, if the programmer hovers the mouse cursor over the variable State, a small pop-up box appears showing the contents of the variable, which is IN. This is a very useful technique to figure out the values in the variables during the program execution. One can also right-click on the variable and click on QuickWatch as shown in Figure A.6.

```vb
Private Sub btnProcess_Click(sender As Object, e As EventArgs) Handles btnProcess.Click
    ' Declare Variables
    Dim State As String

    'Validate if something is selected
    If cboStates.SelectedIndex = -1 Then
        MessageBox.Show("Select a state.", Application.ProductName, MessageBoxButtons.OK,
                        MessageBoxIcon.Information)
        Exit Sub
    End If

    'If it is selected, assign the value in the combobox to the variable
    State = cboStates.Text
            State  Q ▾ "IN"
    'Display selected output into a label
    lblOutput.Text = State
End Sub
```

Figure A.5 *Hovering the mouse over a variable*

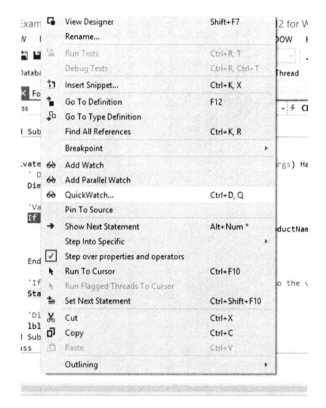

Figure A.6 *Selecting Quick Watch at runtime*

Figure A.7 *Quick Watch dialog*

When QuickWatch is clicked, the Form, as shown in Figure A.7, gets displayed to the programmer.

 It is recommended to use QuickWatch when debugging arrays in a program. QuickWatch will display the contents of the array items along with their respective indices, improving the process of debugging.

The Graphical User Interface

After completing of Appendix B, students should be able to:

❑ Define graphical user interface (GUI)

❑ Understand the importance of GUI standards

❑ List and state the general rules of thumb for GUI standards

❑ List and understand the importance of the various Windows GUI design guidelines

B.1 Introduction

The graphical user interface (GUI) is the part of a computer program in which the end user observes and interacts with while the program is in execution. Over the last twenty years, there have been major improvements in the usability of programs. The first user interfaces were generally referred to as Command Line Interfaces (CLIs). These are different from GUIs because they have no graphical aspect. The end user interaction with the program was solely based on textual input received via keyboards. They were difficult to use, and end users had a difficult time learning how to use them. Since such user interfaces were hard to use, computer scientists devised new ways of interacting with a computer program, especially after the invention of mouse. Currently, most computer operating systems (OS) have a GUI. One of the most popular operating systems is Microsoft Windows. A user is able to interact with the operating system using various input peripherals such as a mouse and a keyboard. The focus of this chapter is to introduce various standards that a Windows programmer should adhere to, when designing a GUI for a Windows-based application.

B.2 Importance of GUI Guidelines

Having a standard to adhere to for designing GUIs is important. To give you an idea on the importance of following proper GUI standards, think of the following situation. You are a regular Windows user and you use various programs like Microsoft Excel, Microsoft Word, etc. You then purchase or download a new program and install it in your computer. Once you install it, and start using it, you discover that the look and feel of that program is very new to you. For example, when a MessageBox appears, it is round, with a purple background and white text. Furthermore, as a user, you are accustomed that when the Exit Button is clicked, a MessageBox pops up asking if you would like to save the changes before you exit. However, as you click the Exit Button, the program execution simply ends without confirming with you. Such differences can be confusing or annoying. These are just two small examples of why GUI standards are crucial. When end users get accustomed to certain features that deal with GUIs, they expect to see these features when they use other applications as well. Programmers should be fully aware of these standards so as not to confuse the end users.

B.3 General Rules of Thumb for GUI Development

There are a few rules of thumb that should be adhered to when dealing with GUI design.

Rule 1. Always aim for the ease of use, not for how pretty your program should look

Your program should be user friendly. Some developers spend a lot of time on making the application look pretty and colorful. Instead, the colors make things more difficult to read, and may decrease the overall usability of the program.

Rule 2. Always attempt to have a program that has a standard look and feel

Programmers are advised to create a program that has a common look and feel. If one Form in the program has Buttons with hot keys, the end user would expect that other Forms would have hot keys as well. Programmers should keep this in mind.

Rule 3. When programming in a Windows environment, the standard Windows GUI guidelines should be followed

Different operating systems have different GUI guidelines. The programmer should understand the environment he/she is developing in. The guidelines for Windows that should be adhered to when developing in VB .NET are explained in the next section.

Rule 4. Always follow the proposed GUI standard guidelines. However, sometimes a programmer might have to deviate from the norms for certain reasons

There are scenarios in which a programmer might have to deviate from using the proposed GUI guidelines. The reasons for which a programmer should deviate from the guidelines should ultimately depend on whether or not that deviation is going to benefit the end user. A programmer should not let his/her own GUI preference override the end users preference.

B.4 Windows GUI Development Guidelines

1. **Font usage**

    The standard Windows GUI system font is 8pt MS Sans Serif. The standard color for the font is black. This font is recommended by Microsoft's GUI guidelines.

2. **Color usage**

    Color may be used when it seems appropriate to mark things and make them look clearer in the GUI. Try to use colors that are of varying degrees of brightness. This can be helpful for people that are color-blind. Additionally, the use of graphics such as Icons can help in making the message clear rather than using color and shading to convey a certain message.

According to GUI standards control's BackColor should be set to Control as shown in Figure B.1. This is a default for colors in VB .NET's Integrated Development Environment.

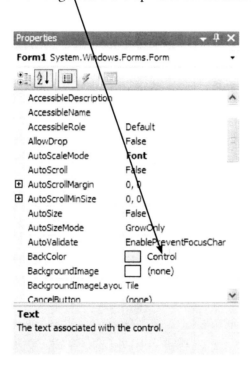

Figure B.1 *Control color setting*

Note: For some controls like a TextBox, control's standard BackColor is set to Windows. Windows is the default white color for a VB .NET control.

3.   **How to lay out controls on a Form**

The general rule is to space out controls equally from one another. A programmer should eliminate unneeded space from the GUI. Figure B.2 shows an example of a well-designed GUI versus a badly designed GUI in Figure B.3.

Figure B.2 *Well-designed GUI*   **Figure B.3** *Poorly designed GUI*

4. When to use ComboBoxes and RadioButtons

Both of these controls are used to offer different choices to the user. The user may select only one of the available choices. The general rule is to use a DropDown/ComboBox when there is a large list. When there is a potential for making only one choice from two to six items, perhaps RadioButtons can be used. Also numerous RadioButtons take up more space on the Form than a single ComboBox. ComboBoxes should be used when the amount of space to be used on a Form is limited.

Note: It is easier to programmatically implement a ComboBox in VB .NET because you can use the Text property of the ComboBox to get the selected item. With a RadioButton, you have to write the code to check which RadioButtons has been selected. This part is discussed in more detail in the Appendix D for Additional Controls.

5. How to indicate processing

Generally, when there is a long process, the programmer should change the mouse cursor to an hour glass to indicate that a lengthy process is taking place. This is performed by setting a Form's Cursor property to Cursors.WaitCursor. To return the cursor back to its default look, the programmer has to set the Forms's Cursor property to Cursors.Default. Below is a sample code for two Buttons. When the first Button is clicked, it changes the cursor to an hour glass and when the second Button is clicked, the cursor changes back to its default look. Note that in the code below *Me* refers to the current form.

```
Private Sub btnHourGlass_Click(...) Handles btnHourGlass.Click
    Me.Cursor = Cursors.WaitCursor
End Sub

Private Sub btnDefault_Click(...) Handles btnDefault.Click
    Me.Cursor = Cursors.Default
End Sub
```

6. Disabling controls

If a control is not going to be used, it is usually a better idea to disable the control rather than hide it. This can be accomplished by setting the control's Enabled property to False in the code. To enable the Button again, the control's Enabled property needs to be changed to True. Once a control is disabled, it automatically gets shaded in a different color to indicate that it cannot be used. An example with the Button control is shown in Figure B.4.

Figure B.4 *Enabled vs disabled button*

A programmer can also hide the control by changing the Visible property to False, but that is typically not a good idea. It is usually a better idea to disable the control as not to confuse the end user.

7. Always set the proper Tab Order

Setting the proper Tab order for the controls is crucial. The Tab Index property of a control defines its Tab order. By setting the proper Tab Index for the control, the user can move to the next control simply by pressing the Tab key on the keyboard. If an object on the Form has a zero Tab Index, it gets the focus when the Form gets loaded into memory. Pressing the Tab key on the keyboard, moves the focus to the object with Tab Index of 1, and etc. Tab indices can be changed in two ways. One way is to change the Tab Index property of each object in the Properties Window. Another way is by clicking on View ⟶ Tab Order, as shown in Figure B.5.

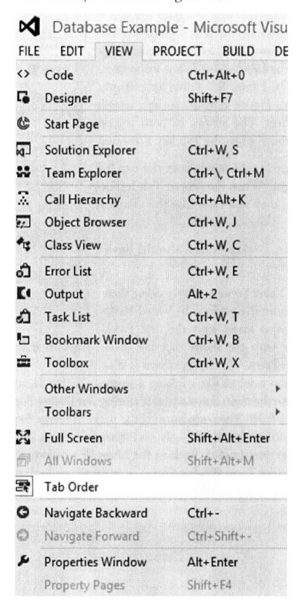

Figure B.5 *View ⟶ Tab Order*

Once the Tab Order submenu item is clicked, the Tab Index for every object on the Form is displayed as portrayed in Figure B.6.

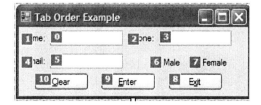

Figure B.6 *Tab indices*

Once a screen similar to Figure B.6 is shown, the Tab Index indices can be set by clicking consecutively on the numbers that appear on the objects. The first object clicked will have the index of zero assigned to it, the second one will have the index of one assigned to it, and so on. Generally it is a Windows OS standard that the cursor should jump from left to right, and top to bottom. The Tab Index of the Label object is not important, since Labels never get the focus. Figure B.7 shows an example with well-defined Tab indices. Figure B.8, shows an example with badly assigned Tab indices. The arrows in both images illustrate how the cursor will move when the Tab key is pressed.

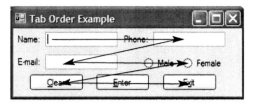

Figure B.7 *Well-defined Tab indices*

Generally speaking, the cursor should move from the top left of the Form to the bottom right. When the proper Tab Indices are set for the above example, they will look like the image as shown in Figure B.9.

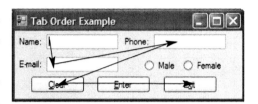

Figure B.8 *Poorly defined Tab indices*

8. In multiform projects, Dialog Forms should have special characteristics

Typically, a Windows Dialog Form is a Form other than the main Form in a programming project. In Visual Basic .NET, the program execution starts with the first Form created in the project, or with the Form that has been designated as the Start Up Form. The Dialog Form is dis-

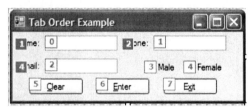

Figure B.9 *Properly set Tab indices*

played when a certain action is taken like clicking a Button. Dialog Forms are unique because the end user is not able to go back to the main Form without closing the Dialog Form. Such Forms are referred to as modal Forms. See Figure B.10. The main Form is the major Internet Explorer (IE) window. A sample Dialog Form appears when the user clicks Tools → Internet Options. Note, after the Internet Options Form opens, if the end user tries to click back to the Main IE window, it won't work. The user has to first close the Internet Options Form (Dialog Form) in order to get back to the main Form.

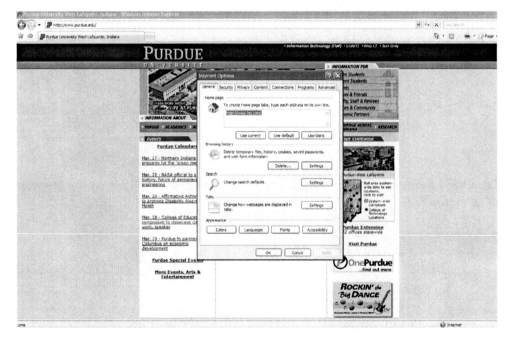

Figure B.10 *Main Form and Dialog Form*

Notice a couple of things that are unique about the Dialog Form depicted in Figure B.10.

 a.   The Dialog Form cannot be resized

 b.   The Dialog Form cannot be maximized or minimized

 c.   Typically, a Dialog Form should also pop up in the center of the Main Form

These settings can be easily set in the Properties window of a Form. To change these graphical settings, change the following properties for a Dialog Form (as shown in Figure B.11):

 a.   Change the MinimizeBox's value to False (this hides the MinimizeBox at the top right of the Form)

 b.   Change the MaximizeBox's value to False (this hides the MaximizeBox at the top right of the Form)

 c.   Change the StartupPosition's value to CenterParent (this forces the Form to start in the middle of the Main Form)

 d.   Change the FormBorderStyle's value to FixedDialog (this makes the Form to acquire a fixed size)

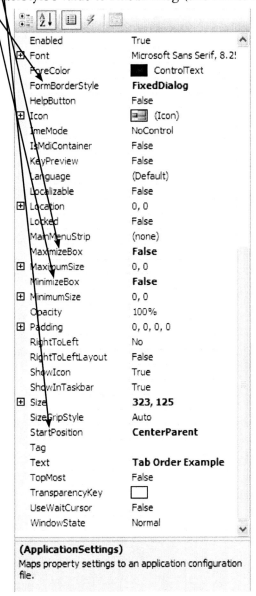

Figure B.11 *Dialog Form properties*

9. When displaying a MessageBox, make sure that it complies with the Windows GUI guidelines

There are numerous ways that a MessageBox could be displayed by changing things such as the icon and the Buttons on the MessageBox. There are two major types of MessageBoxes that have been discussed in this book. Refer to Chapter 5 for their respective properties.

10. Using the appropriate Button properties

Buttons are widely used in visual programming environments. In the Windows GUI environment, Buttons can be typically categorized into four major categories (this is a hasty generalization, but also a general assumption). Refer to Figure B.12.

 a. OK Button

 b. Cancel Button

 c. Edit Button

 d. Apply Button

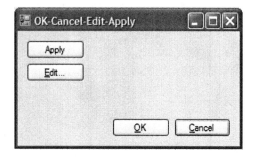

Figure B.12 *OK, Cancel, Edit, Apply*

Note, in Figure B.12, how the Cancel button is on the right-hand side, and the OK button is on the left-hand side. The OK and Cancel buttons are typically placed on the bottom right of a Form. They also typically appear on Dialog Form as shown in Figure B.10. By looking at the GUI in Figure B.12, a Windows user will intuitively think that the Edit button is going to open a new Form because the Button is labeled with three "...". This is also a Windows GUI standard. A good programmer should adhere to these Button standards so as not to confuse the end user with the program's functionality. The Apply Button is usually used to apply any changes that are made by the end user.

11. Access keys

Access keys are important in Windows GUI development. Access keys provide an alternative way for clicking a Button by using the keyboard. Note in Figure B.12, how all the Buttons have one letter underlined. The underlined letter is used to gain key access to the Button by simultaneously clicking the Alt key on the keyboard with the underlined letter. For example, in Figure B.12, if the end user clicks the Alt key along with the O key on the keyboard, the OK Button will be clicked. This is important because a programmer should never assume that all computers have a mouse. If a computer does not have a mouse attached to it, and there are no shortcut keys for the Buttons, the end user might find it difficult to access these Buttons.

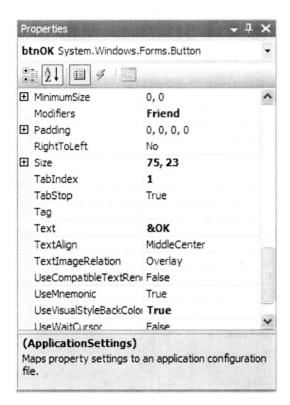

Figure B.13 *Designate a hot key for OK Button*

To create an access key for a Button, a programmer simply has to change the Text property of the Button by adding an "&" before the letter that is going to be designated as the access key. For example, Figure B.13 illustrates how the letter O of the OK Button in Figure B.12 is underlined. The "&" before the O, underlines the letter O during the program execution and designates the O as a hot key.

12. The AcceptButton and CancelButton Form properties

Typically, Windows OS users expect the processing Button of an application to be clicked when the Enter key is pressed on the keyboard. Additionally, the end user expects a Form to close when the Esc key is pressed on the keyboard. A programmer can perform this task by simply changing a Form's AcceptButton and CancelButton properties as shown in Figure B.14 and Figure B.15, respectively. When the drop-down arrow for either of the properties is clicked, the available Buttons on the Form are displayed in a dropdown box. The programmer then has a choice to bind the AcceptButton and CancelButton properties to any of the Buttons that are placed on the Form. After these changes are made, when the end user presses the Enter key on the keyboard, the OK Button gets clicked. Additionally, when the end user presses the Esc Button on the keyboard, the Cancel Button gets clicked.

Figure B.14 *AcceptButton property*

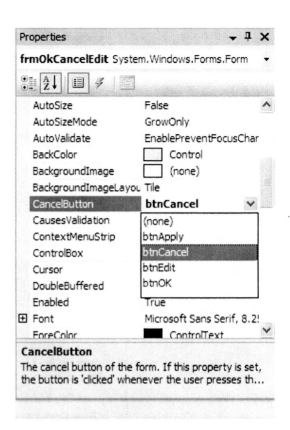

Figure B.15 *CancelButton property*

Coding Standards

After completing Appendix C, students should be able to:

- [ ] List and understand the reasons why coding standards are important
- [ ] List and understand the proposed coding standards
- [ ] List the various prefixes that are used for naming controls

C.1 Introduction

Most of the big corporations with numerous programmers have instantiated programming standards for their application developers to follow. It is usually the case that more than one programmer works on a single project, and at some point these programmers have to collaborate. If individual programmers use their own style of coding, it would be rather difficult for them to collaborate and understand each other's code. Because of the increased value of coding standards in the Information Technology (IT) industry, this Appendix has been added to the book.

Coding standards exist for all programming languages; however, some of the standards such as naming a variable vary from one language to another. For example, in the C programming language, programmers typically tend to use underscores in their code, however, in VB .NET they do not. Additionally, programmers tend to start their variable names with a lowercase letter in the C programming language, whereas in VB .NET, programmers tend to start their variable names with a capital letter. The coding standards offered in this chapter are the ones that people in the industry typically use when programming in VB .NET. They might vary from one company to another, but the purpose is to give the introductory programmer a structure to follow when programming.

C.2 Why Coding Standards?

Coding standards are important for a couple of reasons. Below is a list of the reasons for why coding standards are important.

1. They improve collaboration amongst programmers when working on a single project. Programmers will be able to understand each other's codes.

2. It improves the readability of a program. Consider two programs that accomplish exactly the same task. In one of them the programmer has followed the coding standards, and in the other no standards have been followed. It is much easier to read and understand the one that is written with proper standards. Most likely the program written by a developer will be used or modified by others in the real world, therefore following the proper coding standards is crucial in writing useful and meaningful programs.

3. Coding standards enforces including comments in the code. When programmers comment their code properly, it helps them remember their train of thought when they look back at their code. Additionally, when working on large projects, programmers can read the comments in the code, and understand what other programmers were doing with the code.

C.3 Suggested Coding Standards

This section offers the reader with the authors' suggested VB .NET coding standards based on their experience. Take this section as a guideline that could be followed whenever writing a VB .NET program.

Rule 1: Declarations: Always Declare Variables at the Top of the Sub Procedure or Function

Do not declare variables within the body of routines mixed with other statements; always declare them at the top. This avoids declarations being encased within conditional statements and might decrease program bugs. It also means declarations are easier to find, being located at one place.

Recommended Way:

```
Dim FirstName As String
Dim LastName As String
Dim FullName As String
FirstName = txtFirstName.Text
LastName = txtLastName.Text
FullName = FirstName & " " & LastName
```

Wrong Way:

```
Dim FirstName As String
FirstName = txtFirstName.Text
Dim LastName As String
LastName = txtLastName.Text
Dim FullName As String
FullName = FirstName & " " & LastName
```

Rule 2: Declare Each Variable on a Separate Line

This improves program clarity and makes it easier to maintain and modify the code in future.

```
Dim Variable1 As Integer
Dim Variable2 As Integer
```

Instead of:

```
Dim Variable1, Variable2 As Integer
```

Rule 3: Use the Following Guidelines for Naming a Variable

- Variables should NOT be named using Hungarian Notation (ex: intCount).

- Underscores should not be utilized as not to confuse the variable name with event procedures inherent to VB .NET

- Use CamelCase when naming a variable, i.e., start with an uppercase letter and follow with lowercase letters. If the variable name has more than one word, start every new word with an uppercase letter.

- When declaring variables, use a descriptive name (something meaningful, unlike X, Y, Z).

- The following are some examples of proper variable names:

```
Dim FirstName As String
Dim Name As String
Dim Counter As Integer
Dim NumberOfTickets As Integer
Dim SalaryPaidAfterTax As Decimal
```

When declaring a class/module/form scope variable, use the prefix m to specify that the variable is a module scope variable. (see examples below)

```
Private mFirstName As String
Private mName As String
```

When declaring a global/project scope variable, use the prefix g to specify that the variable is a global scope variable. (see examples below)

```
Public gFirstName As String
Public gSalaryPaidAfterTax As Decimal
```

Rule 4: Variables Should Be Defined with the Tightest Scope Possible

Variables should be declared with the tightest scope possible. Do not declare a variable with module scope unless there is a good reason for such declaration. Likewise, global variables should be avoided, unless the variable is needed in several Forms or classes. Excessive use of module scope or global scope variables results in programs that are very difficult to debug and maintain.

Rule 5: Always Indent Code Properly

Proper indetation adds to the clarity of the program, but is, completely ignored by the compiler. Luckily, the editor in VB .NET helps in indenting the code properly. The rule of thumb is to indent the code inside a procedure, a function, loops, and selection structures by four to five spaces. Code indentation improves program's clarity. The following depicts a sample of code indentation:

```
Private Function ValidateData() As Boolean
    If txtEmployeeID.Text = "" Then
        MessageBox.Show("Enter an employeeID", ...)
        txtEmployeeID.Focus()
        Return False
    End If
    If txtFirstName.Text = "" Then
        MessageBox.Show("Enter a first mame", ...)
        txtFirstName.Focus()
        Return False
    End If
    Return True
End Function
```

When continuing a long line of code across several lines, indent the subsequent lines:

```
lblShow.Text = "Name: " & txtName.Text & vbCrLf & "ID: " &
        txtID.Text & vbCrLf & "E-mail: " & txtemail.Text &
        vbCrLf & "Address: " & txtAddress.Text
```

Rule 6: Include Introductory Comments

Always start the code window with a few lines of introductory comments, specifying the programmer's name, date, and purpose of the program. The authorship and initial purpose of the program can always be tracked that way. For example:

```
'Programmer's Name
'Date: ##/##/##
'Brief description of the program
```

Rule 7: Include Inline Comments Whenever Needed

Add comments between the lines of the code for clarification. Also, you may add comments following the declaration of variables to describe their purpose.

```
Dim Ctr As Integer   'Loop Counter
Dim MonTax As Single 'Monthly Tax
```

Rule 8: Use Prefixes When Naming Controls

As used by most VB .NET programmers, and recommended by Microsoft, we suggest using Hungarian Notation for naming the controls placed on the Form. There is a specific prefix for each control which is a three-letters in lower case derived from the name of the control, such as lbl for Label, and btn for Button. For example, when naming a TextBox used for entering an address, it should be prefixed with txt, and named txtAddress. Table C.1 shows prefixes for some of the common controls used in VB .NET applications.

TABLE C.1 Control prefixes

CONTROL TYPE	PREFIX	CONTROL TYPE	PREFIX
TextBox	txt	List View	lvw
Button	btn	Menu	mnu
ListBox	lst	RadioButton	rad
CheckBox	chk	GroupBox	grp
CommonDialog	dlg	PictureBox	pic
Form	frm	Timer	tmr
ComboBox	cbo	Month View Calander	mvw
DatePicker	dtp	RichTextBox	rtf
Tab	tab	Progress Bar	prg
Label	lbl		

APPENDIX D

Additional Controls

LEARNING OBJECTIVES

After completing of Appendix D, students should be able to:

☐ Understand how to incorporate the following controls in their VB .NET application

- CheckBox
- RadioButton
- ComboBox
- DateTimePicker
- PictureBox

D.1 Introduction

This Appendix covers some useful VB .NET controls. Various controls can be used to either minimize the amount of data validation needed, or to increase the usability of an application.

D.2 CheckBox Control

The CheckBox control is used to provide the user with a number of choices and allow him/her to select zero, one, or more of these choices by checking the corresponding CheckBox. If you have ever filled a Web application on a Website, you have, most likely, experienced a CheckBox control. Table D.1 shows some important properties of a CheckBox control.

TABLE D.I Important CheckBox properties

Property	Description
Name	The three-letter prefix for naming a CheckBox is chk.
Checked	The Checked property is of type Boolean. Its value is True if the CheckBox is selected (checked), and False otherwise. The Checked property can also be used in the code to clear the selected CheckBox by setting the property's value to False.
Text	The Text property is the text that is displayed next to the CheckBox placed on the Form. It has to be changed to a descriptive text.

Figure D.I *CheckBox Example*

CheckBox Example

Consider the GUI presented in Figure D.1, where the user is allowed to choose the type of TV channels that he/she would like to subscribe to. To simplify this example, when the user clicks the Select Button, all the selected channels are displayed in the Selected Channels Label. Primarily, the program checks to see if at least one of the CheckBoxes is selected. Normally there is no need to make sure that at least one of the CheckBoxes is checked, but the nature of this example requires such validation. The Clear Button is used to clear the selections made by the user; basically, the CheckBoxes will become unchecked when the Clear Button is clicked.

Below is the code written for this example:

```
Private Sub btnSelect_Click(...) Handles btnSelect.Click
    Dim SelectedChannels As String = ""

  'Make sure that at least one of the checkboxes were selected:
    If chkSports.Checked = False And chkNews.Checked =
        False And chkHistory.Checked = False Then
        MessageBox.Show("Select at least one of the channels.",
            Application.ProductName, MessageBoxButtons.OK,
            MessageBoxIcon.Information)
        Exit Sub
    End If

  'If chkSports is selected, assign Sports to the string:
    If chkSports.Checked = True Then
        SelectedChannels = "Sports"
    End If

  'If chkNews is selected, concatinate News to the string:
    If chkNews.Checked = True Then
        SelectedChannels = SelectedChannels & vbLf & "News"
    End If
  'If chkHostory is selected, concatinate History to the string:
    If chkHistory.Checked = True Then
        SelectedChannels = SelectedChannels & vbLf & "History"
    End If
```

```
 'Display the string in Label:
   lblSelectedChannels.Text = SelectedChannels
End Sub

Private Sub btnClear_Click(...) Handles btnClear.Click
   'Clear all the CheckBoxes:

     chkSports.Checked = False
     chkHistory.Checked = False
     chkNews.Checked = False
End Sub
```

D.3 RadioButton Control `⊙ RadioButton`

The RadioButton control is used to make a single choice out of several choices. The reason how the RadioButton got its name, is because of the old radios that had buttons. When one of the radio's buttons was pressed, the others would flip back up and the button that was pressed would stay down, thus enabling the user only to make a single choice. Table D.2 shows some important RadioButton properties.

TABLE D.2 Important RadioButton properties

Property	Description
Name	The three letter prefix for naming a RadioButton is rad.
Checked	The Checked property is of type Boolean. Its value is True if the RadioButton is selected, and False otherwise. The Checked property can also be used to clear the selected RadioButton by setting the property's value to False.
Text	The Text property is the text that is displayed next to the RadioButton placed on the Form. It has to be changed to a descriptive text.

For RadioButtons to work properly, they have to be added to the same container element. For example, a Form is regarded as a container element. To create another container element within a Form, the programmer has to add a GroupBox `[x⁵] GroupBox`, from the ToolBox, under Containers category. When there are more than one set of RadioButtons on the Form, you must place each set in a separate GroupBox.

To check if a RadioButton is selected, you have to check the Checked property of that RadioButton. If the Checked property is equal to True, the RadioButton is selected, otherwise it is not selected. To clear a RadioButton in the code, simply change its Checked property to False.

RadioButton Example

Consider the GUI in Figure D.2. Three RadioButtons are added to a GroupBox on the Form, and the user can choose only one of the provided choices: Sports, News, or History. When the Process Button is clicked, the selected subject is displayed in the output Label. Additionally, when the Clear Button is clicked, the selection made in the RadioButtons will be cleared.

Figure D.2 *RadioButton Example GUI*

Below is the code written for this example:

```
Private Sub btnProcess_Click(...) Handles btnProcess.Click
    'Inform the user if none of the RadioButtons is selected
    If radNews.Checked = False And radSports.Checked = False And
        radHistory.Checked = False Then
        MessageBox.Show("Select at least one of the RadioButtons."
        Application.ProductName, MessageBoxButtons.OK,
        MessageBoxIcon.Information)
        Exit Sub
    End If

    If radNews.Checked = True Then
        lblOutput.Text = "News"
    ElseIf radSports.Checked = True Then
        lblOutput.Text = "Sports"
    ElseIf radHistory.Checked = True Then
        lblOutput.Text = "History"
    End If
End Sub

Private Sub btnClear_Click(...) Handles btnClear.Click
    radHistory.Checked = False
    radNews.Checked = False
    radSports.Checked = False
End Sub
```

D.4 ComboBox Control

The ComboBox control is used to allow the user make a single selection from many available choices. Table D.3 shows some important properties when working with a ComboBox.

For example, if a person had to choose the state where he/she lives in, the programmer can use a ComboBox that is filled in advance with the names of states. Let us assume that the states in the ComboBox are IN, IL, KY, and CA. First, you must add the control to the Form. The next step is to populate the ComboBox with the state names. The Items property needs to be selected as shown in Figure D.3. Once the Button ⊡ is clicked, Figure D.4 is shown to the programmer. The developer can then enter the values on separate lines as shown in Figure D.4.

To allow the user to enter a choice that is not included in the ComboBox, change the ComboBoxStyle property to Simple. This way, the user can enter a state other than available choices into the ComboBox as shown in Figure D.5.

TABLE D.3 Important ComboBox properties

Property	Description
Name	The three-letter prefix for naming a ComboBox is cbo.
SelectedIndex	The SelectedIndex property exists during the runtime. Its value is a zero-based index of the item that is selected in the ComboBox. If the first item is selected, the SelectedIndex is 0, if the second item is selected, the SelectedIndex is 1, and so on. If nothing has been selected then this property equals to −1.
Items	The Items property is a Collection (similar to an array) that contains all the items that are displayed in the ComboBox. The Items property can be populated during the design time of the project or during the runtime through VB .NET code.
DropDownStyle	This property can be set to DropDownList to disallow the user from entering text other than available choices into the CombBox.
Text	During the run time, when the user makes a selection from the ComboBox, the selected item gets stored in the Text property of the ComboBox.

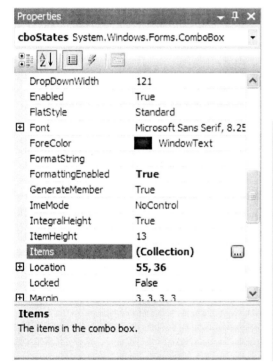

Figure D.3 *ComboBox Properties*

Figure D.4 *Items property at design time*

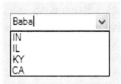

Figure D.5 *Allow other choices*

To disallow the user from typing a different choice into the ComboBox, change the DropDownStyle property to DropDownList as shown in Figure D.6.

Figure D.6 *DropDownStyle Property*

The best way to check whether an item in the ComboBox has been selected or not, is to check the SelectedIndex property of the ComboBox. It is equal to negative one, if nothing has been selected. A ComboBox's SelectedIndex property is the index of the item selected at runtime. For example, in Figure D.5, if "IN" is selected, the SelectedIndex property would be 0 (zero). If "IL" is selected, the SelectedIndex would be 1 (one), etc. To get the selected value in the ComboBox, simply use the Text property of the ComboBox. This is more elaborately explained in the example below.

ComboBox Example

Let us design a simple program that allows the user make a selection in a ComboBox, and click on the Button to get the selected item displayed in a Label. If no selection has been made from the ComboBox, a message would be displayed to the user. The GUI is shown in Figure D.7.

Figure D.7 *ComboBox Example*

The click event procedure of the Process Button is shown below.

```
Private Sub btnProcess_Click(...) Handles btnProcess.Click
    'Validate if something is selected, if not inform the user.
    If cboStates.SelectedIndex = -1 Then
        MessageBox.Show("Select an item from the ComboBox.",
            Application.ProductName, MessageBoxButtons.OK,
            MessageBoxIcon.Information)
        Exit Sub
    End If

    'Display SelectedItem in the Label:
    lblOutput.Text = cboStates.Text
End Sub
```

Figure D.8 *DateTime Picker Calendar Pop Up*

D.5 DateTimePicker Control

The DateTimePicker control is used to allow the user select a date/time. It looks like a ComboBox when placed on the Form, but when the drop-down arrow is clicked, a calendar pops up (as shown in Figure D.8) to ease the process of the date entry. This helps minimize the amount of erroneous data entry. There are different formats in which the date and time can be displayed in the DateTimePicker. Table D.4 shows some important DateTimePicker properties.

TABLE D.4 Important DateTimePicker properties

Property	Description
Name	The three-letter prefix for naming a DateTimePicker is dtp.
Value	The Value property is of data type Date, and its value is the selected date.
Format	The Format property can be used to change the way the date and time are displayed in the DateTimePicker. This is explained in detail in the following section.

The display format of the picked date can be changed through the Format property of a DateTimePicker as shown in Figure D.9. The date shown in the DateTimePicker Control in Figure D.10, is in Long format.

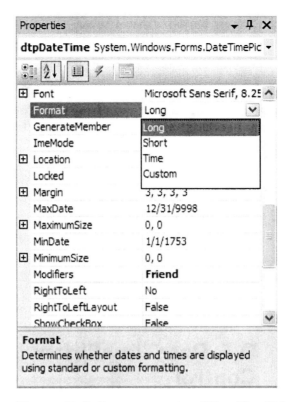

Figure D.9 *Format property of DateTimePicker*

Example of how date will be displayed in the DateTimePicker when the respective Format is selected:

Long: Wednesday, May 09, 2013

Short: 5/9/2013

Time: 5:09:11 PM

Custom: If the custom field is chosen then a custom Format has to be entered in the CustomFormat property. For example, if dd/yy was entered in the CustomFormat property, and the Custom field is chosen for the Format property, the DateTimePicker will display 09/13 for the date 05/09/2013.

DateTimePicker Example

Given below is an example of how to use a DateTimePicker in a program. Consider the GUI as shown in Figure D.10. The program should simply display the selected date in the output Label.

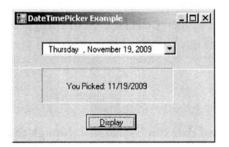

Figure D.10 *Screen capture at runtime*

The click event procedure of the Process Button:

```
Private Sub btnDisplay_Click (...) Handles btnDisplay.Click
    Dim InputDate As Date
    'Assign the value selected in the DateTimePicker to the variable. Notice, there is no need for
    'explicit type conversion, the DateTimePicker's value is already of type Date

    InputDate = dtpDate.Value
    'Display the selected date in the output label
    lblOutput.Text = "You Picked:" & InputDate.ToShortDateString()
End Sub
```

 To display a date in Long format, use Date.ToLongDateString() method.

D.6 PictureBox Control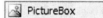

A PictureBox control is useful if a picture is to be shown on a Form. A PictureBox is added to the Form and then a picture/image is selected from the hard drive or the Internet resources to be displayed. Table D.5 shows the important properties for a PictureBox.

TABLE D.5 Important PictureBox properties

Property	Description
Name	The three-letter prefix for naming a PictureBox is pic.
Image	This property allows the programmer to choose the picture that will be displayed in the PictureBox.
SizeMode	This property gives the programmer the ability to have the image being displayed auto-stretch to the size of the PictureBox. This is discussed in the section below.

Choosing a picture can be done during the design or execution of a program. Once the PictureBox is added to the Form and an appropriate name is given to the box, an image can be added at design time through the Image property and clicking on the ⬚ as shown in Figure D.11. The screen as depicted in Figure D.12 shows up and an appropriate picture is chosen from the storage medium. The Local Resource RadioButton is then selected, and the Import Button is clicked.

When the Import Button is clicked, Figure D.13 is shown to the programmer and an appropriate image is chosen from the storage medium. The Open Button shown in Figure D.13 is then clicked, and the OK Button shown in Figure D.12 is also clicked. It is recommended to set the SizeMode property of the PictureBox to StretchImage as shown in Figure D.14. Once that property is set, the picture will be properly displayed in the PictureBox as shown in Figure D.15.

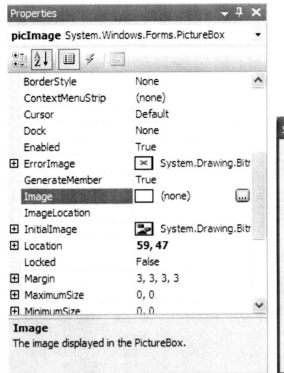

Figure D.11 *PictureBox properties*

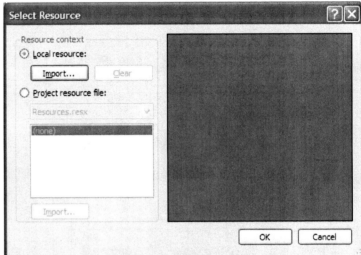

Figure D.12 *Selecting an image*

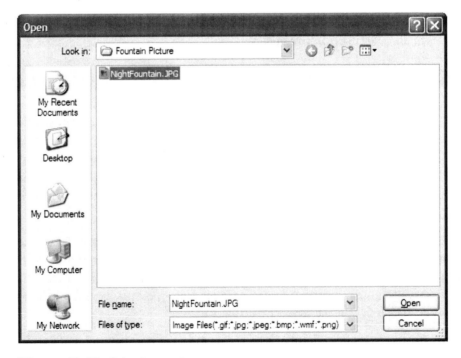

Figure D.13 *Selecting a picture*

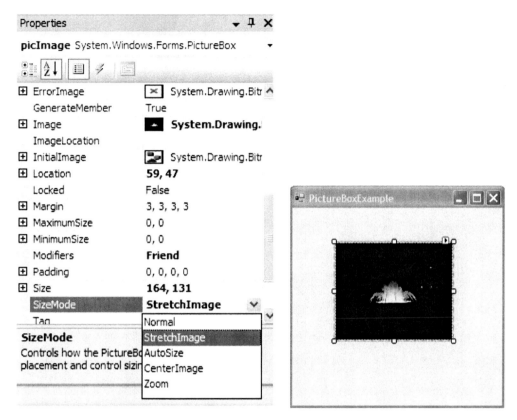

Figure D.14 *Changing the SizeMode property*

Figure D.15 *Fountain image being displayed in PictureBox*

Integrating Excel into VB .NET

LEARNING OBJECTIVES

After completion of Appendix E, students should be able to:

❑ Add a COM Reference to a VB .NET Project

❑ Open an Excel spreadsheet from a VB .NET project

❑ Create an Excel spreadsheet from a VB .NET project

❑ Copy a two-dimensional array content to an Excel spreadsheet

❑ Retrieve a range of values from Excel spreadsheet into a two-dimensional array

E.1 Introduction

Visual Basic for Application known as VBA is a programming language very similar to Visual Basic but with slightly different syntax. Unlike Visual Basic, one cannot create an executable program using VBA. This language has been developed by Microsoft mainly to automate Microsoft Office applications. Using VBA, a programmer may add Buttons, Textboxes and other objects to an Office application, and write the code to have the application perform desired tasks, hence add to the functionality of the application.

In this appendix we will not discuss VBA; instead we show the reader how to integrate an Excel spreadsheet into a Visual Basic .NET project. This is useful if the programmer needs to create an Excel file, or programmatically open an Excel file from a VB .NET project. This way one can save the data generated in a VB .NET project or retrieved from a database, in an Excel spreadsheet, or open an existing Excel spreadsheet. Automation is the answer to such integration. In general automation is a process that allows an application to control objects in another application.

E.2 Adding Reference to a COM Object

Microsoft supplies several Primary Interop Assemblies (PIAs) that contain the official description of the most commonly used types that are defined in COM libraries. These PIAs allow the managed code (i.e. VB .NET) to bind to the COM types at compile time and provide information to the common language runtime (CLR). In other words, PIAs make interoperability easier between the managed code and Office component type libraries, such as Excel object library.

To access Excel from a VB .NET project, the programmer should add a reference to the Microsoft Excel Object Library. By adding the reference, the VB project can work with all the classes and objects that are provided in the Excel library. Below are the steps for adding a reference to Excel in a VB .NET project.

1. Create a VB .NET Windows Application and name it "Automation" or any name you wish.

2. Choose Project on the menu bar, and click on Add Reference in the submenu. The Add Reference dialog box opens up.

3. Click on the COM tab on the left side and scroll down the list until you find the right Excel Object Library reference.

4. Click on Microsoft Excel Object Library, as shown in Figure E.1. Notice that there can be more than one Excel Object library in the list; make sure to select the one that is compatible with the Excel version installed on your computer. For example, Excel 2010 requires Microsoft Excel 14.0 Object Library, Excel 2007, requires Microsoft Excel 12.0 Object Library, Excel 2003, requires Microsoft Excel 11.0 Object Library, Excel 2002 requires Microsoft Excel 10.0 Object Library, and Excel 2000 requires Microsoft Excel 9.0 Object Library to be added as reference.

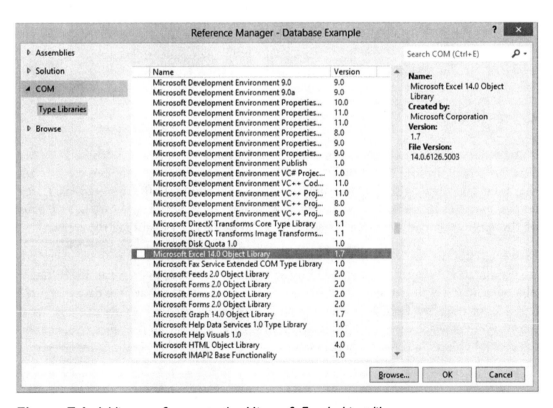

Figure E.1 *Adding a reference to the Microsoft Excel object library*

E.3 Excel Objects

Once the reference to Microsoft Excel Object Library is added in the VB .NET project, one can use the classes, objects, properties and methods that are provided in that library in order to create, open, and manipulate an Excel file. There are four objects used when working with Excel:

- The Application Object
  The Application object is like a container for all the program objects and refers to the application as a whole. It provides many useful methods and properties that will be discussed next.

- The Workbook Object

- The Worksheet Object

- The Range Object

To manipulate an Excel file in a VB .NET project, one has to include the required Imports statement to the code, declare few objects and activate the Excel application. The basic steps for working with Excel from within a VB .NET project are as follows:

1. Declare an Excel Application object with local or module scope:
   ```
   Dim ExcelObj As Excel.Application
   ```

2. Since an Excel application has a workbook and at least one worksheet, declare a Workbook and a Worksheet object. A Range object can also be declared if working with a range of values:
   ```
   Dim WorkbookObj As Excel.Workbook
   Dim WorksheetObj As Excel.Worksheet
   Dim RangeObj As Excel.Range
   ```

3. Create an instance of Excel application on the disk using the Application object:
   ```
   ExcelObj = New Excel.Application
   ```

4. Using the Add method of ExcelObj.Workbooks, add a workbook to the application and assign it to the workbook object.
   ```
   WorkbookObj = ExcelObj.Workbooks.Add
   ```

5. Using the Add method of Workbooks.Worksheets, add a worksheet to the workbook and assign it to the worksheet object.
   ```
   WorksheetObj = WorkbookObj.Worksheets.Add
   ```

E.4 How to Access an Excel Spreadsheet

Assume that the goal is to have a VB .NET project access and display an Excel spreadsheet at runtime. The first step is to add a COM reference to the VB .NET project. For Excel 2010 add a reference to Microsoft Excel 14.0 Object Library. You need to know what version of Excel has been used to create the Excel file on the disk. You might need to add an Imports statement to the VB .NET project as well. The following example has been created in Visual Studio .NET 2012 and requires *Imports Microsoft.Office.Interop,* before the Windows generated code.

EXAMPLE 1

Design a VB .NET 2012 project, add a Button to the Form; name it btnOpen, and change its Text property to "Open Excel File", as shown in Figure E.2. Create an Excel file named "test.xls"; store some random data in the file and save it in the C:\Temp folder. The project should open up the Excel spreadsheet once the Button in clicked at runtime. Exception handling has been added to handle possible exceptions at runtime:

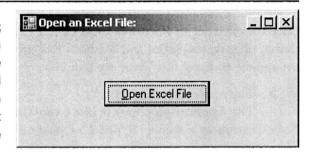

Figure E.2 *GUI for Example 1*

```vb
Imports Microsoft.Office.Interop
Public Class Form1
    Private Sub btnOpen_Click (. . .) Handles btnOpen.Click

        'Declare required objects:
        Dim ExcelObj As New Excel.Application
        Dim WorkbookObj As Excel.Workbook
        Try

            'Instantiate an Excel Application:
            ExcelObj = New Excel.Application

            'Open the Excel file and assign it to the workbook object:
            WorkbookObj = ExcelObj.Workbooks.Open("C:\Temp\test.xls")

            'Make the Excel file visible:
            ExcelObj.Visible = True

            'Give the control to the user:
            ExcelObj.UserControl = True

            'Release the objects:
            ExcelObj = Nothing
            WorkbookObj = Nothing
        Catch Ex As Exception
            MessageBox.Show (Ex.Message, . . .)
        End Try
    End Sub
End Class
```

In this example, notice that the `Excel.Workbooks.Open` method is used to open an existing Excel file. After opening the file, the `Excel.Visible` method is used to make the data visible on the screen. Furthermore, the control of the file is given to the user by means of the `Excel.UserControl` method. At the end, the objects are set to nothing in order to release the memory allocated by these objects.

To test this simple project, run the VB program and click btnOpen. The Excel spreadsheet will be displayed on the screen, as shown in Figure E.3. Try to change some of the data in the Excel file, click on the disk icon on the toolbar of the Excel to save the changes and close the file the same way you would work with a stand alone Excel spreadsheet. The user can click on btnOpen to access the Excel spreadsheet as many times as needed. Make sure to close the spreadsheet each time before clicking on the Button again, otherwise several copies of the Excel file will be opened on the screen which may lead to data inconsistency.

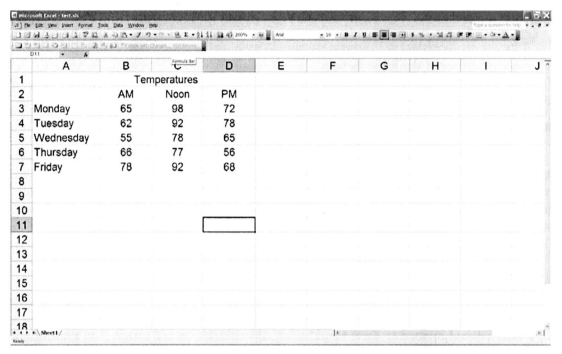

Figure E.3 *Excel spreadsheet accessed via VB. NET Project*

E.5 How to Create an Excel Spreadsheet

To create an Excel spreadsheet from a VB .NET project, one has to add the Excel Object Library reference to the project and then use the objects and methods provided in the Excel library to create and open an Excel spreadsheet. Let us look at an example:

EXAMPLE 2

Design a VB .NET project to store the name and score of an unknown number of students in a dynamic array of structure; At the end of the program execution, save the data to an Excel file. Figure E.4 is a possible GUI for this project.

Data Structure: Let us declare a structure with two members for name and score, and declare a dynamic array of a structure to store all the students' data. The data structure should be declared with module scope.

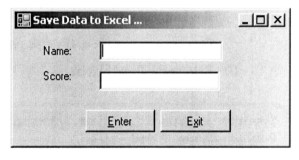

Figure E.4 *GUI for Example 2*

```
'Data Structure:
Private Structure mRecord
    Dim Name As String
    Dim Score As Short
End Structure

Private mStudent() As mRecord
Private mCount As Short = -1
```

The Buttons should respond to the click event, and the Form should respond to the Form Closing event. Below is the logic for each event procedure.

a. Click event procedure of the Enter Button:
   When clicked, this Button is responsible for storing the entered data in the dynamic array of structure. The logic of this event procedure is similar to the examples discussed in chapter 10.

b. Click event of the Exit Button:
   When clicked, it should end the project by closing the form.

c. Form Closing event procedure:
   Form Closing event of the Form takes place right before the Form is unloaded from the memory. The data stored in the dynamic array should be saved to an Excel file in this event procedure. Below is the pseudo-code for this event procedure:

   1. Declare an Excel application, workbook and worksheet objects.

   2. If array is empty, do nothing.

   3. Otherwise, create a new instance of an Excel application; assign it to the Excel object.

   4. Using the Add method of Excel.Workbooks, add a workbook and assign it to a workbook object.

   5. Using the Add method of Workbook.Worksheets, add a worksheet and assign it to the worksheet object.

   6. Using the Cells method of the worksheet object, add column headers to the columns in the spreadsheet. The rows and columns in the spreadsheet are numbered from 1.

   7. Start a loop to iterate through all the array elements
      a. Assign each student's name and score to the next row in the spreadsheet in columns 1 and 2.

   8. Make the Excel file visible and give the control to the user.
      This will open the Excel file on the screen, as shown in Figure E.5. The user can view, modify the data, and save it to the disk the same way one would do with a standalone Excel file.

   9. One can save the file to the disk programmatically.

   10. Release the Excel objects.

```vb
Imports Microsoft.Office.Interop
Public Class Form1
    'Data Structure:
    Private Structure mRecord
        Dim Name As String
        Dim Score As Short
    End Structure
    Private mStudent() As mRecord
    Private mCount As Short = -1

    Private Sub btnEnter_Click(. . .) Handles btnEnter.Click
        'Assume the entered data is valid.
        'Store data in the dynamic array:
        mCount = mCount + 1
```

```
        ReDim Preserve mStudent(mCount)
        mStudent(mCount).Name = txtName.Text
        mStudent(mCount).Score = Short.Parse(txtScore.Text)
        'Get ready for the next data entry:
        txtName.Clear()
        txtScore.Clear()
        txtName.Focus()
    End Sub
    'Save data stored in the array to an Excel file.
    Private Sub Form1_FormClosing(. . .) Handles Me.FormClosing
        'Declare required objects:
        Dim ExcelObj As Excel.Application
        Dim WorkbookObj As Excel.Workbook
        Dim SheetObj As Excel.Worksheet

        Dim Ctr As Short
        Dim Row As Short

        If mCount = -1 Then 'Check for empty array
            Exit Sub
        End If

        ExcelObj = New Excel.Application
        WorkbookObj = ExcelObj.Workbooks.Add
        SheetObj = WorkbookObj.Worksheets.Add
        'Create column headers in Excel file:
        SheetObj.Cells (1, 1) = "Name"
        SheetObj.Cells (1, 2) = "Score"
        'Save array content to the Excel file
        For Ctr = 0 To mCount
            Row = Ctr + 2      'Find the proper row number
            SheetObj.Cells(Row, 1) = mStudent(Ctr).Name
            SheetObj.Cells(Row, 2) = mStudent(Ctr).Score
        Next Ctr
        'Make Excel file visible. Refer to Figure E.5:
        ExcelObj.Visible = True
        ExcelObj.UserControl = True
        'Save the workbook object to the disk:
        WorkbookObj.SaveAs("C:\Temp\students.xls")
        WorkbookObj.Close()
        'Release the objects:
        ExcelObj = Nothing
        WorkbookObj = Nothing
        SheetObj = Nothing
    End Sub
    'End the program execution.
    Private Sub btnExit_Click(. . .) Handles btnExit.Click
        Me.Close ()
    End Sub
End Class
```

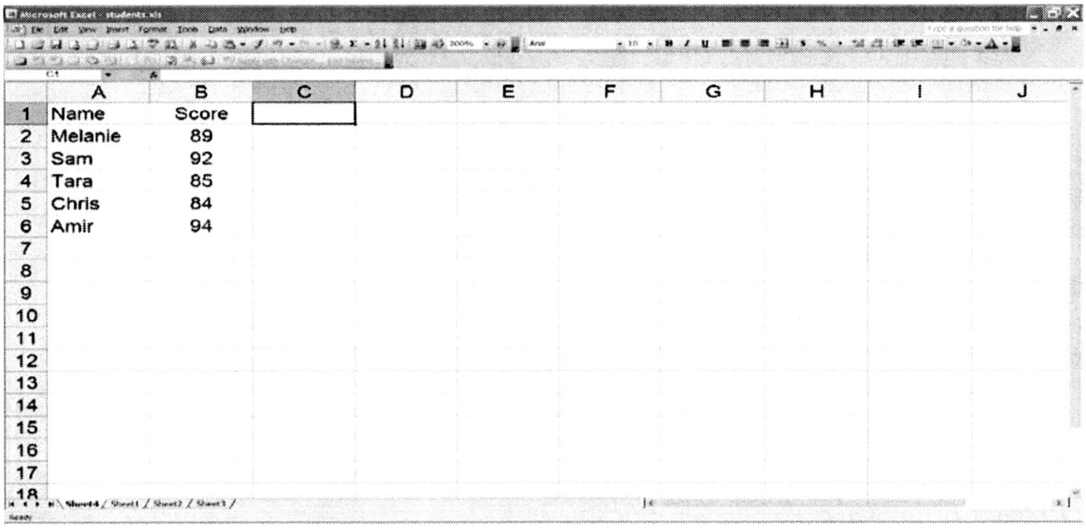

Figure E.5 *Excel file with array content saved to it*

E.6 How to Manipulate Data in an Excel Sheet

Let us work out a simple example and demonstrate how to change the data stored in a cell, or how to retrieve the data from a cell of an Excel sheet. Assume that an Excel file named "test.xls" has been created and saved in folder C:\Temp.

EXAMPLE 3

Design a VB .NET project with one TextBox, one Label, and two Buttons. Name the objects: txtName, lblShow, btnChange and btnRetrieve. Assume that btnChange when clicked, will open an Excel file, and change the data stored in the cell at row 1 and column 1 to the name entered in txtName. btnRetrieve when clicked, will open the same Excel file, and retrieve the data stored in the cell at row 1 and column 1 and display it in lblShow. Figure E.6 is the screen capture at runtime when the user has entered Robert in txtName, clicked on btnChange, and then clicked on btnRetrieve.

Before writing any code make sure to add a reference to the Microsoft Excel Object Library, and add the Imports statement before the Windows generated code.

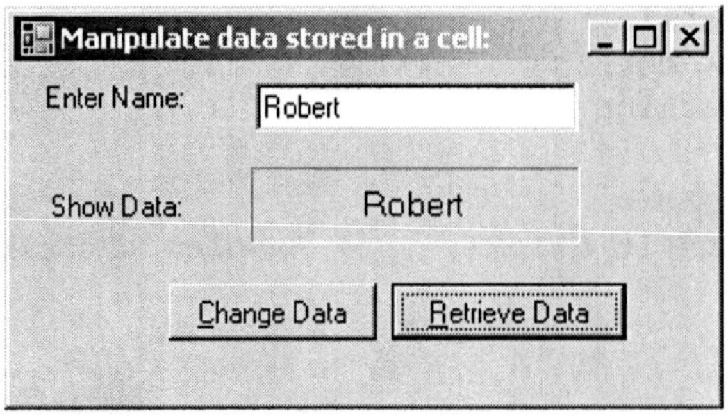

Figure E.6 *Change | Retrive data in a Cell*

```vb
Imports Microsoft.Office.Interop
Public Class Form1
    'Open an Excel file, retrieve data from a cell, and close it.
    Private Sub btnRetrieve_Click(. . .) Handles btnRetrieve.Click

        'Declare required objects:
        Dim ExcelObj As Excel.Application
        Dim WorkbookObj As Excel.Workbook
        Dim SheetObj As Excel.Worksheet

        ExcelObj = New Excel.Application
        WorkbookObj = ExcelObj.Workbooks.Open("C:\Temp\test.xls")

        'Access the first worksheet
        SheetObj = WorkbookObj.Worksheets(1)
        'Retrieve data from a cell (1, 1), display it in the Label:
        lblShow.Text = SheetObj.Range("A1").Value.ToString

        'Close the Workbook:
        WorkbookObj.Close()

        'Release the objects:
        ExcelObj = Nothing
        WorkbookObj = Nothing
        SheetObj = Nothing

    End Sub

    'Open an Excel file, change a cell value, save and close it.
    Private Sub btnChange_Click(. . .) Handles btnChange.Click

        'Declare required objects:
        Dim ExcelObj As Excel.Application
        Dim WorkbookObj As Excel.Workbook
        Dim SheetObj As Excel.Worksheet

        ExcelObj = New Excel.Application
        WorkbookObj = ExcelObj.Workbooks.Open("C:\Temp\test.xls")

        'Access the first worksheet:
        SheetObj = WorkbookObj.Worksheets(1)
        'Change data in cell(1, 1) to the name entered in txtName
        SheetObj.Cells (1, 1) = txtName.Text

        'Save and close the Workbook:
        WorkbookObj.Save ()
        WorkbookObj.Close ()

        'Release the objects:
        ExcelObj = Nothing
        WorkbookObj = Nothing
        SheetObj = Nothing

    End Sub
End Class
```

E.7 Two Dimensional Array and Excel

One can save the content of a two-dimensional array to an Excel file by means of the Range object. Let us look at an example.

EXAMPLE 4

Design a VB .NET project with only one Button, named btnSave. In the click event of the Button, declare a two-dimensional array, fill the array with some random values, save the array's content to an Excel file and display the file on the screen. The GUI is shown in Figure E.7.

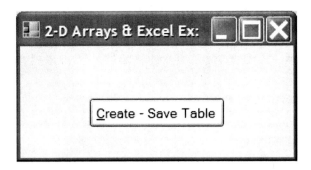

Figure E.7 *GUI for Example 4*

Before writing any code make sure to add a reference to the Microsoft Excel 12.0 Object Library.

Pseudo code of the Click event procedure of btnSave:

1. Declare required objects, variables and the two-dimensional array

2. Fill the array with some values

3. Instantiate a new Excel object

4. Add a workbook object to the application

5. Add a worksheet to the workbook

6. Initialize and resize the Range object to fit the 2-D array

7. Assign the two-dimensional array to the Value property of the Range object

8. Release all the objects.

Translate to VB .NET code:

```
Imports Microsoft.Office.Interop
Public Class Form1

    Private Sub btnSave_Click(. . .) Handles btnSave.Click
        Dim Excel As Excel.Application
        Dim Workbook As Excel.Workbook
        Dim Worksheet As Excel.Worksheet
        Dim Range As Excel.Range
```

```
'Declare a 2-D array with 6 rows and 4 columns:
Dim Table (5, 3) As Integer

'Declare loop variables to traverse the array:
Dim Row As Integer
Dim Col As Integer
'Fill the array with some values:
For Row = 0 To 5
    For Col = 0 To 3
        Table(Row, Col) = Row
    Next Col
Next Row

Excel = New Excel.Application
'Add a workbook to the Excel:
Workbook = Excel.Workbooks.Add
'Add a worksheet to the Excel:
Worksheet = Workbook.Worksheets.Add
'Define the range objects from A1 to . . .
Range = Worksheet.Range("A1", Reflection.Missing.Value)
'Resize the range object to 6 rows and 4 columns:
Range = Range.Resize(6, 4)
'Assign the 2-D array to the Range object:
Range.Value = Table
'Display the Excel file:
Excel.Visible = True
Excel.UserControl = True
'Save and close:
WorkbookObj.Save()
WorkbookObj.Close()
'Release the objects:
Excel = Nothing
Workbook = Nothing
Worksheet = Nothing
Range = Nothing
    End Sub
End Class
```

Start the VB .NET project and click the Button. The spreadsheet shown in figure E.8 will be opened.

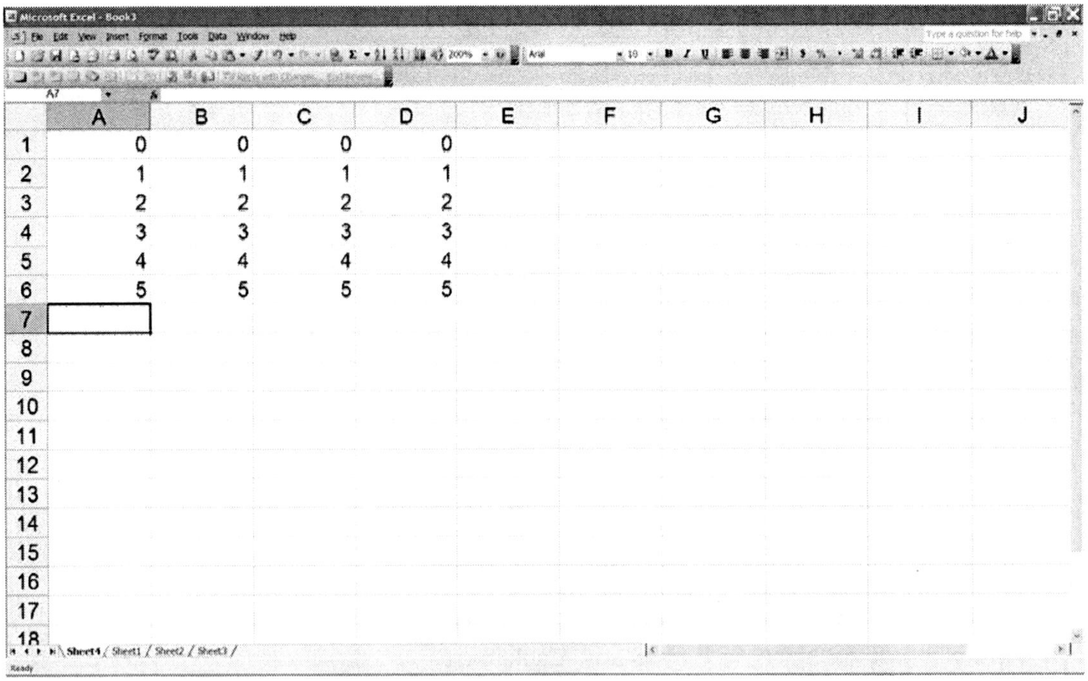

Figure E.8 *Excel file with 2-D Array content saved to it*

E.8 Saving Data to a CSV File

Another way of saving data to Excel from a VB .NET project is saving the data to a Comma Separated Values (CSV) file. You can open a CSV file as an Excel file. Saving data to a CSV file is similar to saving data to sequential access files. When writing to the file, use comma as the delimiter character. A Tab delimited file is another option. Refer to chapter 12 to review sequential access files.

Answers to Review Questions

Chapter 1

1. A TextBox control.

2. The AutoSize Property.

3. The Label control is used to display the program's output and to describe other objects placed on the Form.

4. To clear the Label object, the following code is used:
    ```
    lblOutput.Text = ""
    ```

5. There are two ways to clear a TextBox. To clear txtName:
    ```
    a)  txtName.Text = ""
    b)  txtName.Clear()
    ```

6. Use the Focus method of the TextBox, i.e. txtName.Focus()

7. An event is something that happens during the program execution, e.g. clicking on a Button.

8. To make the VB .NET program respond to an event, one has to write the code in the corresponding event procedure of the object.

9. The Tab order is the order in which the objects get focus when the user presses the Tab Key during the runtime

10. One way to change the Tab order of the object is via the TabIndex property.

Chapter 2

1. Variable is a place holder in computer's random access memory (RAM). Variables are declared to store data values that can be changed or referenced in the program.

2. Dim is the keyword.

3. Decimal is the recommended data type for storing monetary values.

4. Byte is the smallest data type in VB .NET. It consumes one byte in the memory.

5. Single, Decimal, and Double are used to store numbers with a fraction part.

6. Declare a variable...
```
Dim Population As Integer
Population = 125000
```

7. `Dim MyName As String = "Guity Ravai"`

8. A variable to store your address:
```
Dim Address As String
Address = "124 Kent Ave." & vbLf & _
"West Lafayette, IN. 47906"
```

9. Yes, it is a legal name, but it is not a good name.

Chapter 3

1.
```
a.  23 * 2 / 5 —>9.2
b.  3 + 5 * 2 —> 13
c.  2 * (12 + 5) Mod 9 —> 7
d.  1200 \ 2 ^ 3 —> 1200 \ 8 —> 150
e.  -10 ^ 2 —> -100
```

2. `Z = (X^2 + X * Y)/(3 * Y)`

3.
```
Dim Name As String
Name = txtName.Text
```

4.
```
Dim Size As Short
Size = Short.Parse(txtNumber.Text)
```

5.
```
Dim Area As Single
Dim Radius As Single
```

6. `Radius = Single.Parse(txtRadius.Text)`

7. `Area = 3.14 * Radius ^ 2`

8. `lblOutput.Text = Area.ToString ("n")`

Note: Any of the following parameters "n", "N", "n2", "N2" will result in a numeric string with two digits after the decimal point.

Chapter 4

1. The relational operator for equality is: =

2. The relational operator for less than is: <

3. Here is the If statement:
```
If Score > 60 Then
    lblOutput.Text = "You passed the test!"
End If
```

4. The If statement to check employee's salary:
```
Dim Salary As Decimal
Salary = ...
If Salary >= 4500 And Salary <= 7000 Then
    lblOutput.Text = "Salary is within the proper range."
End If
```

5. False

6. True

7. An If statement to check if the user has entered a valid department name.
```
Dim Department As String
Department = txtDepartment.Text.ToLower()
If Department = "cgt" Or Department = "met" Then
        'Department name is valid.
    ...
Else
        'Invalid department name
End If
```

Chapter 5

1. MessageBox function is a good way to inform the user.

2. Perform an existence check for txtData.
```
If txtData.Text = "" Then
  MessageBox.Show("Enter a value.", Application.ProductName,
      MessageBoxButtons.OK, MessageBoxIcon.Information)
  txtData.Focus()
  Exit Sub
End If
```

3. Perform a numeric check for txtData.
```
If IsNumeric(txtData.Text) = False Then
  MessageBox.Show("Enter a number.",
  Application.ProductName,
      MessageBoxButtons.OK, MessageBoxIcon.Information)
  txtData.Focus()
  Exit Sub
End If
```

4. False

5. False

6. Exit Sub ends the procedure execution.

7. True

8. A runtime error occurs, the program execution stops, and the system displays a diagnostic error message highlighting the erroneous line.

9. The MessageBox will display "Enter a whole number." and then 0 will be displayed in the Label. The reason is that Integer.TryParse, cannot parse "ten" into an Integer, therefore, it does not change N, and returns False. The correct code should include an Exit Sub before End If.

Chapter 6

1. Two advantages of modularity are:
   a) Eliminates redundant code
   b) Improves clarity of the program

2. A general procedure is a segment of code that is written to accomplish a certain task. It has to be called to do its job.

3. The click event procedure of a Button is not a general procedure, it is an event procedure.

4. IsNumeric is an example of an intrinsic function in VB .NET.

5. A general function is the right choice, because a general function does the calculation and returns the calculated area as its output.

6. This is a general function.

7. Call/Invoke the module given in the previous question:
```
Dim N1, N2, SumUp As Integer
N1 = 203
N2 = 874
SumUp = Sum (N1, N2)
```

8. Below is the general procedure that displays instructions for making scrambled eggs:
```
Private Sub ScrambleEggsForOne ()
   Dim Recipe As String
   Recipe = "1) Break 2 eggs into a bowl " & vbLf _
            "2) Add a tsp of water to the eggs" & vbLf _
            "3) Beat the eggs with a whisk for 1 minute." & vbLf _
            "4) Heat 2 Tbsp of oil in a small frying pan." & vbLf _
            "5) Pour the eggs in the frying pan, and cook." & vbLf _
            "6) Add salt and pepper for taste. Enjoy!"
   lblOutput.Text = Recipe
End Sub
```

Chapter 7

1. In a pretest loop, the condition of the loop is examined at the beginning of the iteration, whereas in a posttest loop, the condition is examined at the end of the iteration. Therefore, in a posttest loop, the body of the loop gets executed at least once.

2. b

3. a

4. d

5. a

6. c

7. a

8. d

9. b

10. b

Chapter 8

1. 0

2. 1

3. `Dim Student(119) As String`

4. `Student(4) = "Robin Hood"`

5. `Dim Salary(1000) As Decimal`

6.

a. `Const cSize As Integer = 20`
b. `Dim Score(cSize) As Integer`
c.
```
Dim Index As Integer
For Index = 0 To cSize Step 1
   lstShow.Items.Add(Score(Index).ToString)
Next Index
```
d.
```
Dim Index As Integer
Dim Sum As Integer = 0
Dim Avg As Single
For Index = 0 To cSize Step 1
   Sum = Sum + Score(Index)
Next Index
Avg = Sum / (cSize + 1)
```

7. Stores 0, 1, 2, ..., 10 in Data(0), Data(1), ..., Data(10), respectively.

Chapter 9

1. A dynamic array is an array that can be resized during the program execution.

2. Once memory gets allocated, the lowest index is always 0.

3. `Private SSNO() As String`

4. `ReDim SSNO(5000)`

5. Array content after the first pass of bubble sort: `6, 23, 50, 44, 17, 90, 33, 96`

6. The difference between ReDim and ReDim Preserve is that: ReDim re-sizes a dynamic array, resetting all the previously stored values to the default value (0 for numeric arrays); ReDim Preserve, on the other hand, re-sizes a dynamic array, while preserving the existing values.

Chapter 10

1. By using a MessageBox function.

2. By using an InputBox function.

3. Below is a structure defined to store information about a college football team:
```
Private Structure mFootballTeam
    Dim CollegeName As String
    Dim TeamName As String
    Dim Coach As String
    Dim PlayersCount As Integer
End Structure
```

4. `Dim Team As mFootballTeam`

5. Store given data in variable Team:
```
Team.CollegeName = "Purdue"
Team.TeamName = "Boilermaker"
Team.Coach = "Darrell Hazell"
Team.PlayersCount = 46
```

6. Array of structure to store ten football teams:
```
Private mTeam(9) As mFootballTeam
```

7. Store variable Team in the first element of this array.
```
mTeam(0) = Team
```

8. Store the given data at index # 4 of the array.
```
mTeam(4).CollegeName = "Michigan"
mTeam(4).TeamName = "Wolverines"
mTeam(4).Coach = "Brady Hoke"
mTeam(4).PlayersCount = 32
```

Chapter 11

1. Two applications of multiform projects are:
   a. To display the program output
   b. To display instructions on using the program

2. A modal Form is a Form that has to be closed, before the user can click outside of it.

3. A modeless Form is one that the user can click in and out of it.

4. Form load event takes place when the Form gets loaded into the memory.

5. Form closing event takes place when the Form is getting unloaded from the memory.

6. Public 7.   True

Chapter 12

1. False

2. True

3. False

4. File.Exists()

5. StreamReader's Peek method

6. FormClosing Event procedure

7. Form_Load Event procedure

Chapter 13

1. Exception handling is mostly used to handle unexpected errors. Data validation is used to handle user input errors.

2. System.DivideByZeroException and System.OverflowException.

3. A Try block is used to encapsulate the portion of the code that could potentially generate an exception (runtime error).

4. A Catch block is used to catch the exception generated in the Try block.

5. A Finally block is useful in file processing. One can close the file in Finally block; this ensures that the file closes, even if the file processing fails in Try block.

6. True

7. It is useful to have more than one Catch block so that the program can catch more specific exceptions.

8. True

9. The Message property

10. System and Application.

Chapter 14

1. A database is a repository of data in which data can be easily queried from, added, updated, and deleted.

2. A database is made up of one or more tables. Each table is made up of rows (records) and columns (fields).

3. A primary key is a unique identifier for the data stored in a table.

4. True

5. Currency.

6.   A Row is generally referred to as a record and is made up of all the fields of data for one object.

7.   All the values of certain field form a Column.

8.   A DataSet is an ADO .NET object that stores the data retrieved from the data source, into VB .NET application's memory.

9.   A Data Adapter is a .NET object that provides methods for retrieving data from the Data Source.

10.   An Excel file and MS Access .mdb file are both examples of Data Sources.

INDEX